THE FISHERMAN'S NET

Michael Collins

The Fisherman's Net

THE INFLUENCE OF THE POPES ON HISTORY

HiddenSpring

Cover design by Liam Furlong

Book design by Bill Bolger

This revised and updated edition is published by arrangement with The Columba Press, Ireland.

Cataloging-in-Publication Data is available on request from the Library of Congress.

ISBN: 1-58768-033-5

Published by
HiddenSpring
an imprint of Paulist Press
997 Macarthur Boulevard
Mahwah, New Jersey 07430

www.hiddenspringbooks.com

Printed and bound in Ireland by
ColourBooks Ltd, Dublin

Contents

AUTHOR'S NOTE

There are so many books on the papacy, it is hard to see how there could be room for another. Most of us understand the papacy purely in religious terms. But there is more to the papacy than that. In writing this book, I wanted to examine a few of the major and minor ways in which the pontiffs have shaped our past and indeed still mould our present. The calendar, the Crusades, the division of the New World, the arts are just some of the areas which have been influenced by the popes. While some readers may have the time and inclination to read much more scholarly books, *The Fisherman's Net* is written for those of you who may not have sufficient leisure or patience. The title was suggested to me by Nick Kelly to indicate the wide cast of the net.

During the final illness of Pope John Paul II, his funeral and the conclave to elect Pope Benedict XVI, many people were amazed by the interest in the papacy. The enormous media coverage reflected the impact the papacy continues to have to this day on Catholics and non-Catholics alike. I hope you enjoy this book and perhaps find some interesting angles on this fascinating legacy.

PROLOGUE

We know frustratingly little about Peter. Even the gospels, on which we must rely as primary sources, contradict the way in which Peter and Jesus met. St Matthew records: 'As Jesus was walking beside the Sea of Galilee, he saw two brothers, Simon called Peter and his brother Andrew. They were casting a net into the lake, for they were fishermen. "Come, follow me," said Jesus, "and I will make you fishers of men".' At this enigmatic invitation, the brothers followed Jesus. St John's gospel, written much later, has a variation. John tells us that it was Andrew who first saw Jesus being baptised in the river Jordan by his cousin. Andrew was already a follower of the fiery John the Baptist, who fiercely denounced the civil and religious rulers for corruption. When Jesus appeared at the river and asked for John's baptism, John saluted him as the Lamb of God. Andrew and his companion were mystified by such a greeting and wondered what it meant. Following the stranger, Jesus turned round and asked them what they wanted. Unable to put their request into words, they simply asked Jesus where he was staying. In answer to this question, Jesus invited them to come and find out. They accompanied him to an unknown destination. His very presence enchanted them and they spent the rest of the day with him. At dusk, Andrew hurried to tell his brother of the strange event. 'We have found the Messiah,' he blurted and insisted that he come with him to meet Jesus. With its typical economy of words, John's gospel gives us no account of the meeting and leaves us with bundles of unanswered questions. John simply observes that Jesus gave Simon a nickname, Peter, or 'rock', by which he would henceforth be known.

Nevertheless, it is obvious from the gospels that Peter was soon nominated the leader of a little band of 12 men called individually by Jesus to be his special helpers. He became the spokesman for the group and indeed was seen as a special insider within the group.

The little band found it difficult to express the fascination Jesus held for them. There was something they could not quite identify. On one occasion, Jesus put the question to them: 'Who do people say that I am?' We can imagine them shuffling the dust with their sandals, their eyes afraid to meet Jesus. 'Some say you are John the Baptist come back from the dead, others say Elijah, still others Jeremiah or one of the prophets.' Jesus pressed on. 'Who do you say I am?' It was impetuous Simon Peter who spoke up. 'I say you are the Christ, the Son of the Living God.' He was the first to make such a public confession, and Jesus assured him that this was not achieved by human reasoning, but revealed by his Father in heaven. 'And I tell you that you are Peter,' continued Jesus, 'and on this rock I will build my church, and the gates of Hades will not overcome it. I will give you the keys of the kingdom of heaven; whatever you bind on earth shall be bound in heaven and whatever you loose on earth shall be loosed in heaven.' With this imagery, Jesus seemed to hand Peter a share in his authority, which he claimed came from God the Father.

When Jesus spoke of his impending death, Peter tried to talk him out of accepting it willingly. Jesus seemed to know that when the time came, Peter would not stand by him and would even deny ever having known him. During the trial of Jesus, Peter and John waited outside in the courtyard. A brazier stood in a corner, full of charcoal, where they warmed their hands. The dropping temperatures and their own fear made them cold. A young serving girl recognised Peter's rustic accent and accused him of being Jesus' disciple. Peter was startled and, without thinking, he denied that he had even known Jesus. On the third furious denial, a cock crew and Peter suddenly recalled the strange prophesy of Jesus that he would deny even knowing him. Peter rushed headlong from the atrium, weeping bitterly.

When Jesus was crucified, the gospel accounts mention that his mother Mary and two other women were at the foot of the cross. The only male disciple was a young man called John, with whom Jesus seemed to have a special friendship. There is no mention of Peter.

Yet on Sunday morning, two days after Jesus had died on the cross, some women went to anoint the body of Jesus which had been hastily buried before the sundown heralding the Sabbath. Finding the tomb empty, one of their number ran to tell the apostles that the body had been stolen.

John, who had stood by Jesus as he was dying, and Peter met the distraught women. They themselves ran to the tomb to verify the event. Although John outstripped Peter, out of respect he allowed Peter enter the empty tomb first. Within hours people reported seeing Jesus, whom they believed had risen from the dead.

One morning at dawn, Peter and some of the other apostles were returning to shore after a night spent fishing. Peter may well have had some sort of co-operative in the village on the lakeside. It had been a disappointing catch. As they pulled towards the quay, a man called to them to throw the nets to the far side of the boat. Perhaps they supposed him to be a fisherman like them who had seen a shoal darting towards the deep. With nothing to lose, they accepted the tip and cast their nets. The fish swam in, so many that the dumbfounded apostles could hardly pull the bursting net to shore.

It was John who recognised Jesus first and Peter clambered to pull the net from the sparkling waters.

As they breakfasted with Jesus, Peter was given the chance of retracting the three occasions he had denied his Lord on the night of his trial. 'Do you love me?' Jesus asked innocuously. Peter responded that of course he loved him. 'Feed my lambs,' Jesus urged Peter, 'feed my sheep.' Then he added an ominous prophecy. 'When you are old you will stretch out your hands and someone else will dress you and lead you where you do not want to go.' It was clearly understood that this was to refer to the manner of Peter's death.

Peter's faith was re-kindled. Within days, he became the enthusiastic spokesman for Jesus' followers. Despite opposition from the local Jews, and perhaps the Roman authorities, he preached publicly about the risen Jesus. The Acts of the Apostles, a first-century document possibly written by St Luke, recounts the breathtaking pace at which the Christian community developed. At some unknown time, Peter left Jerusalem and set out to preach the message of Jesus to the scattered Jewish community. Tradition tells us that he lived for a while in Antioch before moving to Rome, the capital of the empire. Of his residency in the city there are no traces. But the last years of his life were seen to have been spent in Rome, which was home to the oldest Jewish colony outside Palestine.

CHAPTER I

St Peter and the Early Bishops

PETER · LINUS

CLETUS · CLEMENT

EVARISTUS · ALEXANDER

SIXTUS · TELESPHORUS

ANICETUS

The emperor Augustus (27 BC-AD 14) boasted that when he came to power, Rome was a city of brick but by the time of his death, it was a city of marble. It all started with a spark.

One of his successors, the ill-fated Nero (54-68), was not happy with the shabby wooden buildings he found in the city. All around the Palatine, near his imperial residence, lay the untidy hovels of the poor. He told friends that he wanted to demolish these slums and expand his palace, the Golden House. Few believed, or wanted to believe, that the emperor would really carry out his threat.

On the night of 19 July, in the year AD 64, a fire broke out around the area where the emperor lived. The dark dank houses of the poor were the first to go up in flames. The fire raged until dawn. As the sun rose, it fought with the orange flames for attention. The citizens were devastated at the destruction. The fire brigade, under the special command of the emperor, had been ineffective. Eyewitnesses would later swear that they saw the emperor high on the plinth of his palace stroking the strings of his lyre and singing a lament for the city.

Nobody ever found out what happened. Perhaps a spark falling from an unattended lamp, perhaps a torch deliberately thrown in a window landing on the straw bedding caused the conflagration. Whatever it was, soon the citizens were blaming their emperor. Mad as he may have been, Nero was no fool. He realised that he had to find a scapegoat, and chose a newly-arrived religious group in the city. They were related to the Jews. They claimed that their leader, a certain rabbi called Jesus, had been crucified, and had risen from the dead. And so he gave the order that all followers of this sect should be arrested. The Roman writer Tacitus gives us some more details:

> To scotch the rumours, Nero charged and tortured some people hated for their evil practices – the group popularly known as the Christians.
>
> In their deaths, they were made a mockery. They were covered in the skins of wild animals, torn to death by dogs, crucified or set on fire, so that when night fell, they burned like torches. Nero opened up his own gardens for this spectacle and gave a show in the arena, where he mixed with the crowd, or stood dressed as a charioteer on a chariot. As a result, although they were guilty of being Christians and deserved death, people began to feel sorry for them. For they realised that they were being massacred not for the public good, but to satisfy one man's mania.

Among the casualties of this pogrom, we are told by PETER tradition, was a Galilean called Peter. He had been living quietly in the city for some years. As a close friend of Jesus of Nazareth, he was seen as the leader of the little group of Christians in Rome. And so he had to die. Late one autumn evening, he was brought to the Circus of Nero, which lay in the valley between the Vatican and the Janiculum Hills. According to legend, one of the soldiers had heard how Jesus, his leader, had been executed. Peter was condemned to perish in the same way, crucified as a common criminal. In a moment of zeal for martyrdom, he begged to be crucified upside-down, claiming not to be worthy to die in the same manner as Jesus. And so the wooden cross was slammed into the ground headfirst. As the blood rushed to his head, Peter may have heard the agonised screams of his friends, or seen their contorted faces disappear behind grey plumes of acrid smoke. The smell of burning flesh was everywhere. How could it all have ended like this, he must have thought desperately. How could the promises of the Messiah perish and curl away like dried-up parchment?

And so it had come to pass. When it was all over, those who had survived the round-up took Peter's bruised body away for burial. At least, they comforted themselves, he had been spared the indignity of being burned alive. The little band snaked its way across the road, the Via Cornelia, and into the cemetery which lay alongside Nero's gardens. There, under a little red wall they buried him, a tiny flagstone to mark his grave. Years later, Gaius, a Roman presbyter wrote to pilgrims: 'If you want to see the trophy of the apostles, go to see Peter at the Vatican and Paul at the Via Ostiense.'

The effect of this event must have been traumatic. We have no reliable information from within the Roman community. We do not know for how long Peter lived in Rome. Later traditions claim that he lived 25 years in the city, but it was more likely less than half that time. He had previously been leader of the community at Antioch, the Syrian city where the followers of Jesus were first called Christians. The early followers of Jesus were almost all Jewish. Gradually, the disciples realised that they would have to spread their net further. Surely Jesus had not just wanted the conversion of the sons of Abraham? Was not his instruction to go to the whole world and baptise everybody in the name of the Father, the Son and the Holy Spirit? It was a clear indication that Peter, the leader of the disciples and apostles, decided that the message of Jesus was for everybody, Jew and Gentile alike.

There are no contemporary records of Peter's life in

Rome – some scholars even question whether he ever lived there at all – but it seems that his memory was venerated by the Roman Christians. Archaeologists continue to find graffiti scratched on the walls around the tomb underneath St Peter's High Altar, 'Peter, pray for me!'

Another great figure of the early church, Paul of Tarsus, had met the executioner's sword in Rome. A native of Cilecia , Paul had converted from Judaism and travelled extensively throughout modern-day Greece and Turkey. He founded small communities and kept in touch with them by brief letters when he moved on.

Denounced to Rome, Paul was held under house arrest for several years before he was executed. Although we cannot be certain, he must have met Peter during that time. He also was to die under the persecution of Nero. These events must have almost destroyed the Christian community in Rome.

Little by little, the Roman church sought to reorganise itself. A successor was elected to Peter, and the community regrouped as a tight little band, anxious to avoid the public gaze. The terrible persecution ordered by Nero ended when the emperor committed suicide in AD 68. None the less, the Christians in Rome had learned a salutary lesson and were determined to keep as much as possible to themselves. News that the temple in Jerusalem had been destroyed by Roman troops in AD 70 must have confirmed their fears of renewed persecution. The Roman writer, Tacitus, although writing 50 years after the event, refers to the Christians' 'crimes' and their 'hatred of humanity'. A contemporary of Tacitus, the Roman historian Suetonius, remarks with evident distaste on 'the new and criminal superstition'. Both Tacitus and Suetonius used earlier documents on which to base their assertions. The educated classes evidently little understood the Christians with whom they often confused the Jews.

We know virtually nothing but the names of Linus (c. 66-c. 78) and Cletus (c. 79-91), the successors of Peter as leaders of the Christians in Rome. Whatever they achieved evidently disintegrated into the dust. Although a third-century list of the popes name Cletus after Linus, it is possible that the two may have worked as a team. Certainly there was no tradition at this early stage of a monarchical bishop ruling alone. For the first several centuries, the clergy and people of Rome met to elect a leader, or bishop, from among the deacons and presbyters. Not infrequently these elections were marred by factions that sought, even violently, to have their candidate elected. In time, the position of bishop of Rome was to be as highly prized as it was lucrative. The Roman clergy were anxious not to be identified with the pagan priests who presided over the temple worship, where the office was often handed down from father to son.

Most of our knowledge of the early popes comes from a catalogue compiled sometime in the sixth century. The anonymous author of the *Liber Pontificalis* – the Book of the Popes – probably worked at the papal court on the Caelian Hill overlooking the Coliseum and seems to have had access to documents written centuries earlier. These manuscripts have since perished, and the information contained in the catalogue is thus invaluable. Although an indispensable aid to the study of the development of the papacy, the book is not without its limitations. The writer often attributes events and happenings to various popes who evidently lived after the events had happened. Given the precarious nature of the Christian community in Rome, it is easy to understand how detailed records were not kept. Often we read of the Tiber overflowing, of earthquakes and invaders who destroyed all they could in the city. The *Liber Pontificalis* lists the popes in a chronological order, but the precise dates of the reign of any one bishop are often inaccurate. It is also true to say that the concept of history in the sixth century is vastly different from our modern-day understanding. Writers saw themselves as chronologers, setting down events of which they had heard. Myth and legend were often recorded indiscriminately. Hearsay was sometimes relayed as faithfully as fact, gossip as undeniable truth.

We have only the briefest information concerning Clement (c. 91-c. 101), the third successor of Peter as head of the Roman Christian community. Most of our knowledge is contained in a letter that he wrote sometime around the year 91. Having heard of some turbulence within the Christian community in the Greek city of Corinth, Clement addressed them, lamenting that a few

> rash and self-willed persons have inflamed you into such madness that your venerable and illustrious name, worthy to be loved by all men, has been greatly defamed.

Excusing his tardiness in sending the letter of reprimand, Clement shows that he considered it his clear duty to bring the upstarts to order, no matter what the distance. He mentions the city as having previously carried on a correspondence with 'the apostle Paul'. As with the letters of Paul, there is no trace of a reply from the unruly Corinthians. Perhaps, as we have no further word from Corinth, the troublemakers changed their ways and obeyed Clements's instruction.

Of the 12 emperors who ruled during the first century, six of them met violent deaths at the hand of zealous assassins. One can easily understand how the nervous Roman legislators would seek to outlaw secret meetings, especially those that took place under the cover of darkness. Conspiracies and plots to assassinate the emperor, hatched and developed in the glow of an oil lamp, were all too often successful. The inward-looking Christian community was an understandable target of imperial agents.

The pagan Roman historian Suetonius has left us a vitally important book, *The Lives of the Emperors*. Written in elegant prose, it remains our most important source of information for these emperors. Their coins and statues give us a glimpse of what the men looked like. Circulating from hand to hand around the empire, the coins were an important source of propaganda. Marble and bronze busts of the reigning emperor adorned courts and temples throughout the empire. Men from Britain to Africa studied the latest portrait of their ruler and styled their beards and hair in the same manner. But Suetonius describes them, their passion and actions, and brings them to life. He relates how a plot to kill the emperor Diocletian was discovered in the year 95. Among those to be rounded up were the consul of that year, Flavius Clemens and his wife. They were accused of 'godlessness, for which many others also were condemned because they had drifted into the practices of the Jews'. Retiring to their bathing room, the couple entered a sunken bath filled with warm water. Having bid farewell to each other with a kiss, they opened the veins of their wrists and watched their lifeblood ebb out. How often in the future centuries would people sacrifice their lives in this world in the hopes of an immortal life in the world to come. The Romans probably did not distinguish too clearly between Jews and Christians, and it behoved both groups to avoid seeking undue attention. This may account for the fact that we have such scant information about the next bishops of Rome. Certainly persecutions of the Christians were reported from as far away as the provinces of Bithynia and Pontus.

Around the year 117, the legate Pliny the Younger wrote to the emperor Trajan for advice concerning accusations against some Christians living in the region. The legate may well have wished to ingratiate himself with the emperor, and prove that he was determined to root out any conspirators against the state. Pliny informed the emperor that he had rounded up the accused. Some claimed that they had never been Christians, while others declared that they had left the community as much as 20 years previously. To put them to the test, Pliny obliged them to address prayers to the gods and offer a pinch of incense to the image of the emperor. To seal the pact, he demanded that they curse the name of Christ. A true Christian, he had been informed, would rather die first.

In case the emperor was not familiar with the practices of the Christians, Pliny summarised their activities:

They were accustomed to meet on a fixed day before dawn, to say an antiphonal hymn to Christ as to a god, and to bind themselves with an oath – not for performing any crime but for abstaining from theft, robbery, adultery, the violation of oaths, and the refusal to repay deposit on demand. After this they were accustomed to meet again for a meal which was ordinary and harmless.

It is tempting to read into this account the soft-heartedness of the governor. None the less, he carried out the emperor's order that required punishing as necessary. Pliny adds that with the round-up and persecutions there was general satisfaction at the pagan temples. The contented meat vendors reported brisk business as people returned to make burnt offering as sacrifices to please their gods. Rising smoke around the temple precinct and the scent of sizzling meat was always a sign of good business.

The emperor replied, praising Pliny for the course of action that he had taken so far. He counselled against a general round-up of Christians, and especially against listening to anonymous charges. However, where Christians were tried and convicted, they were to be punished. Recantation would result in full pardon.

IGNATIUS   Some five years earlier, Ignatius, bishop of Antioch in Syria, was condemned to die in the arena at Rome. The old man saw himself as the central lynchpin of the Christian community in the Syrian town. On his journey from Antioch to Rome, he wrote seven letters to the communities he was to visit on his way. He seems to have been quite resolved to die as a martyr. The Greek word *martyr* means witness, and Ignatius saw himself as an innocent if willing victim. Greeting the Romans shortly before his arrival, he wrote:

> Allow me to be eaten by the beasts, which are my way of reaching God. I am God's wheat, and I am to be ground by the teeth of wild beasts so that I may become the pure bread of Christ.

How did the Roman Christians anticipate the arrival of this zealot in the city? All we know is that the elderly bishop's will was fulfilled and he perished in the arena.

In view of the activity in the provinces, it is not surprising that the leaders of the Roman community would seek to protect the members by staying on the right side of the law.

EVARISTUS,   The bishops Evaristus (c. 101-109), Alexander (c. 109-c.
ALEXANDER,   116), Sixtus (c. 116-125) and Telesphorus (c. 125-136)
SIXTUS,   appear and fade like the morning mist. There are no
TELESPHORUS   traces of their stewardship apart from their names.

While the community was seeking to avoid the public gaze, the Christians had to contend with internal differences. Irenaeus, the bishop of Lyon in Gaul, tells us that during the administration of the bishop Hygenus (c. 136-c. 142) a certain Valentinus came to Rome from the provinces. He was greeted with suspicion and branded by the locals as a heretic. The Christians had up until recently been proud of the fact that they were new, fresh, enthusiastic. Now, however, they came to distrust people without a pedigree.

This type of visitor was the worst of all. Valentinus was a Gnostic, one of the groups that claimed to have secret knowledge. Nobody likes to be on the wrong side of secrets, and Christians, above all, should have known that. Hygenus set about making Rome an uncomfortable place for the Gnostic Valentinus and his companions, urging the Christians neither to offer the visitors hospitality in their homes nor to welcome them to the liturgy on Sundays. Valentinus outlived Hygenus and went on to win more and more converts to his doctrines.

How loyal were the Christians to their bishop? It is an intriguing question which, almost 2,000 years later, eludes a response. The fact, however, that some Christians were won over to the Gnostic faith evidently rankled the loyal Christians and goaded them to denounce them, sometimes in violent terms.

Who then were these Gnostics that caused such anxiety for the community? GNOSTICS

The Christian faith was still in a process of development, trying to come to an ever-clearer understanding of the message of Jesus. Paul, writing in the first century, had warned against those who sought to offer a definitive interpretation that would not be in accordance with their Lord's teaching. Those who claimed to have a secret knowledge were labelled as Gnostics (*gnosis* in Greek means knowledge), as knowledge was seen to be the key to understanding humanity's relation to the universe and its creator.

Although such elitism was not peculiar to the Christians, it nevertheless became a strong branch in the Christian community. Different groups sprang up both in the Middle East and further westwards towards the heart of the Roman Empire. The basic tenet of the Gnostics (all led by different founders) was that the world was invented, not by the Supreme Being, but rather by a demiurge, or spirit, who sought to enslave humanity. A small number of people were fortunate enough to realise that they could escape this world and be united to the demiurge. The pathway, taught the Gnostics, was through knowledge. Anyone who claimed to have some esoteric knowledge which united them to the demiurge was sure to be sought after. Various teachers set themselves up as masters of the new way. Much of the church's theology was a reaction against Gnostic heresy. When the Gnostics argued that the spiritual was good and material was bad, a response was called for from the orthodox Christians. When they argued that Jesus was only a phantom, the Christians had to think out an intelligible reply. That the Gnostics had articulate spokesmen is obvious by the amount of Christian authors who railed against them. This had the effect of forcing the orthodox Christians to define the tenets of their belief. Church leaders, the bishops being chief amongst them, saw this as their ministry.

The Gnostics rejected the Old Testament and most of the New Testament, as well as basic beliefs such as the resurrection. The orthodox Christians were forced to define their own canon of scripture. None the less, the Gnostics continued to have similarities to the Christian Church. Several Gnostic branches had an episcopate, and, if they had not entirely rejected the sacraments, they celebrated baptism and Eucharist.

Marconian of Pontus, a rich merchant, was one of the most influential Gnostic leaders. In 140 he left Bithynia and, arriving in Rome, began a popular school of teaching. Soon his sect rivalled the mainstream church at Rome. His influence spread, but as the church more carefully defined itself, it became less of a threat. There was always a willing audience for the teachers who sought to found new ways of faith, loosely modelled on the Christian Church. Eventually the Christian community tired of Marconian and expelled him from the city.

The Eucharist became more and more important in Eucharist the lives of the Christians. In the mid-150s, Justin, a Palestinian who had settled in Rome and taught philosophy there, wrote an account of how they met once a week to celebrate the Eucharist, as a symbol of communion with each other and with God. It still echoes down the centuries and strikes us with its immediacy.

On the day called after the sun there takes place a meeting of all who live in towns or in the countryside. The memoirs of the apostles are read, as are the writings of the apostles, in so far as time will allow. When the reader has finished, the president, in his speech, admonishes and urges all to imitate these worthy examples. Then we all stand and pray together aloud. When the prayers are ended, we greet one another with a kiss. At that point, as we have already said, bread is brought, with wine mixed with water to the president. Prayers are offered, giving 'praise and glory to the Father of the Universe, through the name of the Son and the Holy Spirit'. The bread and wine is then distributed to those present by the deacons, and also brought to the sick in their homes.

The Sunday Eucharist provided a sense of community and solidarity in a harsh and difficult world.

Around the middle of the century, a venerable visitor arrived in Rome to consult with the bishop of the city. Polycarp was bishop of the Turkish town of Smyrna. His claim to fame rested on the fact that he was a disciple of the apostle John the Evangelist, and indeed a friend of several of the other disciples of Jesus. Ignatius of Antioch had also addressed a letter to him as he made his way to Rome to meet his death. Polycarp's purpose in making the difficult journey by sea and land was to discuss with the bishop of Rome the date of Easter.

ANICETUS The bishop, Anicetus (155-166) received his noble visitor in his small villa outside the city walls. The two men talked of various problems besetting the Christian communities throughout the world. Anicetus listened politely as the white-haired Polycarp begged the bishop to change the date of celebrating Easter. Anicetus was in favour of celebrating the feast on the Sunday after the 14th day of the Jewish month of Nisan. Polycarp hoped to persuade Rome to celebrate the feast of the resurrection of Jesus according to the eastern tradition, that is, the fourth of Nisan. What a wonderful thing it would be, he urged Anicetus, if all Christians could celebrate the feast of the resurrection of Jesus together. Anicetus excused himself, pleading that the weight of tradition forbade any such change from the Roman way of doing things.

This journey shows that Polycarp must have attached importance to visiting the Roman community. Polycarp pressed him, perhaps referring to his prestigious teacher, John the Evangelist. But it was to no avail, and after exchanging prayers and blessing one another, Polycarp departed from Rome to return to Smyrna. There, in his 86th year, he was burned to death during renewed persecutions. As the flaming hemp torch was lowered to the stake in the arena of the city, the prefect offered the old man the chance of recanting. 'I have served Christ as my Lord for 86 years,' came the dignified reply, 'and I can do no other.'

CHAPTER TWO

The Barque of Peter

VICTOR • ZEPHYRINUS

CALLISTUS • HIPPOLYTUS

URBAN • PONTIAN

ANTERUS • FABIAN

CORNELIUS • NOVATIAN

The emperors were busy either fighting Rome's enemies, or shielding themselves from the assassin's knives. Few since the time of Augustus have left anything of literary merit. Modern readers of the Meditations by the emperor Marcus Aurelius (161-180) will be impressed by his sagacious and tolerant views. Indeed, his writings have enjoyed renewed publicity in recent years. Unique among the Roman rulers, the morose emperor also was practical, setting up schools, orphanages, hospitals and institutions for the poor of the empire. The fair treatment of slaves was a particular passion of Aurelius. Despite all the values which Marcus Aurelius and the Christians shared, the philosopher emperor was deeply intolerant of the Christians, on whom he blamed the moral disorder of his day.

Most of his 19 years as emperor were spent defending the northern borders from the attacks of the barbarians. While planning a campaign to extend the empire northeastward beyond the Vistula river, Marcus Aurelius was struck down by plague. Before he died, he called for his son, Lucius Aurelius Commodus and grudgingly bestowed the imperial purple on him.

Of all the emperors to sport the laurels of power, Commodus was one of the most depraved. Even his father regretted that his son would one day succeed him. Physically like his father, with wide protruding eyes, a small chin and mop of curly hair, Commodus shared none of his intellect. The 18th-century historian, Edward Gibbon dryly observes of Commodus:

Nature had formed him of a weak, rather than a

wicked disposition. His cruelty, which at first obeyed the dictates of others, degenerated into habit, and at length became the ruling passion of his soul.

Following an assassination attempt in 183, Commodus ensconced himself in a den of bodyguards and sycophants, avoiding further threats. When the corn prices rose dramatically in 189, a mob of protesters tried to storm the palace, and only the intercession of Marcia, his mistress, averted catastrophe.

Marcia was a Christian, and it has been suggested that it was due to her influence over the emperor that a truce was made between the Christians and the government. However true this may have been, the same Marcia was held responsible for drugging the emperor following a hunting expedition. As Commodus slumbered, a young and robust wrestler was smuggled into the emperor's chamber, whereupon he strangled his sovereign with his bare hands.

Rome was at this time a melting pot of different cultures. Tacitus referred to it as 'the common receptacle of all that is vile'. Romans loved anything that was novel. If an intriguing cult were discovered in the provinces, they would happily bring it to the capital, and open a temple in honour of the exotic deity. The more gods they worshipped, the happier they felt. The Christians with their one dour god were of little interest to them. Among the gods that fascinated the Romans most were those imported from the Egyptian provinces. They realised that the gods worshipped by the pharaohs were ancient. That was important for the Romans. As long as anything had a pedigree, they liked it. The Romans also built temples to those emperors that had been deified, a shrewd means of increasing loyalty to the state. The citizens were obliged to attend extravagant rituals, whether they believed in the existence of these gods or not. In addition, the Romans continued to worship the household gods, the Lares and Penates, as well as venerate their own ancestors.

The modern visitor to Rome will find, in its quieter moments, a city line punctuated by graceful cupolas and serene campaniles. Almost every street boasts the stately façade of a church dedicated to a local saint. In the first centuries, it was not so. Only the pagan temples were built on public highways to be frequented by the populace. The pagan priests dedicated themselves to their task of offering gifts to the gods on behalf of the suppliants. Animals of all descriptions were sacrificed, their entrails burnt on an altar before the temple which the crowds thronged to see. Over the centuries, the ceremonial was developed down to its minutest detail. Certain phrases had to be recited by the priest and replied to by the attendants. If at any time the ceremony was interrupted, or if an incorrect response was offered, the whole ceremony had to start from the very beginning. If a bull pulled away from the slaughter knife, the omens might be bad. Before any great event, the commencement of a battle, the choice of the legions, the sacrifices would be made and, depending upon the priest's interpretation of the entrails, the action would be considered. These entrails were later burned as a fragrant offering to the gods. The smell of blood and burning flesh must have been at times overpowering for the spectators.

The early Christians at Rome had no buildings that we would recognise as churches. Instead, they met in each other's houses. Most of these were the equivalent of the modern apartment blocks, using the largest room to accommodate visitors. Archaeologists have discovered that in some cases adjoining houses were converted, doubling the available space. Such restricted quarters fostered a sense of intimacy, something entirely lacking in the official rituals performed in the temples. In a society that tolerated the exposure of infants to wolves, the Christian concern for the poor and defenceless must have been alluring. In a culture that lauded success, the Christian support for the weakest members of society must have been all the more attractive. The Christian theologian Tertullian, writing in the third century, gleefully reported that the pagans were often overheard remarking, 'See how the Christians love one another.'

From which strands of society did the Christians originate? As a port and as the capital, Rome was an obvious destination for people arriving from different parts of the empire. From the earliest inscriptions in the catacombs, their place of burial, it seems that the first Christians came from the lower, Greek-speaking classes. The dark corridors of the Roman catacombs preserve secrets of ages long since past. Simple inscriptions light up briefly in a torchbeam. 'Flavia, rest in the Lord! Eutherius, take your well-earned rest! Claudius, rest in peace!' A crudely scratched dove with an olive branch reminds one of Noah's delivery from the flood. For the early Christians who felt that they were wallowing in the surrounding waters of paganism, this was a reassuring comfort of paradise.

As the second century progressed, many Romans were converted to Christianity. As with all small groups, loyalty and fidelity were paramount, and we can easily imagine with what pride they saw the advancement of their little community.

The peace must have been shattered in the spring of 177 with the report that 48 members of the Christian community had been slaughtered in Vienne, in southern Gaul. Their crime was vaguely described as 'immorality'. Gruesome reports relate how the victims were strapped to wooden poles and set alight as the citizens of Vienne looked on. Three years later, 12 Christians were killed in Scilli, in northern Africa. The Christians soon gave these fallen comrades the title martyr. They died, they argued, bearing witness to their faith. The growing strength of the Christian community in the empire was a cause of worry to the Roman authorities and in 202 the emperor Septimus Severus (193-211) issued an edict, prohibiting conversion to Christianity. The peace-loving Christians were affecting the morale of the army. Proof of the emperor's determination came the following spring when a group of catechumens, preparing to be baptised as Christians, was arrested and put to the sword.

VICTOR

The question of the date of Easter continued to be a source of friction between East and West. At the end of the second century, Victor (189-198), the bishop of Rome, wrote to all the churches telling them that Easter could only be celebrated on the Sunday following the Jewish Passover. In 196, bishops throughout the empire had met to discuss a uniform date for Easter. Several Asian bishops resented his autocratic stance, but the determined Victor would not stand for any opposition. Those who did not agree with him were excommunicated. Victor won moral authority, and may well have set the bishops of Rome on the road that would carry them over the threshold of the third millennium as the oldest monarchical system in the world. But, as with everything, there would be a price to pay.

ZEPHYERINUS

The continued threat of imperial persecution under Septimus Severus must have placed the date of Easter in the shade. The leader elected to succeed Victor on the latter's death in 198 was the Greek-speaking Zephyrinus (199-217). A contemporary source, the Roman presbyter Hippolytus, refers to him as 'ignorant and greedy, a receiver of bribes and lover of money'. Hippolytus was intensely jealous of Zephyrinus, and considered setting

himself up in opposition to the bishop. But Zephyrinus
seems to have commanded the loyalty of the majority of
the Christians. Hippolytus bided his time. In 217, following the bishop's death, the clergy and people of Rome
met and by ballot chose a successor. They decided to elect
Callistus (217-222), the senior deacon of the city. Hippolytus contested his election and succeeded in having
himself elected a bishop in opposition by a small faction
of dissatisfied clergy and people. He thus became the
first of a handful known in history as anti-popes.

The seven deacons of Rome were highly important in
the community. They were in charge of the public funds,
and were open to accusations of profiteering. Hippolytus
related a story concerning the newly-elected bishop, Callistus.

According to Hippolytus, Callistus was the slave of a
Greek-speaking master, Marcus Aurelius Carpophorus,
who worked at the imperial court. Given his talent for
managing his master's money, Carpophorus put Callistus in charge of his funds. Moreover, he asked his slave
to invest some money for him. This the slave obediently
did and made a handsome profit. Other members of the
Christian community, recognising his entrepreneurial
flair, also entrusted Callistus with large sums. Instead of
returning the money to the community members, Callistus absconded. He was captured at the port of Rome on
the mouth of the River Tiber while embarking on a cargo
ship and sentenced to death.

The Christian community pleaded for his release and
instead his sentence was commuted. Frustrated by his
guardians, Hippolytus tells us, Callistus went to the synagogue one Sabbath, where he ranted at the congregation
until he was arrested once more. This time, he was sentenced to forced labour in the mines of Sardinia. His
plight reached the ears of Marcia, the mistress of the

emperor Commodus. She intervened on his behalf with the emperor, and Callistus was once more released, but this time into the care of the bishop, Victor, who exiled him from the city.

When Zephyrinus succeeded Victor, Callistus made headway in his ecclesiastical career with Zephyrinus as his new patron. He was appointed a deacon, in charge of one of the deaconries and given charge of the catacombs.

Hippolytus, the author of this story may be reporting fact, or may be embroidering fiction. Even after Callistus' death in 222, Hippolytus continued as bishop in opposition, contesting the elections of Urban (222-230) and Pontian (230-235) until his own death in exile in Sardinia.

The Christians had to walk a taut tightrope with the emperors. One might be favourable, but his successor was liable to order a fresh persecution. The emperor Alexander Severus (222-235) during this period seems to have been quite tolerant of Christianity. His mother, Julia Mammaea, attended lectures given by Origen in Antioch and the historian Lampridius tell us that the emperor eclectically embraced elements from various religions. Roman eclecticism was quaintly displayed by Alexander as he covered his head in prayer.

(He would).... perform his devotions early in the morning, in his Lararium. There he had carefully selected statues of the deified Caesars, only those of good repute and of particularly holy spirits, including Apollonius of Tyana ... and also Christ, Abraham and Orpheus.

The accession of Maximinus Thrax (235-238) to the imperial throne put an end to the relative peace that the Christians in Rome had enjoyed for over two decades. Fighting on the borders against the Persians occupied the time of the emperors and they were constantly alert for an assassin's blade. The swarthy Maximinus led a revolt on the banks of the Rhine, near Mainz and had himself elected by the troops. The mutinous troops then turned on the former emperor, Alexander Severus and ran him through with a sword. Maximinus was only the second emperor to date not to have come from the senatorial aristocracy, and his nickname, the Thracian, indicated his lowly origins. The new emperor immediately rounded up the leaders of the Christians in the city and deported them to Sardinia. Pontian, who had been validly elected bishop of Rome, and Hippolytus the anti-pope were both arrested and exiled. Tradition reports that the two rival bishops met in the salt mines of the island and were reconciled under the burning sun. Believing that he would never be released, Pontian resigned his position as bishop of Rome, the first pope in history to abdicate. This allowed the clergy and Christian people of Rome to meet and elect a new bishop of the city. His successor, Anterus (235), died after only 43 days as bishop, and was then succeeded by the Roman presbyter, Fabian (236-250).

The new bishop managed to steer clear of imperial observation. The little we know of him suggests that he was a wise and careful administrator, expanding the cemeteries, setting the number of deaconries at seven and appointing notaries to codify the archives of the diocese.

In early 238, an uprising took place in the Province of Africa, led by wealthy landowners. Following a revolt, they met in Carthage, where they elected the elderly governor, Gordian, as the new emperor in place of Maximinus. When news of this startling uprising reached the senate in Rome, the senators even more surprisingly embraced the revolt. Wintering in Syrmium, Maximinus ordered a march on Rome, where he intended to teach the senate who was in charge. Gordian died suddenly and the terrified senators elected two of their number, Balbinus and Pupienus, as co-emperors. Maximinus was furious and laid siege to Aquileia on his way to Rome. The siege proved more difficult than he had expected and his own troops turned on him. Surrounding his tent one day, the soldiers ran their emperor through with a sword. His son, whom he had recently named Caesar and heir, was also murdered. The severed heads of father and son were sent in a canvas sack to Rome.

The Romans were on their guard again. The first days of a new emperor's reign were days of insecurity and the Christians realised how closely their fate was entwined with the civil leader.

Philip of Arabia (244-249) was elected emperor by the troops in early 244. The former Prefect of the Praetorian Guard which protects the emperor, he had been responsible for inciting a mutiny against the emperor Gordian III (224-244). He immediately set about ending the costly war in the East, even if it meant signing a humiliating treaty with the barbarians.

In April AD 248, Rome celebrated a thousand years since its foundation. The Secular Games, last held 44 years previously under Septimus Severus, were celebrated with great pomp and style, with lavish spectacles in the arena for the populace. The games must have brought back haunting memories to the Christians, whose recent ancestors had died in the circus. The shrill blast of the trumpets, which had recently heralded the persecutions, led the legions from the Colosseum to the Circus Maximus. There charioteers raced around the oblong tracks, dust flying as the chariots rounded the corners at terrific speed. Prostitutes, pimps, clowns, acrobats, gladiators and children all mixed in the joyous atmosphere induced by the celebrations. The Roman Christians and indeed

Christians throughout the empire were relieved to have Philip as their emperor. During his reign, Christianity was tolerated and Christians were protected from persecution.

Writing some 75 years after the death of the emperor, the first Church historian, Eusebius of Caesarea, hailed Philip as the first Christian emperor. Eusebius was a great favourite of Constantine, who had regarded himself as the first Christian emperor. Apart from Eusebius' report, there is no evidence that the emperor was a Christian. Philip may have known and respected Christianity but he continued to adorn temples and strike coins with pagan motifs.

So impressed was the emperor Constantine by Eusebius' learning that he authorised the bishop to write a history of the world down to the year 324. It was quite a daunting task but the document is invaluable for the information it provides us today. Most of his sources have unfortunately been destroyed by time.

Philip had to deal with several revolts against his authority. The most serious was the final one. In order to quell disturbances in Pannonia (modern-day Hungary), Philip appointed a young native of the area, Decius (249-251) as commander. It was to prove a foolish and ultimately fatal move as the popular Decius spearheaded a revolt against the emperor. In the early summer of 249, the infuriated Philip led an army northwards from Rome and engaged with Decius' troops outside Verona. The emperor was either killed in battle or struck down soon afterwards by his own bodyguard. Thereupon the exultant soldiers proclaimed Decius emperor, hoisting him on a leather and brass shield to hail the troops. The Senate in Rome quickly and prudently added its approval to the selection.

The Christians in the empire would soon have reason

to lament the choice of emperor. Despite the impending collapse of the frontiers, Decius dedicated much of his prodigious energy to a systematic persecution of the Christians. The new emperor argued that the empire's misfortune was a direct result of the people abandoning the gods of their ancestors. Decius called for a return to the old ways and ordered them to offer regular sacrifice to the ancient gods.

For the Christians, this was impossible. The emperor devised an ingenious method that would weed out his disloyal subjects. All who offered a pinch of incense in front of a pagan statue, and prayed for the emperor's health, would be issued with a *libellus*, a papyrus parchment confirming their loyalty. People scrambled to obtain this passport to continued freedom.

One of those who refused to subscribe to a libellus was a deacon of Rome, Laurence. For his pains he was stretched on an iron grid and burned alive by the Roman soldiers. A medieval biographer later attributed to him the statement: 'Turn me over now, I am done on this side.'

Fabian appears to have ran foul of the emperor Decius. It was most likely for his refusal to offer the required incense that he was arrested and thrown into prison. After caring for the Roman community for 14 years, Fabian was dispatched by decapitation in January of the year 250, the first and most prestigious victim of the persecution. Although the emperor Decius fell in battle against the Goths in that same year, his sons continued the ferocious persecution.

Roman Christians were unable to assemble in safety to elect a new leader for 14 months. During that time, a committee of the presbyters governed the Christian community. One of these was a certain Novatian. Intolerant of those who sought to accommodate themselves to the imperial regime, the austere Novatian penned a letter to the Christian community of Carthage in North Africa, who, he argued, had betrayed their faith. The accusation was that, in the face of persecution, Christians had conformed and returned to worship of the pagan gods. These unforgivable actions, Novatian claimed, put such feeble people outside the Christian community. When the people and clergy of Rome finally elected Cornelius as their new bishop, Novatian set himself up as a bishop in opposition. In the autumn of 251, a synod of bishops and presbyters in Rome excommunicated him. Charity and forgiveness, they reminded Novatian and his followers, was the first hallmark of a Christian.

By the middle of the third century, the administration of the church in Rome was firmly centred on the bishop. Despite the persecutions ordered by the emperor, in a letter dated 251, the bishop Cornelius refers with pride to '46 presbyters, seven deacons, seven sub deacons, 42 acolytes, 52 exorcists, lectors and porters.'

Furthermore, he notes with evident satisfaction, the incidence of 1,500 cases of charity towards widows and the poor in Rome. Cornelius had an excellent relationship with Cyprian, the bishop of Carthage in North Africa. Shortly after Novatian had had himself elected a bishop in opposition to Cornelius, Cyprian wrote a sympathetic letter to Cornelius condemning the heretics. It was intolerable, he maintained, to have such rogues,

... carry letters from schismatic and blasphemers to the chair of Peter and to the principal church, in which sacerdotal unity has its source.

The underlying message was one of support for the beleaguered bishop of Rome.

In the June of 253, Cornelius was exiled to the port of modern-day Civitavecchia, outside Rome, where he died. Novatian meanwhile continued as a rival bishop in the city. It was becoming more and more obvious that there had to be one bishop and one source of authority in Rome. Otherwise there would be confusion and factions would continue to form. The Roman mob in history was famous for its partisanship and often violent actions.

After a brief period of peace, the Christians were to face the fiercest persecution at the hands of the Roman authorities.

CHAPTER THREE

Early One Morning

SIXTUS • MARCELLINUS

CONSTANTINE

MILTIADES • SYLVESTER

DAMASUS • URSINIUS

On a bright summer's morning, on 4 August 257, Pope Sixtus and three of the deacons were celebrating Mass in the cemetery of Callistus. By then it had become an established custom to meet in the cemetery and offer prayers for the dead who lay buried there. A troop of soldiers arrived and arrested the bishop and his deacons on the orders of the emperor Valerian. The emperor had initially tolerated the Christians but now decided that they had to be excised from view. The group was charged with sedition and the soldiers drew their swords and beheaded them on the spot. The Christian onlookers were paralysed with fear. Sixtus had been leader of the Christians for just one year. As the soldiers marched off, the Christians recovered his body. They wrapped their martyred bishop in a linen shroud and his severed head was placed in a silk pouch. When the funeral rites were over, the Christians nervously elected a new leader, in the knowledge that the imperial sword was never far away.

The Roman Empire was experiencing trouble due to its sheer size. The senate and the army reacted as swiftly as they could when trouble broke out, but it was obvious that the empire was now too large to be ruled successfully. The empire was slowly collapsing from within.

Who can tell what may have happened had it not been for the arrival of a new contender for the imperial diadem, a man of lowly rank who aspired to save the empire from its woes?

The son of poor parents, Gaius Aurelius Varerius Diocletianus (284-305) joined the army on his father's advice. Born in a the Roman province of Dalmatia, Diocletian was hugely ambitious and showed great bravery in battle against the Persians. Rewarded by the emperor Numerian, Diocletian was made commander of the prestigious corps that guarded the emperor. When Numerian died in 284, under suspicious circumstances, Diocletian was proclaimed by the troops. The assembled soldiers accused the leader of the Praetorian Guard, Arrius Aper, of having murdered the emperor, whose failing sight had rendered him almost blind. In his first act as emperor, Diocletian called for Aper to be dragged before him in chains. Drawing his sword, he plunged it into the astonished Prefect's breast. 'This man,' he said, as he withdrew the bloodied blade, 'is the murderer of Numerian.' This decisive action was just what the troops wanted. With a roar of approval, the newly-acclaimed emperor was lifted shoulder high and carried round the camp.

Despite popular acclaim, Diocletian struggled for years with the unwieldy, far-flung territories. Realising that it was now impossible for one man to rule the empire on his own, Diocletian came up with an ingenious solution. Having assigned himself an assistant, in 296 he introduced a two-tiered government. From now on there would be two Augusti and two Caesars. The empire was split into four administrative regions, two in the East and two in the West. Each would be governed by an Augustus, effectively one of two emperors, and by a Caesar, the vice-emperor. The 101 provinces were divided into 12 sections, each called a diocese. Rome was no longer considered the centre of the empire. Milan became the first city in Italy, assigned to the Augustus Maximian. Constantius the Pale, (because of his pallor) was designated Caesar and given an imperial residence in Trier. The third ruler, the Caesar Galerius, resided in the city of Sirmium, in modern-day Hungary. Diocletian ruled his quarter of the empire from his palace in Nicodemia, in Asia Minor. Concord between the rulers was maintained by the necessity that all four sign documents and edicts before they could be promulgated.

The portly Diocletian considered himself a statesman, but he was equally a shrewd military tactician. During his reign, the Roman Empire enclosed every shore of the Mediterranean Sea. From Spain to Palestine to the north of Africa, the sea was almost a Roman lake. *Mare nostrum*, or Our Sea, was how the Romans proudly referred to the waters surrounded by Roman provinces. The sea was rid of pirates, the countryside liberated from bandits. Order was restored and the economy improved dramatically. Busts of the emperor, with his protruding chin and squinting eyes, were erected in every public building.

For all the good he may have accomplished, the Christians in the empire had cause to curse the name of Diocletian. In 303, he issued an edict prohibiting Christians from practising their faith in public. This time not even a *libellus* could save them. In particular, the soldiers in the army were obliged to declare their religious sensibilities or face martyrdom.

MARCELLINUS Pope Marcellinus (296-304) did not die a martyr's death. He stood accused of handing over to the imperial authorities the Bible to be burned. Moreover, according to the Donatist heretics in northern Africa, Marcellinus was believed to have offered a pinch of incense before a pagan idol. For a Christian that was worse than selling one's grandmother to the pirates. Ironically, a year or so before the persecutions, a marble tablet had been set up in the catacombs, referring to the bishop Marcellinus of Rome for the first time by the title 'pope'. Several bishops had used the title, a diminutive of father, but this was the first time the bishop of Rome was specifically referred to as 'pope'. The first to use the title was thus the first to renege on his vows of consecration. This was a serious blow to the Christians in Rome. After a line of faithful bishops stretching back to Peter, they now had a leader who had capitulated to the treat of torture. It is unlikely that Marcellinus would have been permitted to continue as bishop of Rome, and indeed, after the persecution, Marcellinus disappears from history.

At the age of 60, Diocletian unexpectedly retired, forcing Maximian to follow suit. By 305, he had been 21 years emperor. The rulers Constantius and Galerius were promoted with the title Augustus, the positions that he and Maximian had occupied, and were left to rule alone. Part of his reason for retiring may indeed have been the public outcry against the bloodbath and slaughter of Christians. By now, the numbers had steeply risen and many people may have had friends or family members of the sect.

For nine years, Diocletian resided peacefully in his palace that he had built in Salonia, in Dalmatia. A delegation from the restless Maximian, his former co-emperor, came to find the retired emperor in his home. The ambassadors urged him to emerge from his retirement. The new Augusti were incapable of governing wisely, they argued. The former emperor shook his head and replied: 'If you could see the wonderful cauliflowers I am cultivating in my garden, you would not implore me to leave them.'

Maxentius, son of the retired emperor Maximian, was created one of the four rulers in 307. Shortly afterwards he ended the persecutions of Christians within his territories, although for whatever reason is lost in history. On 30 April 311, the co-emperor Galerius wrote to the Christian community, invoking the aid of their god in the face of a fatal illness. The Christian God did not appear to heed the frightened emperor's prayers, for Galerius died six days later.

On the horizon of history was soon to appear the man who would shape and mould Christianity irrevocably. His name was Constantine.

Born about the year 280 in what we now call Siberia, Constantine was the son of Constantius Chlorus, a military official who had been appointed Caesar by the emperor Diocletian. In 305, Contantius was promoted to be the Augustus by the emperor. He did not enjoy the new position long, for in the summer of 306, he died suddenly while on a mission to Britain. Upon his death, the troops, stationed at modern-day York, elected his 26-year-old son Constantine as Augustus.

The young Constantine decided to set up his palace in the town of Trier, at the foot of the southern Alps, where his father had ruled as Caesar. He put away his mistress and made a strategic alliance by marrying the daughter of the emperor. Constantine was now brother-in-law to Maxentius but would grow to mistrust him as the years went by. Constantine decided to go to war against his brother-in-law as rumours of Maxentius' desire to usurp his power reached his ears.

As Constantine crossed the Alps and descended with his troops into Italy, Maxentius rode out to meet him. It was the early autumn of 312. Just eight miles north of the city, at a place called Saxa Rubra, Constantine confronted his rival. Lactantus, whom Constantine later appointed tutor to his son, described how on the eve of the battle, on 27 October, Constantine had a strange dream. An unrecognised voice urged him to place a cross on the shields of his soldiers. A Christian in the army may have helped him interpret the strange portent. Years later, the official biographer of the emperor, Eusebius of Caesarea, gave a more detailed account. In broad daylight, a cross appeared in the sky, and underneath the words, *In hoc signo vinces* – under this sign you shall conquer. 'Then in his sleep the Christ of God appeared to him,' recounted Eusebius, 'with the same sign which he had seen in the heavens, and commanded him to make a likeness of that sign which he had seen in the heavens, and to use it as a safeguard in all engagements with his enemies.'

Inspired by the strange vision, Constantine placed his army under the protection of the mysterious Christ and engaged in battle.

Constantine's troops outmanoeuvred those of Maxentius, and after only a few hours of combat, the battle turned in favour of Constantine. The sturdy horses that Constantine had brought from Gaul outran the feeble horses of Maxentius, and many Numidean foot soldiers turned and fled at the sight of Constantine's ferocious troops. Maxentius raced across a bridge that began to collapse with the weight of his fleeing soldiers. As he charged, a javelin caught him in the chest. He tumbled off the bridge and his body was carried a short distance by the water, before it sank into the mud of the river bank, weighed down by the silver breastplate. A day passed before the turbulent waters subsided and Maxentius was found face downwards in the mud. The head was cut from the bloated body and stuck on a spear. The victorious Constantine entered the city.

The Senate and the Praetorian Guard had sided against Constantine, and now received the victor with apprehension. He ordered the bodyguard of the fallen emperor to disband and confiscated their barracks. To the faithful soldiers he distributed a generous bounty of money and confiscated lands.

When he had dispatched the affairs of state, he turned his mind to matters of religion. Constantine had, as early as 306, ended the persecution of Christians in his territories and restored some of their properties. He himself was at that time a sun-worshipper, a devotee of the *Sol*

Invictus, the unconquered sun. Already in 310, he claimed to have had a vision of Apollo, the sun god. Inquiring as to who might be the leader of the Christians of Rome, he was informed that it was the elderly Miltiades who had come many years earlier from Africa..

The 32-year-old emperor summoned the bishop to his lodgings in the city and assured him that he need not worry. He may have confided in the old man the story of his vision the day before the battle. Now Constantine wanted to reward this Christian God for his help, or at least show his appreciation. He assured the pope that the persecutions were over for good, both in Rome and throughout the empire. Furthermore, as a pledge of his good faith, he gave Miltiades the barracks of the imperial guard as well as contingent lands that he had received in his wife's dowry. The old residence of the Laterani family was to be transformed into his new palace, a residence worthy of the bishop of Rome. He endowed the pope with an income which would eventually amount to several million euro in today's terms. The transformation of hounded criminals into millionaires in less than a decade was astonishing, and assured the position of the popes forever at the centre of western civilisation.

In addition to an annual income and pension, the emperor may have declared his intention to build several churches in honour of the Roman saints to be built outside the city walls, over their tombs. In order not to provoke the pagans, the emperor shrewdly decided to maintain the old pagan temples. All the property confiscated seven years previously was to be restored. The stamp of the imperial ring upon the melted wax would have sealed the pact.

Miltiades did not last long. Just three months later he was dead. The perplexed Christians met in late January to elect one of their number to succeed the recipient of such singular imperial grace. The choice fell to Sylvester, one of the presbyters of the city. For the next 23 years, Sylvester seems to have charmed the emperor into ever-more generous concessions to the Christian faith.

The *Liber Pontificalis* relates with a mixture of pride and wonder the magnanimous gifts which the emperor bestowed on the new churches. Although compiled from the sixth century onwards, the 'Book of the Popes' is a collection of papal biographies. It lists the gifts of the emperor to his new ally, Sylvester. Gold and silver chalices, candlesticks, jewelled shrines and marble altars were just some of the gifts the grateful pontiff received from the emperor. Constantine made sure that his precious churches should have nothing but the best.

And yet, the emperor did not become a Christian. There were a number of reasons for this decision. In those days, many people were not baptised until near their death. There was a belief that once one was baptised there could be no excuse to sin. If one did sin, then there could no be forgiveness. Better then to live *like* a Christian, than to actually be one.

Constantine also maintained his devotion to Apollo as the sun-god, the unconquered sun, a typical characteristic of his Roman education. His mother, Helen, was a Christian and must have had some influence on her son. Indeed, mother and son were very close, as is evidenced by his support for her and his provision of a magnificent residence in the Sessorian Palace near the Lateran.

There is a medieval story that Constantine was baptised by Sylvester after being cured of leprosy, but is more likely to have been a symptom of a storyteller's over-fertile imagination rather than an accurate account of the truth. Of course, there may have been a more pragmatic reason for Constantine's hesitation to be baptised. The new emperor may not have wished to antagonise the pagan majority in the Senate, nor the large segment of the population that had chosen to continue to worship the ancient gods. With shrewd political acumen, the churches were built far from the city centre, and often outside the city walls.

In the spring of the following year, 313, Constantine met in Milan with his co-emperor Licinius (311-324), the emperor of the East. Here they devised a protocol, which ended the persecutions of the Christians and restored the properties that had been confiscated in 305. Wisely, they also granted religious liberty to any shade of belief in the empire. The pact between the two emperors was sealed by the marriage of Constantine's half-sister to Licinius. The pact was not to endure, for three years later civil war had broken out between the two emperors.

Constantine may have wished to use religion as a uniting force within the empire. He must have been dismayed when, in April of 313, a delegation arrived from the province of Africa, begging an audience with the emperor. The embassy was composed of a group of hardliners who had survived the last of the imperial persecutions. Kneeling in front of the emperor, they begged him to intervene in a dispute. Some Christians, they argued, were too lenient with those who had betrayed their faith in the face of persecution. These *lapsi*, or lapsed ones, had reneged on their faith. Rather than face excommunication or other penalties, they were absolved of their sin after a desultory penance. That, the rigorists argued, was simply not fair. After all, they had suffered and remained steadfast, regardless of the pain. Why not the others?

Constantine was initially unsure as to how he should proceed and summoned a group of bishops to Rome to debate the issue. Caelian, the bishop of Carthage, had been accused by these hardliners of being unduly soft on these *lapsi*. Constantine may have asked the bishop of

Rome for advice, but he himself presided over the assembly, and upheld the decision of the bishops when they voted in favour of Caelian. The rigorists, led by bishop Donatus from Africa, appealed the decision of the assembly of bishops. Constantine responded by summoning 33 bishops to meet in the Gallic town of Arles in August of 314. Once more the faction of Caelian won the case. Constantine was obliged to suppress the opposition, this time with force.

In 321, a law was passed, allowing the church to inherit lands and goods from bequests. This marked a significant leap forwards and augmented the already generous income from the emperor. But the emperor was facing further problems from within the Christian community. In 319 Arius, a presbyter from Alexandria in Egypt, was excommunicated by Alexander, the bishop of the city. Jesus of Nazareth, Arius argued, was created by God the Father, and therefore was inferior. In Arius' opinion, Jesus was nothing more than God wearing a human mask. Although Arius' teaching caught on in Alexandria, it caused consternation in the wider Christian world. Contemporary accounts relate that even the sailors in the port sang sea shanties which Arius had composed for them. One ecclesiastic from Alexandria grumbled:

Ask a baker for a loaf of bread and he will tell you how Father is greater than the Son. Try to buy fish and the fisherwoman will tell you the Son is obedient to the Father. There is nothing but madness in the city.

Eventually Constantine was obliged to intervene. He had no desire to see his newly-adopted religion rent asunder by faction fighting. The emperor realised that the local synods of bishops that he had convoked at Rome and Arles had been fruitless. This time he summoned the bishops of the whole empire to Nicea, in modern-day Turkey, to discuss and resolve the issue. To ensure their swift and safe passage, Constantine accorded them the travel rights reserved to the senatorial class. They could travel by litter and have fresh horses at every changing post.

The bishops, over 250 of them, hurried to the council at which the emperor had chosen to preside. The emperor arrived at Nicea in June, two weeks after the bishops had commenced their meeting. Packed into a large hall, they awaited the audience to be granted by Constantine.

Dressed in a purple mantle and with a crown of gold laurels on his head, the emperor rose from his gilt throne. Enormous fans of peacock feathers stood on either side of him. 'Dissent within the church,' he told the assembled bishops, 'is worse than war.' In clear terms, he elaborated his desire that the Arian controversy be resolved immediately. There would be little patience with the philological arguments that had caused this rift.

Leaving the debate to the bishops, under the presidency of Hosius, the Spanish bishop of Cordoba, the emperor impressed on them his desire for a swift resolution of the matter. Six months earlier he had executed Licinius, the co-emperor, for suspected treason. Now, at the age of 45, Constantine was the sole ruler of East and West. Still, he was beset with problems. In 326, he had his wife Fausta and their son Crispus strangled for some crime, now lost to history. Rumours at the time hinted at an incestuous affair. He had already named the old city of Byzantium on the Bosphorus as his capital, and in 327 he sailed to his new city, renamed Constantinople. Three years later, amid glorious pageantry, the city of Constantine was dedicated. The emperor was never to set foot in Rome again.

In Rome, Pope Sylvester tried to hide his dismay. But there was little he could do. Constantine was gone, and it was important to make the best of it.

On the last cold day of the year 335, Sylvester ended his pontificate. As he looked back over his stewardship, he could be proud of the manner in which he had wooed and courted the emperor. Not only had his diocese benefited financially, but also Sylvester's tact and forbearance had ensured that the Arian and other heretics had been almost vanquished. It may have been as well for Sylvester to die when he did. The city of Rome had been embellished by several new churches, most notably the basilica which rose over the shrine of Peter's grave on the Vatican Hill. Constantine himself had dictated that the basilica was henceforth to be the model of a Christian church for worship, its long rectangular shape housing the people who looked eastwards towards an altar where the priests offered the Eucharist.

Assuming the title *Pontifex Maximus*, the high Priest, Constantine gave orders, as only the emperor could, to close the cemetery at the Vatican Hill. He set his soldiers to fill in the small cubicles that covered the lower slopes of the hill. On top of these, Constantine's solders built a huge platform on which to build the great edifice. The modern-day visitors to St Peter's are scarcely aware, when they enter the imposing basilica, that they are walking over the necropolis, or city of the dead, destroyed by Constantine.

The following year, in 336, the rift with the Arians was about to be concluded. Agreement had been reached between Arius' supporters and the orthodox Christians. On the day before Arius was to celebrate his first Mass in public for over a decade, he unexpectedly dropped dead. Although rumours of poisoning circulated, nothing was proved. This dramatic turn of events was to have tragic consequences for several centuries to come. The rivals regrouped and this time their opposition to each other was even fiercer.

While on a visit to Helenopolis, in April of 337, a city he had founded in memory of his mother, Constantine began to feel unwell. For years he had worn a wig and make-up, a style adopted from the Eastern rulers which he admired. The make-up camouflaged his pale complexion. The seriousness of his condition was made evident when he decided that the time had come for his baptism. Throughout his life, theological niceties had largely been lost on Constantine. He started back for Constantinople, but upon arriving at Nicodemia, he summoned Eusebius, the bishop of the city, and in the presence of the imperial court, descended into the pool of baptism. The fact that Eusebius was Arian was of little importance to the emperor, who was clearly dying. Eight days later, on the Feast of Pentecost and still wearing the white garment of the newly baptised, Constantine expired. He was 57 years old.

The whole empire joined in the official mourning. The rule of Constantine had lasted 31 years. His body was placed in a golden casket and brought to Constantinople. There, at the centre of the great throne room of the imperial palace, the coffin was placed in a position of honour, watched over by his faithful bodyguards. It was to lie there for almost 12 weeks, as the three sons of Constantine vied as to who would succeed their father. Constantius, the eldest son, produced a forged will, purportedly written by his father, claiming that the other sons had poisoned him. The bishop Eusebius had most likely composed the letter. As an Arian sympathiser, he undoubtedly favoured Constantius who shared his Arian beliefs.

Finally, the great games to accompany the burial took place and the body of the emperor was borne to its final resting place, the circular stone Mausoleum of the Twelve Apostles. In 12 niches surrounding the porphyry sarcophagus stood statues of the apostles. Constantine, Eusebius of Caesarea noted, saw himself as the 13th apostle. In the last years of his life, Constantine often referred to himself as Equal to the Apostles. Dressed in garments of purple and gold, the embalmed corpse was lowered into the stone sarcophagus and the lid was pushed into place.

No amount of hyperbole can exaggerate the effect that Constantine had on the Christians. Everyone wants to be associated with success. As the imposing churches with their sumptuous decorations rose around the empire, it was natural that more and more people attached themselves to the community that had won the emperor's favour.

Following the death of the emperor, male members in the line to power were almost all exterminated. Rumours circulated the city that the emperor had been poisoned by his half-brother, Julius Constantus. Within six months, both the brothers of the late emperor, and most of their sons, had been assassinated on the orders of Constantius. The three sons of Constantine survived the bloodletting. Following almost a year of intrigue after their father's death, with both his brothers dead, Constantius was the sole emperor. He realised that he would need a co-emperor to rule in the West. Skirmishes on the Danube frontiers indicated further and more serious trouble. Yet Constantius was obliged to return to the East to continue a war against the Persians. Searching within his family proved difficult, as so many in the male line had been murdered years earlier. Eventually his choice, limited as it was, fell on his 23-year-old cousin Julian.

Flavius Claudius Julianus was the son of Contantine the Great's half-brother, the first to die in the bloodletting of 337. Julian had only been five when his father was murdered. Even if Julian did hold the emperor responsible for his father's death, there was nothing that could be done. At least he should be grateful for this delayed inheritance.

Julian was summoned from Athens, where he had passed two pleasant years studying philosophy. Much to his surprise, he was charged by his cousin with the obligation of defending the empire in the West.

Those who knew Julian were anxious about his ability. The handsome young man was an intellectual with a greater love for Greek philosophy than for Roman military tactics. Indeed, he scarcely spoke Latin at all. Christians were all the more worried by his firm dislike of their faith. There would no longer be the luxury of faction fighting between the orthodox and the Arians. Constantius died in battle against the Persians at the beginning of 361. Now Julian was the sole emperor of the East and West. He immediately renounced his Christian faith and reverted to his devotion to the pagan gods. Julian ordered the reopening of all the pagan temples that Constantine had closed between 324 and his death in 337. The priests of Jupiter and Venus, with their stern entourage, came back from their humiliating exile. Julian himself officiated at public sacrifices, his head covered as a sign of respect for the ancient gods.

Not wishing to create new martyrs, Julian did not outlaw Christianity. Indeed he restored most of their properties. He may well have suspected that, once more allowed to flourish the Christians would destroy each other. But in this he was to be mistaken. 'The Christians look after our poor better than we do ourselves,' Julian complained reproachfully to the members of his court. The Christian community throughout the empire breathed a collective sigh of relief when they heard that the emperor had been killed following a battle with the Persians in Mesopotamia in June 363. Centuries later, a zealous Christian chronologer would have the dying emperor draw his last breath and exclaim, 'So, thou hast won, O Nazarene.' Julian was 32 and had been emperor for one year and eight months.

Julian, called 'the Apostate' by the resentful Christians, was the last of the royal house of Constantine, and had no heirs or relatives to succeed him. The new emperor, Jovian, was an orthodox Christian, and immediately on his accession, abrogated any laws of Julian which were held to be offensive to the Christian community. His reign proved to be brief, and just seven months after his accession, he was found dead in his apartment at Antioch.

In the autumn of the year 366, things changed radically for the Christian community. On 1 October 366, the deacon Damasus was elected. Almost immediately riots broke out, as a group of Christians in the city had wanted the deacon Ursinius to be their bishop. Ursinius was elected by a mob and consecrated in the Liberian basilica, recently favoured by the anti-pope Felix. The followers of Damasus climbed onto the roof of the church, tore off the tiles of the roof and hurled them onto the worshippers below. The walls were splattered with the blood of the injured and the dead. By sunset, 137 corpses were strewn on the marble floor of the basilica. DAMASUS AND URSINIUS

Damasus was forced to petition the Prefect of the City for help, the first recorded incident of a pope requesting help from the civil authorities. The prefect intervened and Ursinius was exiled from the city. A year later he returned, but as street violence broke out, he was expelled from Rome once more.

The Ursinian faction continued to make trouble for Damasus. In 371, the pope was obliged to appeal to the emperor to clear his name from charges of adultery which Ursinius had brought against him. This time the emperor Gratian, who had succeeded Valentinian in 375, exiled Ursinius to Milan, where he lived in confinement until his death in 381. Damasus continued to excite passion amongst his supporters and opponents and 44 bishops were summoned to a synod where he was acquitted of the crime of adultery. The contemporary pagan writer, Ammianus Marcellinus, referred to Damasus acidly as 'the ladies' ear-tickler'.

Damasus proved to be an able administrator. As his secretary, he chose a young priest, Jerome, and after only two years assigned him an enormous task. Realising that the majority of people could no longer understand the Greek scriptures, nor indeed the Hebrew scriptures, Damasus commissioned Jerome to translate the scriptures into Latin, the language of the people in the West.

Pleading his need to consult the sources directly and indeed to learn Hebrew, Jerome set sail from Italy with a group of aristocratic ladies for the Holy Land. There he worked for the remaining years of his life, eventually settling in Bethlehem where he remained until his death. For the next 12 centuries, the Latin text produced by Jerome was to remain the definitive version in the West. In the meantime, malicious tongues in Rome put about the rumour that the handsome Jerome had been banished by Damasus, jealous of his success with the ladies. Certainly, even in Bethlehem, people noted the close relationship Jerome had with a certain widow, Paula, who had accompanied him from Rome.

For almost 1,500 years, Jerome's majestic Latin would be used in every liturgy of the church. Where monks and nuns gathered in stone vaulted chapels, or exuberantly carved churches, they sang the psalms painstakingly translated by Jerome on the sandy fringes of the Judean desert. As his Latin Bible was copied in countless monasteries throughout Europe, the slip of a quill often ensured that small inaccuracies crept into the text. One famous example was the description of how Moses descended from Mount Sinai having received the Ten Commandments from God. The original text described the radiant face of Moses. Jerome's text misinterpreted the word *ray* for *horn*. In depictions until the 16th century, artists continued to show Moses, as in Michaelangelo's famous statue for the tomb of Julius II, with two innocuous horns sprouting from his forehead.

When, in the 16th century, the reformer Martin Luther realised how many errors there were in the scriptures, he undertook to do for the German people what Jerome had done for the Latin speakers of his day. Luther worked rapidly to present the Bible in the German language that people of his day could understand. Just as the monks had diffused the 'Vulgate Bible', so now the recently invented printing press ensured wide dissemination of Luther's Bible throughout German-speaking lands.

Damasus meanwhile continued to pour his energy into the reorganisation of the diocese, building churches and amplifying the papal archives. In order to increase devotion to the martyrs, Damasus repaired several of the galleries of the Roman catacombs, where for almost three centuries Christians had been buried.

Like their pagan ancestors, the Christians of Rome considered the burial of their dead a most sacred duty. For reasons of hygiene and space, the law prohibited burial within the city precincts. The Christians of the early centuries adopted the pagan practice of burial in underground chambers, or in cemeteries above ground. While the pagans cremated their dead, the Christians, respecting the body as the creation of God, chose the practice of burial. At first the Christians, prizing their equality before God, buried their dead in narrow tunnels or galleries. Little served to distinguish the wealthy from the poor – all were the same in death. In the third century, the wealthy families of the community constructed small chambers, or *cubiculae*, where several members of one family could be buried together. Due to the dark, cramped space, art was simple and perfunctory. It served, however, to record the memory of the dead, and with simple biblical scenes, to encourage the living.

From the earliest times, records tell us how burial of the dead was a duty of the whole community. Tertullian, the third-century theologian from Africa, relates how collections were made regularly to pay for the burial of members of the community. At the beginning of the third century, Pope Zephyrinus placed his deacon Callistus in charge of a large underground cemetery. The administrator oversaw a team of *fossores*, or gravediggers. These men were responsible for the excavation of the burial places, and often combined their energy with engineering skills, so that several galleries could be laid one above the other. Although not unique to Rome, the greatest number of catacombs is found at the precincts of the imperial city and to this day over 60 have been explored systematically by archaeologists.

In general, such cemeteries were excavated below the property of wealthy Christian families. Most cemeteries contained the body of several martyrs venerated for the witness of their lives to the point of death. Such tombs became the sites of pilgrimages. In time, after the end of the imperial persecutions of Christians in the early fourth century, special churches or funerary halls were built above or near the saints' tombs. The majority, however, of those buried in the catacombs were simple Christians, little distinguished in death but all united in a hope of eternal life. In order to deepen devotion to the Roman ancestors, who almost by definition had been faithful to the bishops of Rome, Damasus composed various inscriptions in their honour. The names of the martyrs Felicity, Perpetua, Alexander, Agnes, Marcellus, Crysogonos amongst others were almost household names and Damasus commemorated the tales of their martyrdoms in simple Latin epitaphs. So impressed was he by his own efforts that he commissioned one of the finest stone-cutters in Rome, Filiocalus, to carve his poems on marble tablets which he then placed in the catacombs.

The number of pilgrims from outside Rome was continually increasing. The shrewd Damasus may have used the verses that he wrote to impress the visitors. Veneration of the saints could inspire admiration of the present-day bishop of Rome, who took such care of their mortal remains. As the visitors filed passed the tomb of a 12-year-old martyr, Agnes, they could read the marble tablet on which was inscribed a poem commemorating her heroic virtue. Damasus recorded that, during an imperial persecution, the young maiden ran from her nurse's lap to embrace martyrdom.

> Fame tells that, while her parents were carrying her off with lugubrious songs, the young girl broke away from her mother's apron strings upon hearing the trumpet sound which heralded the rage and threats of the tyrant.

Perhaps because of the way in which his episcopate had been contested, Damasus robustly developed his claims to primacy within the Christian community. There could only be one bishop in a diocese, he wrote, and the thought must have occurred to him that one overall bishop in charge of the bishops would be no bad thing either. It would certainly do away with the need to appeal to the civil authorities in dealing with internal matters.

Nonetheless, Damasus continued to court the emperor. He was astute enough to realise the importance of having the emperor on his side. With the election of Theodosius as emperor of the East in 379, Damasus found an enthusiastic ally and supporter for his papacy. A native of Spain, Theodosius took the side of the orthodox Christians against the Arians. Damasus pressed his advantage, and took every opportunity to meet with the emperor and flatter him for his support. On 28 February 380, the emperor issued a decree that established Christianity once and for all the state religion:

> Let all the inhabitants of the empire follow the form of religion handed down by the apostle Peter to the Romans, and now followed by Bishop Damasus and Peter of Alexandria.

Christianity became the official religion of the empire. In the East however, where they were most numerous, Theodosius actively persecuted the Arian Christians.

The occasion for rejoicing in Rome was rather spoilt by a declaration of the bishops at the Council of Constantinople held a year later by imperial decree. The city was named as the second most important See, or diocese, in the empire after Rome. Damasus was wise enough not to complain too loudly, as the emperor had given his approval to the declaration. None the less, he was aware that the emperor paid less and less attention to Rome, the former capital of the empire. He took consolation in composing more verses in honour of St Peter and St Paul, from whom he claimed to inherit his apostolic authority. Damasus expired on 11 December 384, in his 80th year. Although he believed that Rome was the centre of the Christian Church, he must have realised that the most influential bishop now lived in Milan.

When the Arian bishop Auxentius died, the Christians in Milan gathered to choose a new bishop who would reconcile the Arians with the orthodox Christians. Among the clergy, they sought in vain. Almost in desperation, they turned to Ambrose, the City Prefect of Milan. The young official protested that he had not yet been baptised, but that did not deter them. Within a week, he had been baptised, ordained a presbyter and consecrated a bishop. The choice was a happy one. Ambrose combined his civic skills and pious devotion with dedication to the

Christians he served. He was outstanding in his service to the poor, especially in times of pestilence. A persuasive orator, he successfully urged the wealthy to support those in need. People responded to his gentle character. An eloquent orator, he also became a popular preacher, and the cathedral was packed on the occasions that he celebrated Mass.

All the good that he had achieved was almost wiped out in an unfortunate brush with the co-emperor Theodosius.

Late in the autumn of 389, in the Greek city of Thessalonica, the captain of the imperial guard was killed during an outbreak of mob violence. Upon hearing the news at Milan, Theodosius ordered the troops to retaliate, and make an example of the ringleaders. When Ambrose came to hear of the emperor's decision, he pleaded with him to be lenient. The emperor did in fact countermand the order but it was too late. Some weeks later, when crowds gathered in the Hippodrome in Thessalonica, the garrison attacked the spectators. Seven thousand people were massacred in one day.

There was outrage throughout the empire as the story spread. Ambrose wrote to the emperor, informing him that as a result of his action, he was excommunicated, 'for,' he noted, ' the emperor is not above the authority of the bishop'. Theodosius approached Ambrose privately but the bishop refused to see him until he presented himself on the steps of the cathedral of Milan, dressed in sackcloth, his head completely shaven and covered with ashes.

It was an extraordinary change in affairs that an emperor would kneel at the foot of a bishop, begging forgiveness. Two years later, Theodosius hammered the final nail in the coffin of the old gods when he issued an imperial decree closing all the pagan temples. The Christian Church was given the income and the properties of the pagan places of worship and the temple priests were made redundant.

Theodosius faced grave problems. The following summer, his co-emperor Valentian was murdered, and Theodosius was forced to behead a usurper, Eugenius. This time there was no objection from Bishop Ambrose. These, after all, reasoned the bishop of Milan, were the affairs of state. On 17 January 395, Theodosius died at the age of 50 after only four months as sole emperor of East and West. He was buried in a vast mausoleum overlooking the city of Ravenna.

The end of the Roman Empire in the West was in sight.

CHAPTER FOUR

The Empire Collapses

INNOCENT • LEO I

At his death, Theodosius left two sons to succeed him, the 17-year-old Arcadius and the 10-year-old Honorius. Shortly before his demise, Theodosius placed his sons in the care of Stilicho, the son of a Vandal chieftain, and the husband of Theodosius' niece.

The empire was divided. To Arcadius went the East, while Honorius became the emperor of the West.

Taking advantage of the change in government, the Goths in the empire, led by the 25-year-old chieftan Alaric, revolted. The Goths, like the Vandals, were a tribe that lived just beyond the northern confines of the Roman Empire. The word *vandal* has been handed down to us, echoing through the centuries the destruction wrought by the savage tribe. Stilicho may have bought peace on behalf of his young charges with enormous bribes. Alaric led his troops down through Greece, where they plundered Corinth, Argos and Sparta. The great city of Athens was spared only by the payment of a huge ransom.

Alarmed at the success of Alaric, the emperor Arcadius granted the leader of the Goths the prefecture of Illyrium. Alaric wanted the province as a home for his people and in return for this he promised peace. To further appease the Goths, the emperor Arcadius promised Alaric that he would include him in a planned war against the Persian Empire.

Horses' hooves thundered down the Via Aurelia that led southwards through Italy, headed for Rome. It was early autumn of the year 408. Arcadius had died in the previous May. Alaric was informed that as the emperor was dead, the war against the Persians would not proceed. The infuriated Goths demanded the war and they descended on Rome to pursue their bellicose ambition. They had promised to join the Roman army to fight against Persia from which they had expected rich spoils. Now, since the Romans had broken their part of the bargain, the Goths demanded some form of restitution.

Honorius had executed General Stilicho on 23 August. The paranoid emperor had accused him of conspiring with Alaric to take over the empire. When they arrived outside the Aurelian Walls, the Goths taunted the barricaded Romans and pitched their camp around the city walls. Roman archers picked out the invaders with rapid shots from narrow windows in the walls and turrets. Within weeks, however, the unprepared city began to buckle. Rome had not been invaded for over a thousand years. The threat was as much psychological as physical. By mid-December, plague had been reported in the city and stories spread of mothers eating their offspring. Almost at the point of despair, the Roman Senate sent out two delegates, Basil and John, to negotiate with Alaric.

The envoys were shown into the tent of the Gothic king and they listened incredulously to the terms Alaric offered. He demanded an indemnity for the cancellation of the war against Persia. Indignantly, John the Tribune protested that the people would band together in a defence of their city. 'The thicker the grass, the easier to scythe,' replied the Goth impassively.

There would be no discussion, the king continued. He required 5,000 pounds of gold, 30,000 pounds of silver, 4,000 pounds of silk, 3,000 pounds of pepper and 3,000 hides.

'And what will you give us in return?' asked the envoys.

'Your lives,' came the reply.

The envoys withdrew to report to the Senate. Within a few days, litters loaded with the spoils Alaric demanded were brought to the camp of the Goths.

Two years later, in August AD 410, the Goths returned. This time, they did not have to stay outside for long. The horrific memory of two winters previously was still fresh. A traitor, the familiar visitor of history, was lurking close at hand. Shortly after the midnight hour had been called at the Salarian Gate, an unnamed betrayer slipped out of the city and opened its doors. The unkempt hoards, led by Alaric, swept in. For the first time in 800 years, the city was occupied by a foreign power.

The Goths did not stay in Rome for long. In three days they got what they wanted and left. Their wagons, loaded with gold, silver, jewels and expensive cloths, lumbered northwards.

INNOCENT Pope Innocent (401-417) was not in the city during the attack. He had written to the emperor Honorius holed up in Ravenna, rebuking him for his cowardice in not helping. Believing it his duty to intervene between Alaric and Honorius, Innocent had left for the court of the emperor. Innocent must have wondered which would be the better option, an Arian barbarian as a ruler, or a lazy, incompetent emperor. Deep down he knew the damage could have been much worse. Most of the churches had been spared. The invaders had been Christian Arians who respected things dedicated to God. One story that circulated concerned a Roman matron who was urged to yield herself to a Gothic intruder. Pleading her devotion to God, she begged for protection. The Goth brought her to a church and paid a priest to keep watch over her and restore her to her family when the sack was over.

In Bethlehem, the elderly Jerome, former secretary to

Pope Damasus, was still working on the translation of the Bible into the vernacular. He heard the news from his native city with disbelief. 'Words fail me,' he sobbed. 'The city which took captive the whole world has itself been captured.'

The Gothic army continued their southwards march through Italy. Three times Alaric had brought Rome to its knees. As the Roman scouts watched the barbarians disappear into the distance, they fervently prayed never to see them again.

A few days later, scouts arrived back in Rome with an extraordinary report. While resting at Cosenza, Alaric had taken to bed with a fever. Potions and medicines were of no use. Within days, the king of the Goths was dead. The chiefs placed the corpse in three coffins, one of lead, one of wood and one of gold and prepared a place of burial. They diverted the course of the nearby river, and in the mud laid the body of their king. They then broke the dam, allowing the waters of the river to flow over it, obliterating his resting place.

Rome continued to be a prey to attacks by her enemies. The empire in the West tottered towards a humiliating extinction. In 432, the emperor Theodosius I authorised the payment of a large annual tribute to the Huns, yet another invading tribe from the north. For years, rich families had sent money, rather than sons to the army. As a result, it had grown slack, and lacked the discipline that had made Rome the *caput mundi*, head of the world.

In 452, the Huns, led by Attila, threatened to invade the city once more. Leo I (440-461) had already been pope for 12 reasonably tranquil years. The people turned to him as their leader. The pope left the city and met the Huns 70 miles north of Rome. The papal convoy probably consisted of hoards of gold that the pope hoped would dissuade the invaders. The ruse worked, and Leo

LEO I

returned to Rome triumphant. Somewhere along the way home, a story had begun to circulate that Attila pledged not to invade because Peter and Paul had appeared over the head of the pope, uttering threats of dire recriminations.

Two years later, Attila died suddenly and the power of the Huns was broken. But another barbarian army was ready to attack. Three years later Pope Leo was successful in persuading Gaiseric the Vandal to spare the city.

Pope Leo succeeded in reorganising the Roman church on imperial lines, which was to have far-reaching consequences for the papacy and the church at large. At the Council of Chalcedon, held in Greece in 451, the bishops voted that Chalcedon should be raised to the honour of a patriarchate, equal in status and privilege to Rome. Pope Leo, who had not travelled to Chalcedon to participate in the council, instructed his ambassadors not to sign that particular canon. He was already highly respected by the bishops and won a standing ovation from them when a letter he had written on theology was read aloud. 'Peter has spoken through the mouth of Leo,' the bishops had applauded. Leo decided to bide his time.

The end came in 476. The Germanic tribes that had swarmed through the Italian peninsula were in complete control. Their leader, Odoacer, deposed the 12-year- old emperor, Romulus Augustulus, who had ruled for just one year. The glorious days of the Roman Empire were over.

CHAPTER FIVE

Gregory the Great

JOHN I • GREGORY THE GREAT

PELAGIUS

The terms *dark*, or *middle*, are sometimes used to define the period roughly between the pontificate of Gregory the Great, and the early 15th century Renaissance in the West. They are inaccurate terms, as they do not express the richness and unique qualities of these centuries. During that period, it was the Christian Church that preserved civilisation in mainland Europe. The monasteries came into their own as places of learning. Monasticism was a movement that had its origins in Egypt in the fourth century. People had left the cities in order to spend time, often the rest of their lives, in contemplation and prayer in the desert. For reasons of security, the individuals banded together in small groups that became known as monasteries. In the fifth century, the practice spread to the West. St Benedict of Nursia, founder of monasticism in the West, was born at Nursia in 480, just outside Rome. At the beginning of a rule that he composed for his followers, he stated that his wish was 'to found a school for the Lord's service, where the fainthearted will not be dismayed, and the stout-hearted may still have something for which to strive'.

In the sixth century, the monks founded schools, which were influential in all areas of learning. Developing the art of writing and illuminating manuscripts, they contributed to a flowering of the arts. Not content with simply copying the Bible, they furnished their libraries with the pagan classics as well as Christian writings. In the metalwork shops, the monks made exquisite chalices and ciboria for use in the liturgy.

The barbarian activities in central Europe wiped out

scores of centres of learning. Even the art of writing seemed threatened. Ireland in particular contributed enormously to the restoration of civilisation, as monks built monasteries and abbeys, many of which survive to the present day. Less than 150 years since Patrick brought Christianity – and also writing – to Ireland, Irish monks migrated southwards. The Saxons soon joined them. Where they found villages and towns destroyed by the invaders, they set up a monastery. As the years passed, the monasteries, which were so effectively run, became rich. It resembled a modern co-operative. The pooling of resources not only offered defence from further invasion, but also permitted the people economic growth. The Irish were noted for their zeal, and the Saxons for their practicality. All of these owed their allegiance to their leader, or abbot. But they also proudly boasted that they were the devoted servants of the pope in Rome. Indeed, several popes in history were originally monks. Countless towns and cities in Europe preserve the name of their monastic founders – Gall of Sant Gallen, Killian of Wurtzburg, Feargal of Salzburg who were just some of the lights of the Dark Ages. These men – few women travelled – referred to their self-imposed exiled from their homeland as a white martyrdom and Europe was to remain in debt to these men for centuries to come.

In the second year of his reign, Pope John I (523-526) JOHN I commissioned a Greek-speaking monk, Dionysius Exigous, to compile a calendar of the saints. Dionysius set about his task with enthusiasm and soon produced an up-to-date list of all the feast days of the saints as they occurred throughout the year. When this had been completed, he set about examining the formula of the days and months of the year. Julius Caesar had devised the calendar 500 years earlier. The months were measured by the moon, the year was measured by the sun. Dionysius suggested to the pope that the calculation of the year be changed. Dates were usually given *ab urbe condita*, from the foundation of the city of Rome over a thousand years earlier. He suggested that history be remodelled. Henceforth, all history should be marked as time before the birth of Christ or as time after it. *Anno Domini* was the year of the Lord. Therefore, all time could be measured according to this central event in the history of salvation. In this way Dionysius could calculate the year in which he found himself as the year 525 since the birth of Christ. He had no way of measuring a neutral period and a thousand years were to pass before the Arabs gave the numeral zero to Europe.

When the pope gave his approval for the change to the way in which the years were to be measured, he changed the course of history. From now on, every time a date was written, using Roman numerals, and later Arab numerals, it would be as a result of the permission of the pope, granted to an obscure monk in the year 525 *Anno Domini*.

GREGORY   Waters swirled around the street corners. Citizens scrambled to the roofs of their houses. The muddy brown waters of the river Tiber had flooded Rome. Over one-and-a-half centuries had passed since the emperor had visited the city. The aqueducts had fallen into disrepair. The public fountains and monuments were badly neglected. Nobody seemed to care about the fate of the city, once hailed as centre of the Roman universe.

The citizens flocked to their bishop in place of an imperial administrator. They turned to him for help in times of invasion, and invoked his assistance in repairing the water supply.

In Gregory, they found their best hope so far. Gregory was the great-grandson of Pope Felix III who had died in 492. He was also probably the nephew of Pope Agapetus who had died in 536. More important than family connections was his career prior to becoming pope.

Gregory was born in 540, into a wealthy patrician family. As a young man he enrolled in the civil service and quickly rose through the honorary ranks. In his late twenties he was appointed to the prestigious post of *Prefectus Urbae*, Prefect of the City. In modern-day terms, this would be something akin to being appointed Lord Mayor of New York. Democracy in those days was unheard of in the empire. In his early thirties he decided to resign and become a monk. His family home on the Caelian Hill was converted into a monastery and Gregory founded other monasteries on other family estates. However, he was not long retired from the world when Pope Pelagius asked him to leave the monastery and ordained PELAGIUS him a deacon. The pope wanted him to go as his *apocrisiarios*, or ambassador, to the emperor's court at Constantinople. Reluctantly he departed for the capital, determined never to learn Greek, and his contribution to court life was minimal. He was allowed return to Rome in 586, where he was appointed Secretary of State to Pope Pelagius. On the latter's death in 590, Gregory returned to his monastery. Less than three months latter, he was elected to succeed the pope, the first monk to become pope. It was a post he did not seek, nor want. In fact, he delayed for several months in sending the letter of request to the Emperor Maurice, without which his election as pope could not be confirmed.

Gregory turned out to be a wise ruler. His service as Prefect of Rome stood to him. He was able to deal effectively with the administration of the church. The new pope involved himself in everything, from corn prices in Africa to the appointment of bishops in neighbouring sees. The archives of the Apostolic See contain scores of letters in which Gregory offers detailed advice. He also had a practical interest in the well-being of the city, and when plague and pestilence visited, he organised penitential processions to invoke God's intervention. These were backed up by the distribution of food and clothes to victims of the plague.

An eighth-century Anglo-Saxon text records a story about Gregory, which is most probably apocryphal. It is worth repeating, however, as it allows us into the mind of the English in the Dark Ages.

While he was still abbot of the monastery on the Caelian Hill, he was walking through the market place with his secretary. They saw two fair-haired, blue-eyed youths in chains, waiting to be sold as slaves. Gregory, not perhaps used to seeing fair-complexioned youths among the swarthy Romans, asked his secretary from whence the boys may have come.

'Angles sunt,' came the reply, 'They are from Anglia.'

'Non angles, sed angeles sunt,' quipped Gregory brightly, 'They are not Angles, but angels!'

Taken aback by his superior's benign observation, the secretary hastened to inform him that the people that lived in Anglia, in present-day England, were pagans. Six years after his election as pope, Gregory may have remembered the event. He dispatched his secretary to England to convert the natives. 'Destroy as few pagan temples as possible,' he counselled his assistant. 'Only destroy their idols, sprinkle them with holy water, build altars and put the relics in the buildings.' His advice was well heeded, and may well have guaranteed the success of the mission. The obedient secretary is now venerated in England as St Augustine of Canterbury, the monk who brought Christianity to the south of England.

Although at the beginning of his pontificate Gregory seemed ill at ease with his new responsibilities, gradually he came to assume the role with ease and confidence. In the face of civil unrest, he was forced to intervene on behalf of the population who regularly were subject to raids. Describing himself as the 'servant of the servants of God', he oversaw with considerable success the pacification of Italy and the renewal of prosperity. His firm yet gentle administration enhanced the prestige of the bishops of Rome for centuries to come.

Upon his death, at the relatively young age of 46, he was buried in St Peter's Basilica. On his tomb were incised the simple words, 'The Consul of God'.

CHAPTER 6

A Fire from the East

GREGORY III • STEPHEN II

ADRIAN • LEO III

In the mid-seventh century, the followers of the Prophet Muhammad moved north-westwards from Arabia into central Europe. They were determined to convert the masses to the teachings of the Prophet, as well as conquer new lands. Sweeping through Palestine, Syria, Mesopotamia, Egypt and the north of Africa, the fierce Muslim warriors extinguished the venerable Jewish and Christian communities. They set fire to the great churches and synagogues. Gilt statues of silver and gold were carried off and the sacred books were torn to shreds and burned on bonfires in the town squares.

The monarchs of Europe heard with growing apprehension the fresh dispatches from their scouts. One breathless envoy described the invaders as 'the wrath of God'.

The Prophet Muhammad was born around 570, the son of a poor merchant of the city of Mecca in Arabia. Muhammad's father died before the child was born, and his mother died six years later. The young Muhammad was bought up by an uncle. His earliest task was to care for the camels which crossed the desert with passengers and other cargo. On his trips he came in contact with the Jews and Christians, and listened eagerly to the stories and tales they told of a great God who promised salvation from the selfishness of sin.

Of rather short stature, Muhammad was described by contemporaries as swarthy, with graceful, long fingers. His long dark hair he wore plaited on the crown of his head. At the age of 40, he had a divine experience and was convinced that he had been called to preach the message of Allah to the world. For Muhammad, Allah was the all-powerful God. He traced his religious lineage back to Abraham, the father of the Jews, and Ishmael, one of Abraham's sons.

Muhammad claimed that the Archangel Gabriel taught him about Allah during a series of revelations that would continue for 23 years. These teachings he memorised and later dictated as the Koran, the book sacred to his followers. Muhammad denounced the selfish merchants of Medina, a city 300 kilometres to the north of Mecca. Earnestly he urged them to sell their surplus possessions and give alms to the poor. The merchants were ill-disposed to listen to the ravings of a lunatic who had taken to wrapping himself in blankets to deliver his strange prophecies. Moreover, he had offended them by criticising the temple of Kabul, which he claimed was full of idols.

Early in 622, a band of assassins was sent by some of the merchants to murder the Prophet, probably from the merchants who felt threatened by his message. Alerted to their arrival by a sound from the courtyard of his home, he and his family managed to escape and fled north to the city of Medina. A year later, in 623, Muhammad sent a force to attack a caravan, to provide him with funds for his new mission. Flushed with success and money, Muhammad and his followers undertook a bolder attack on a thousand Meccans at the desert oasis of Badr. A series of daring skirmishes brought him nearer and nearer his native city, which he openly condemned for its public idolatry. In political terms he was also aware of the continued threat of violence to his followers. In 629, an army of 10,000 soldiers faithful to Muhammad laid the city under siege. When after some weeks Mecca fell to him, it became the centre of his new faith. Marching into the temple, he pointed his stick at the 360 statues of idols which stood on plinths. At the Prophet's words of condemnation, the idols fell to the ground smashing into thousands of pieces. The inhabitants were given four months grace to convert to the religion of Muhammad or face the consequences.

Now that the Prophet of Allah, as Muhammad called himself, was a ruler, he needed to apply some regulations to the faith of his followers. He called his faithful companions Muslims, the ones who submit to Allah. Accordingly, Muhammad devised a brief set of rules which were to become the five pillars of Islam.

The devotees of Allah were obliged to acknowledge the might of God. Five times between sunrise and sunset they were to face Mecca and bow their heads to the ground. They were to give alms to the poor and during the autumn month of Ramadan, they were to fast between sunrise and sunset. At least once in their lifetime they were to undertake a pilgrimage to the city of Mecca, birthplace of the Prophet of Allah.

At first Islam was noted for its toleration. The Prophet respected both Jews and Christians as fellow descendants of their common father, Abraham. As long as they were willing to pay a tax, the *jizya*, and contribute to the coffers of Islam the *kharaj* land tax, Jews and Christians could live in peace. Indeed, the Prophet was willing to protect all those who paid such a tax. To underline the close link between Islam and the followers of Jesus, Muhammad had written in the holy book of the Koran that Christians were closest to them 'because they are free'. Slavery was, in the ancient world, the lowest form of degradation possible.

The events of Muhammad's life did not happen in a vacuum. After decades of Persian incursions, the Byzantine Empire was in chaos. The usurper Phocas had taken the throne in Constantinople. The Persians, seizing the opportunity caused by the Byzantines' disarray, had begun making inroads into Palestine. In the spring of 614, the Persian army captured Jerusalem, putting hundreds of citizens to the sword. The victors carried off the most precious relics of Jesus, including what was believed to have been the wooden beams of the cross on which he died.

In 633, Muhammad led his troops into Syria and Palestine, to fight the remnants of the Byzantine army. In rapid succession, Damascus, Antioch, Bethlehem, Jerusalem and Alexandria toppled in the face of the Muslim onslaught. In some places, however, the Muslims were welcomed as more desirable rulers than their Byzantine masters. The nimble nomadic horsemen ripped through the imperial army that tried in vain to protect the ancient towns and cities. Islam's success had changed Muhammad and now he showed less tolerance to the stubborn Christians. The synagogues of the Jews and the churches of the Christians had long fascinated Muhammad. He decided that his followers should have their own meeting place or mosque. From a tall tower, his servants would call out to the devotees of Allah, announcing the hours of prayer. Provided that the Christians paid their taxes, they could keep their churches, although they were forbidden to build anything taller than a mosque. Nor could they have a horse, which limited their travel and commerce. Not only could they never try to convert a Muslim, a Christian was forbidden from even marrying a Muslim. The punishment for any attempt to entice a Muslim from his faith was death.

Muhammad continued to inspire his followers with revelations which continued until his death. On 8 June 632, the Prophet died at Medina, after a short illness. There was no shortage of followers eager to take care of Islam and spread the teachings of their leader.

With the ever-increasing revenues from their con-
quests and taxes, the Muslims rapidly expanded and better equipped their army. With the fall of Alexandria in
September of 642, the entire fertile delta of Egypt, the
land of the Pharaohs and the cornfields of Africa, fell into
Muslim hands.

The plight of the Byzantine Empire proved too much
of a temptation for the followers of Islam. They could
scarcely resist the easy pickings that skirmishes afforded
them. Snaking westwards along the northern coast of
Africa, they conquered the last vestiges of the Roman
Empire. By 711, they ruled everything in sight. At the
rock of Gibraltar, they paused to collect their forces for a
final onslaught into the heart of the Roman Empire. The
Spanish were astonished at the arrival of these dark
invaders, whom they called *moros*, or Moors. In reality,
however, the Moors had been invited by disenchanted
Spaniards who wished to enlist their aid against the king.

By early 732, the Muslims had crossed from Africa
into Spain and were pushing their way across France.
The king of the Frankish territories, Charles the Hammerer, had no intention of letting the invaders arrive
unopposed. The soubriquet vividly illustrated the manner in which he smote the Muslim invaders. In October
of that year, he met them in pitched battle outside the
Gallic town of Poitiers. Among the first to fall was the
Emir, or Muslim ruler of Spain. Within two days
Charles' army had vanquished the foe. His small sturdy
horses easily outran the large but unwieldy Arab stallions. Once more, six years later, the Franks did battle
with the Muslims when they advanced on the French
town of Lyon. Again Charles' army was victorious and
the Muslims were pushed back into Spain. The threat to
Christian Europe was stalled once more, giving hope to a
people terrorised by tales of vicious marauders.

It was 100 years since the death of the Prophet Muhammad.

In Rome, Pope Gregory III (731-741) listened attentively to the impressive reports from his envoys about the prowess of Charles the Hammerer. The Gallic king was, thought the pope, just the person he needed to help ward off the advances of the Lombards, a marauding tribe from the north of Italy. Appalled as he was by the Muslim threat, that posed by the Lombards was closer to home, and so more dangerous. Throughout the summer of 738, Pope Gregory entreated Charles in several gracious dispatches to intervene on behalf of the beleaguered Italians. Charles was fully occupied with the Muslim threat to his own kingdom of Gaul, which prevented him thinking about the Lombard's threat to the pope. However, he did arouse the wrath of ecclesiastics as he confiscated church-owned properties which he did not consider were sufficiently well used and gave them to his own supporters. The incensed ecclesiastics were not in a position, however, to fight the man they realised was protecting their lands from a far worse fate.

It was Gregory's successor, Stephen II, (752-757) who finally gained the ear of the king of the Franks. By the autumn of 741 Charles was dead, but his brother, Pepin the Short, had been elected to succeed him as king of the Franks.

Stephen was greatly impressed by Charles' success in routing the Muslim invaders. The pope reckoned that the new king could just as easily protect him from the threat of the Lombards. His attempts to gain a sympathetic hearing from the Byzantine emperor, Constantine V, had proved useless.

So Stephen began the dangerous journey across the snow-capped Alps to France in order to enlist Pepin's

GREGORY III

STEPHEN II

aid. When the lengthy journey ended in Paris, the pope presented the king with a small wooden casket. Inside was a Latin document that was sure to impress Pepin. The document had been written, claimed the pope, by the emperor Constantine in the fourth century. It purported to be a list of all the territories and tributes which the emperor had given Pope Sylvester. In fact, the document may have been forged some weeks earlier by the pontifical chancellery, or by the monks at the French abbey of St Denis. Although it probably had a slim foundation in historical fact, given Constantine's generosity to the early Christians, the parchment was mainly a devious work of fiction. It was not exposed as a forgery until the 15th century. In all events, Pepin fell for the ruse and weighed in behind the pope. Pepin asked the pontiff who should be king, the one with the title or the one with the power? The pragmatic pontiff replied that the one with the power should hold the royal power. Effectively, this meant that the pope sided with Pepin, who had more power than the legitimate king, Childebert III. Pepin proceeded to depose the king of the Franks and Pope Stephen agreed to consecrate Pepin and his two sons as rulers of the Franks. The elder son was called Charles, later known to history as Charlemange, Charles the Great.

In agreeing to be the protector of the popes, Pepin and his family were buying in to papal power. The pope imposed on Pepin the prestigious title Patrician of the Romans. The papacy, in return, was to gain a much-needed military defence for its territories. At the cathedral of St Denis in Paris, the pope crowned Pepin and his sons rulers of the Frankish empire. In the eyes of the people it was as if St Peter had descended from heaven to approve their choice of ruler. Pepin faithfully carried out his part of the bargain. In the early summer of the following year, he descended into Italy and routed Aistulf who had confiscated the territories outside Rome from which the papacy derived much of its income. Moreover, he also succeeded in routing the Saracens who had taken hold of Narbonne.

After Pepin's death in 768, Charles continued in his father's footsteps, pushing the Muslim threat into northern Spain, and extending his kingdom into what now comprises much of modern Germany. Pepin's son Charles established a particularly cordial relationship with Pope Adrian. The pontiff recognised the importance of ADRIAN maintaining the protection of the king of the Franks, and Charlemagne realised the value of having the pope's personal blessing and support in his political enterprises. The pope regularly supplied liturgical books from Rome so that Charlemagne's scribes could copy them for use within his territories. In this way he increased learning within his realm and used Christianity to unify his kingdom. In one touching letter from Adrian, we read of the pope appealing for long beams to be sent from France to repair the roof of the Constantine basilica of St Peter. Wars had caused the destruction of the woods and forests, and the tallest trees had been felled to enlarge the fleets. The pope and emperor disagreed on the veneration of icons, but remained on friendly terms until the pontiff's death in 795.

In the last months of the year 800, Charles travelled to Rome to settle a violent dispute between the pope, Leo III LEO III (795-816), and the nobles of the city. At Easter 799, the pope had been attacked by a violent mob while riding his horse in a religious procession. The pontiff was dragged to the ground and some clumsy assailants tried to gouge out his eyes. Rescued by his bodyguard, the pope fled to the nearby monastery of San Silvestro, close to the Pantheon. Here he collapsed in front of the high altar while the clergy barred the wooden doors of the church from the assassins.

The cause of the attack seems to have been political. The ruling families of Rome were unhappy with Pope Leo's over-reliance, as they saw it, on the Frankish crown. To blacken the pope's name, they accused him of simony and adultery. Aided by the monks of the monastery of San Silvestro, the pope fled the city to the Umbrian town of Spoleto. There the Duke of Spoleto provided the pope with an armed escort to Paderborn, where King Charles was holding court.

The evidence against Pope Leo seemed to Charles quite strong. However, his trusted adviser, the monk Alquin of York, explained to the king that no power could be above the Apostolic See. Therefore, Charles could not interfere unless to support the pope. Deciding not to make a hasty decision, Charles had the pontiff escorted back to Rome, with the assurance that he would soon come to preside over a synod to clear the pope's name. In preparation for the visit, Leo built a new guest wing at the papal palace of the Lateran where the king would lodge with his court. In the dining hall he placed a large mosaic of Christ flanked by Peter and Paul. The message of the apostolic support for the pope would not be lost on the king.

The Frankish king took his time before he travelled south to Rome. Convening a meeting in St Peter's at the beginning of December 800, Charles instructed the bishops to seek the truth in the allegations against his host. It was obvious that Charles supported his host, the beleaguered pontiff. The bishops, unwilling to incur the king's displeasure, shrewdly found in the pope's favour. On 23 December, the pope was cleared of the charges. The perpetrators and conspirators were condemned to death, although, on the pope's appeal, the sentence was commuted to exile for life from Rome. Two days later, on

Christmas Day, Charles attended Mass in St Peter's Basilica. As he was praying before the tomb of the Apostle Peter, Pope Leo stepped forward and placed a crown on the emperor's head.

The ninth-century entry in the *Liber Pontificalis* paints a gracious picture of the event.

> The venerable and gentle pontiff crowned him with his own hands, with a most precious crown. Then all the Romans, seeing the great love and care which he showed for the Holy Church of Rome and for its vicar, inspired by God and by St Peter who holds the keys of the kingdom of heaven, cried out with one voice: 'To Charles, most pious Augustus, long life!' The pope then knelt, the first and last to do so, to pay obeisance to the Holy Roman Emperor.

The newly crowned emperor feigned surprise, but accepted the honour. In fact, there is every reason to believe that pope and king had planned the event in advance. It was in both their interests to strengthen the link between the imperial crown and the papal tiara. Power was once more concentrated in Rome, at the papal court, and a new empire in the West was established.

Initially, the alliance worked well for both sides. The pope no longer had to look exclusively to Constantinople for help which, in any event, was rarely forthcoming. The new Holy Roman Emperor had the favour of the pope, the most important spiritual ruler of western Europe. He realised, much as Constantine had four centuries earlier, the unifying force of religion. Charlemagne ordered mass conversions among the pagan tribes of the empire, and mass slaughter where there was opposition.

The prestige of the papacy was increased immeasurably. Charlemagne ordered that all liturgies throughout his empire (which effectively corresponded to much of modern-day Central Europe), were to be celebrated in

Latin according to the Roman Rite. Prayers were said in every church in the realm for the Roman pontiff. Not until the Reformation in the 16th century was the position of Latin in the liturgy to be seriously questioned. A further 400 years were to pass by before the Catholic Church permitted Mass to be celebrated widely in the vernacular. In the late 1960s, Pope Paul authorised the Mass to be celebrated in the language of the people.

CHAPTER 7

Of Kings and Popes

JOHN VIII • STEPHEN VII

FORMOSUS • JOHN X

LEO VIII • GREGORY V

SYLVESTER • LEO IX

STEPHEN X • ALEXANDER II

GREGORY V

To be pope in the ninth and tenth centuries was not perhaps the easiest of occupations. Despite the gilded glory of the most important bishopric of Christendom, the stakes for remaining pope were high. Murder or deposition was not an uncommon end for a bishop of Rome.

On a boiling hot day in late August of the year 847, a flotilla of ships turned into the mouth of Ostia, the port of Rome. The townspeople of Ostia may have paid little attention to the wooden vessels which passed the abandoned port and sailed 20 miles up the Tiber. Docking near the Greek quarter, the ships disgorged their content. For three days the surprised Romans were put to the sword by Islamic mercenaries. The tombs of St Peter at the Vatican and St Paul were looted, and gold and silver statues and chalices were carried off. The silver altar which, since the time of Constantine, had stood over the tomb of the apostle Peter was carried off to Africa. The Carolingian emperor, Lothar, sent his son Louis with funds to repair the desecrated shrines and build a wall around the Vatican to protect it from further invasion. The following year, the pope dispatched a fleet to attack the Saracens, who were defeated by Caesare, the Duke of Naples. For the rest of the century, the southern Mediterranian was to be the battleground between the Franks, the Saracens and the Byzantine Empire. The popes consistently supported the Franks as their staunch ally as they sought to defend themselves both from interference from the Saracen and Byzantine invaders.

In 882, the unbelievable happened; Pope John VIII

(872-882) was murdered, the first pope to be assassinated. He died at the hands of a disgruntled entourage. When poison failed to work, he was clubbed to death. Worse was to follow. In the autumn of 896, Pope Stephen VII (896-897) had the body of his predecessor, Formosus (891-896), exhumed from the tomb in which it had lain for 10 months. The decayed corpse was dressed in pontifical vestments and brought before a judicial court held at the Lateran Palace. There it was propped on a throne and a series of invented charges were read against the deceased pontiff. The sentence of *damnatio memoriae*, the damnation of his memory, was passed. All the acts and edicts of his pontificate were annulled. The fingers of the skeleton were cut off and the corpse was stripped of its vestments. The cadaver was then thrown into the Tiber. Stephen was certainly deranged and he also was to meet a violent end. Thrown into prison, he was later strangled by the Roman mob.

The century tottered on towards an uncertain end, whimpering out in relative peace. In 915, Pope John X (914-928) and King Berenger I of Italy formed an alliance to defend Italy from attack. Things did not improve for long, for in 928 the pope was thrown into prison and there he was strangled.

Despite the dangers, the powerful aristocratic Roman families feuded amongst each other to get a member elected to the papacy. In 962, Pope John XII (955-964) begged King Otto 1, the ruler of the East Frankish Kingdom, to protect him from his squabbling enemies in Rome. In return, the pope promised to crown Otto emperor of the Holy Roman Empire. Otto, sensing the political advantage, was quick to oblige, even if he was fully aware of the pope's reputation. The pope was accused of having bought the papal office at the age of 19, and of turning the papal residence at the Lateran into a brothel. John had several enemies, who disliked him because he was the illegitimate son of Prince Alberic II of Rome, and continued to be involved in family intrigues. In return for Otto's intervention, John crowned him Emperor in the West. Almost immediately, Otto was obliged to attack Berenger, the king of Italy, in order to secure his estates.

The pope, meanwhile, changed sides and, supporting the king of Italy, conspired against the new emperor. It was a foolish move. Having discovered the plot, the furious Otto returned to Rome. He deposed John and LEO VIII installed a lawyer as Pope Leo VIII (963-965). But Leo was not recognised as a legitmate pope and was ousted by the mob in Rome. After a brief exile outside Rome, John was restored to the papacy. A few months later, however, John died while, it was whispered by gossiping tongues, in the act of adultery. He was just 27. With the death of Otto in May 973, his son succeeded him as Otto II. The new emperor was too preoccupied to care for the problems of the popes in Rome, who continued to be contested by anti-popes and violent factions. In 996, the new emperor, Otto III, arranged for his 24-year-old Ger-GREGORY V man cousin to be elected Gregory V (996-999). Upon Gregory's death two years after his accession, Otto sponsored the cause of his former teacher, the French Gerbert SYLVESTER who was elected pope.

Gerbert's choice of the name Sylvester (999-1003) may have been symbolic, the name of the first pope to co-operate with the emperor Constantine in his effort to establish a Christian empire. The two-year pontificate was too brief to establish any kind of reform and for almost 50 years, Rome was torn between violent family factions, each vying for lucrative church benefices. Not LEO IX until the election of Pope Leo IX in 1049 (1049-1054), was a true movement for reform launched.

Already since the middle of the 10th century, several monasteries had been clamouring for the eradication of abuses. In France, the abbey of Cluny persistently urged the popes to purge the church of corruption. In particular, the abbots of Cluny and other similar monasteries wanted the popes to abolish the practice of buying and selling church offices. Cluny, founded by Duke William of Aquitaine in 909, was unique, as it was independent of the local lay rulers and dependent rather on the pope. For two centuries, Cluny was to inspire hundreds of new foundations, or to reform older abbeys. These valued their independence from lay rulers and indeed from the interference of local bishops. Obviously, this was going to lead them into conflict. No ruler could afford to leave these communities, with their vast territorial holdings, unchecked. By the turn of the second millennium, there were over 1,000 monasteries loyal to the head house at Cluny. The lay rulers of Europe tried to exercise a restraining hold on the bishopric and abbeys.

Reforming churchmen saw the conferring of the ring and crozier, the so-called 'lay investiture', as an intolerable interference by lay rulers in church matters. With the election of Leo IX (1049-1054), the church finally found a pope willing to take decisive action to abolish abuses and also curb lay interference.

Leo, from Alsace, was related to the imperial family. Determined to address these problems, the pope travelled throughout Europe challenging simony and urging the adoption of celibacy. Church offices were often handed down from father to son and the pope was anxious to break the mould. There were numerous stories of priests' widows and children refusing to leave the parish house and holdings. Flanked by Cardinal Peter Damian, Cardinal Humbert of Selva Candida and Hildebrand, the archdeacon of Rome, the pope had some initial success in convening synods in Italy, Germany and France. However, he made a mistake by leading a badly organised military campaign against the Normans who were attacking southern Italy, an area claimed by Byzantium. During a visit to the south of Italy in June 1053, he was taken prisoner. Within a few weeks, however, the embarrassed Normans liberated their prestigious captive. Leo died the following spring.

The year 1054 was to see the fateful separation of West from East, an event which would sour relations between Christians for almost a millennium. The Patriarch of Constantinople, Michael Cerularius, was enraged by Pope Leo's foray into southern Italy, an area claimed by the patriarch to lie under his jurisdiction. Cardinal Humbert was dispatched to Constantinople to negotiate with the patriarch, who had closed the Latin-rite churches of the city and expelled the clergy. Attempts at reconciliation failed. On 16 July Humbert strode into the church of Hagia Sophia and slammed a bull of excommunication on the altar. That the bull bore the signature of the pope who had died in April was of little concern, as the break had been centuries in the making. The bull was to have been the last resort. Cerularius retorted with an anathema. Relations between West and East were severed. Almost a thousand years were to pass before Pope Paul VI and the Patriarch of Constantinople, Athenagoras I, signed a declaration lifting the mutual declarations of excommunication.

STEPHEN X   Stephen X (1057-1058) continued the papal endeavours at reform started by Leo, but his successors were unable to make much headway. In 1073, Hildebrand was elected as Pope Gregory VII (1073-1085). On the day following the death of Alexander II (1061-1073), during the funeral of the deceased pontiff, the people and clergy began to chant: 'Let Hildebrand be pope!' 'Blessed Peter

ALEXANDER II
GREGORY VII

has chosen Hildebrand the Archdeacon!' Hildebrand was shocked but later that same day, he was brought to the church of San Pietro in Vincoli, and his election was confirmed by the cardinals.

From the beginning, Gregory was determined to achieve reform. He expressed his concern with the state of the church:

> The Eastern Church has fallen away from the faith and is now assailed on every side by infidels. Wherever I turn my eyes – to the west, to the north, or to the south – I find everywhere bishops who have obtained their office in an irregular way, whose lives and conversation are strangely at variance with their sacred calling; who go through their duties not for the love of Christ but from motives of worldly gain. There are no longer princes who see God's honour before their own selfish ends, or who allow justice to stand in the way of their ambition ... And those among whom I live – Romans, Lombards, and Normans – are, as I have often told them, worse than Jews or Pagans.

The year after his election, he published the *Dictatus Papae*, a collection of laws that clarified the official position regarding church discipline. In particular, the pope underlined the independence of the papacy in the face of imperial interference. Gregory was irritated by what he saw as the emperor meddling in ecclesiastical affairs. The *Dictatus Papae* contained the following formulae: 'The Roman Church was founded by God alone', 'Only the Roman Pontiff may dispose or rehabilitate bishops', and even went so far as to claim 'It is licit to depose the emperor'. Gregory was a reformer of exceptional talent and integrity, qualities that had already been recognised by Pope Leo IX some years earlier. His mettle was soon tested.

In 1075, during a synod held at Rome, Gregory

declared 'any person, even if he were emperor or king, who should confer an investiture in connection with any ecclesiastical office is to be condemned'. The practice had grown up that any wealthy landowner could appoint his favourite as an abbot or bishop. The pope opposed 'lay investiture' not so much for the corruption which ensued as because of the weakening of his own authority. In that same year, the emperor Henry IV appointed his own candidate as archbishop of Milan. Gregory threatened the emperor with excommunication. In January of the following year, the emperor retaliated by denouncing the election of the pope as invalid – 'Hildebrand is not the pope but rather a false monk.' The following month the pope responded with a bull of excommunication. Such measures, although seen today as of little impact, indeed were extreme and effectual. The excommunication had political consequences as well as spiritual, for the pontiff released the emperor's subjects from their allegiance to their ruler. The emperor realised his blunder too late and was forced to agree to meet with the pope in Augsburg in the spring of 1077. The emperor was aware of the weakness of his position and instead decided to ask pardon of the pope by the winter of 1076.

By January 1077 the pope had reached Canossa, the residence of Matilde, the Countess of Tuscany. Matilde was a strong supporter of the papacy and had invited the pope to stay in her residence before continuing on to Augsburg. Some weeks later the emperor arrived but he was obliged to wait for the pope for four days. Kneeling in the snow, clad in penitential rags, the emperor had to beg admission to the hall where the pontiff was holding court. Although the pope wanted to extract as much as possible from the emperor at Augsburg, he received Henry sympathetically and absolved him of his excommunication. The emperor's contrition, however, soon proved to be false and in 1080 Gregory was compelled to excommunicate Henry once more. This time, the emperor, who had just survived a civil war in Germany, appointed a priest, Guibert, as anti-pope. Pope Gregory, who had sought protection from the Normans, was forced to take refuge in Castelsantangelo as Rome was sacked by his Norman allies. Gregory fled the city, first to the Benedictine abbey of Montecassino and then on to Salerno, south of Naples. Shortly after he arrived at Salerno, he was taken ill. The doctors were mystified by the pope's condition but soon realised that he would not recover. As he lay dying, the frustrated pontiff must have had bitter thoughts about the way fate seemed to betray him. 'I have loved justice and hated iniquity, therefore I die in exile,' the pope confided on his deathbed.

Disputes between popes and emperors continued for some years until 1122 when, with the Concordat of Worms, the controversy over lay investiture was finally resolved. The emperor agreed that the appointment of bishops would now be in the hand of the church authorities alone, free from secular influence. Although kings were becoming ever more powerful in the face of the weakening empire in the West, the papacy had a number of outstanding popes who defended the church in the face of possible regal interference. The papacy was firmly established as one of the most important political institutions of the medieval world.

CHAPTER 8

For God Wishes it Thus

URBAN II • CLEMENT III

The frail pontiff climbed the wooden platform that had been erected outside the town walls. The damp November of 1095 had begun a harsh winter. Pope Urban II (1088-1099) had travelled for weeks to get to the French town of Clermont-Ferrand. He had received a letter from the emperor Alexius I Comnenus of Byzantium, warning of a Turkish invasion from the East. Imperial scouts had reported the march of thousands of Muslims massing and readying themselves for an assault. He had already informed the bishops meeting in council in the town of the situation. The emperor had appealed to the pope for help. The pope urged the people assembled before him to rally to the emperor's call:

> For your brethren who live in the East are in urgent need of your help and you must hasten to give them the help often promised them. For as most of you have heard, the Turks and Arabs have attacked them and conquered the territory of Romania as far west as the shore of the Mediterranean and the Hellespont. They have occupied more and more lands of those Christians and have overcome them in seven battles. On this account I, or rather, the Lord, beseech you as Christ's heralds to publish this everywhere and to persuade all people of whatever rank, foot soldiers, and knights, poor and rich to carry and promptly to those Christians and to destroy that vile race from the lands of our friends.

In case this hotchpotch of xenophobia and racism was not enough, Urban promised an Indulgence – remission of the temporal punishment of their sins – to all that answered the call. 'All who die by the way, whether by land or by sea, or in battle against the pagans, shall have immediate remission of sins. This I grant them through the power of God with which I am invested. O what a disgrace if such a despised and base race, which worships demons, should conquer a people which has the faith of omnipotent God and is made glorious with the name of Christ!'

Urban had another reason for soliciting support. For the first six years of his pontificate he had been kept out of Rome by the anti-pope Clement III (1080-1100) who CLEMENT III had been selected by the Holy Roman Emperor, Henry IV. Urban was opposed to the investiture of bishops by the emperor and thus was not wanted by the emperor. The pope probably hoped that, by appeasing the emperor of Byzantium, he would eventually regain his throne in Rome.

Clutching his letter from the emperor, and waving it above his crowd, he called out: 'This battle is of God, and we must enjoin it.' Up went the roar of approval: '*Dieu li volt!* – God wants it!'

The enthusiastic response was more than the pope could have hoped for; he retired to the bishop's palace to discuss strategies for the proposed expedition. Adhamer Le Puy, bishop of Clermont-Ferrand, was appointed to be the papal representative. Hundreds upon hundreds of young men offered themselves to train as knights or servants. Some joined in the hope of winning land. In medieval society, only the first-born son inherited property from his father. Others saw the opportunity to get out of town and see the world. Still others were moved by genuine desire to free their fellow-Christians from the terror of invasion. To all of these Adhamer distributed cloth crosses that were to be sewn onto their garments, giving the name 'the crusades'. The old French word *cruz*, meaning a cross, gives us the word crusade.

They would need to be trained to carry arms and indeed form a nimble army.

Little did Urban and the bishops realise at the time that they were playing into the Byzantine emperor Alexis' hands. This was exactly what he wanted, to raise an army from the West that would help him protect his capital, Constantinople, and conquer the East.

The pope left Clermont-Ferrand and traversed France, attending further church synods. He dispatched a letter to the emperor in which he could scarcely hide his pleasure in this success. Throughout the winter, the youths trained and manoeuvred, and the pope drummed up further support wherever he went.

The first to leave for the Holy Land were not the young soldiers, but a mob of men, women and children that had been fired up by the rhetoric of the pope. Tens of thousands formed what is known as the 'People's Crusade'. One such group was led by Peter the Hermit. This mystic had convinced thousands to join him. In the spring of 1096, they left for Constantinople. After almost five exhausting months of travel, they arrived at the gates of the eastern capital in August. They had only a few primitive weapons, and much of their enthusiasm had been dampened by sickness and the journey across an unfamiliar and at times hostile terrain. It came as little surprise when almost all were killed by the arrows of the Turks at Civetot in the Dardanelles.

When the first wave of soldiers left for the crusades the following autumn, many of the volunteers never made it to the East. For most of them, this was the first time that they had been out of their own villages on more than a day trip. Now they had papal approval for all this journeying. For some the temptation proved too great. They raided other towns or villages. In the city of Mainz in Germany, they massacred a large number of Jews.

The main armies sailed with the pope's blessing in the autumn. From the north of France a band set out led by Robert, Duke of Normandy, Hugh, Count of Vermandois and Godfrey de Bouillon.

From southern France the most important army departed, led by Raymond de Saint Gilles. An army of Normans set sail from southern Italy, led by Bohemond, Duke of Taranto. Bishop Adhemar Le Puy accompanied these armies as the pope's personal representative, urging them on with more and more elaborate promises of God's favour.

The forces crossed the Bosphorus and attacked Nicea (in modern-day Turkey) where Constantine had held the first council of the church in 325. The city had been in the hands of the Turks for 10 years. The crusaders laid a siege which lasted two months. Eventually the town surrendered to the emperor Alexis, who had travelled from Constantinople to see the Turks topple from their turrets. The emperor refused to allow the crusaders plunder the ancient city and instead paid them with food and coin.

Flushed with success, the crusaders pushed eastwards towards Antioch in Syria, a city sacred to the memory of St Peter. This time success eluded them. They were ambushed by the Turks, under the leadership of Arstan, Sultan of the Seljuk state of Rhurn. The arrival of Raymond de Saint Giles was in the nick of time, allowing the crusaders regroup and repulse the Turks.

The westerners were temporarily disorientated as they crossed the barren straits of Anatolia. They met serious problems as food and water supplies ran low, as did the temperatures. In desperation they attacked the city of Edessa, which fell to them with surprising ease. It was to prove a boon to them in further campaigns.

By October 1097, the crusaders had arrived at Antioch, where they proceeded to pitch camp and starve the Turks from their lair. The siege dragged on through the winter months, frosting over their initial enthusiasm. Elation gave way to despair, as the Turks gave no sign of evacuating the city. Many of the Christians, worn out by the hardships and disease, fell prey to fatal illnesses. Among the victims was the pope's legate, Bishop Adhemar. As the emperor Alexis marched towards Antioch, his scouts informed him that the Christians had been decimated. Disgusted with their failure, the emperor returned to Constantinople. The crusaders now wondered if the emperor had joined the battle to protect his seat of power.

But the luck of the westerners changed, and soon they were able to break the stronghold and capture the city. Having consolidated their position, the Christian crusaders moved towards the goal of their expedition, the holy city of Jerusalem.

This was the most venerable city, sacred to the Christians, the Jews and the Muslims. The city had an almost mystical hold on the imagination. Here, at least for Christians, was where Jesus had been presented in the Temple, where he had preached and worked miracles. It was in Jerusalem that he had died and had risen again. It was intolerable that the infidel could possess it for one day longer.

After a long siege, the city wall was finally breached on 15 July and the foreigners swarmed in. Raymond d'Aguilers, an eyewitness, takes up the story:

> Now that our men had possession of the walls and towers, wonderful sights were to be seen. Some of our men (and this was merciful) cut off the heads of their enemies. Others shot them through with their arrows, so that they fell from the towers; others tortured them longer by casting them into the flames.

Piles of heads, hands and feet were to be seen in the streets of the city. It was necessary to pick one's way over the bodies of men and horses.

In the temple of Solomon, men rode in blood up to their knees and bridle reins. Indeed, it was a just and splendid judgement of God that this place should be filled with the blood of the unbeliever which had suffered so long from their blasphemies.

Not all the victims were Muslims. Jews also suffered from the frenzy of the invaders. Those who sought refuge in the sanctuary of the synagogue did so in vain, for it was burned to the ground, the Christians' hymns of thanksgiving mingling with the screams of the Jews inside.

The pope was not to hear of the liberation of Jerusalem, as news had not reached Rome before his death on 29 July. He dreamed of the reunion of East and West, but little could he foresee that his action in launching the crusade would result in 200 years of intermittent bloody war, culminating in 1204, when the crusaders sacked the city of Constantinople.

From today's perspective, the period was an epoch of cross-fertilisation of ideas and concepts. Western civilisation, emerging from the Dark Ages, gained immeasurably in the areas of commerce, mathematics, art, music, medicine, philosophy, literature and architecture. The interaction of the knights and their entourages with the Muslims was to bring about advancement in the areas of culture and commerce. Throughout Europe, shrines, cathedrals, and abbeys were built to house relics which had been stolen from the people of the East.

After centuries of barbarian invasions, Europe was no match for the more sophisticated Muslim culture which it encountered in the Middle East. The Arab mind only saw the crusades as local wars, and did not fully appreciate the scale and dedication of the warring parties' efforts. The Westerners, nonetheless, remembered the slaughter and devastation that Muslims had inflicted on Africa in the seventh and eighth centuries, and had no wish that these be repeated. Their initial reaction was of defence, not of destruction. The crusades, none the less, cast a dark shadow on Christian history, as the scale of violence indulged in by the combatants and the misery inflicted could in no sense justify these wars.

CHAPTER 9

The Great Denial

CELESTINE V • BONIFACE VIII

BENEDICT XI • CLEMENT VI

BENEDICT XII • URBAN V

GREGORY XI

The old man gazed from the opening of his tiny cave down into the valley below. The hot August sun beat down on his lined face. He scrutinised the dust rising along the path leading up the mountain. As the cloud came nearer, his astonishment grew all the more. He could make out a line of horses and pack-donkeys. Little could Pietro del Morrone, now in his 80th year, guess that the cardinals and prelates astride the animals had come from Perugia to see him.

The band dismounted, their fine silk robes bathed in perspiration. Bowing before the venerable figure, they delivered their message. The cardinals meeting in Perugia, they explained, had spent 27 months searching for a new pope. The old man knew this as he had sent a letter to those very cardinals rebuking their tardiness and prophesying divine retribution if the stalemate prevailed.

The choice of the conclave was inspired, declared the senior cardinal, by the Holy Spirit. That choice was Pietro del Morrone.

The cardinals and their elegantly attired attendants made a strange contrast to the hermit dressed in a hair shirt wrapped in iron chains. Years of fasting had reduced his gaunt frame to a mere skeleton.

The old man listened in horror. The octogenarian argued that his aged precluded him. The cardinals would not listen. He was a hermit, Pietro protested. That, retorted the cardinals, was what the church urgently needed. The prelates were determined to remain in the barren refuge as long as was necessary to convince the old man to accept the papal throne. Three days passed while Pietro argued volubly against his own election. He considered fleeing his mountain retreat by night, but his plan was foiled by the arrival of Charles II, King of Sicily. The king was determined to see a new pope elected as soon as possible. Overawed by the presence of the king, Pietro finally agreed to accept the papal tiara.

Some days later, mounted on a donkey, Pietro bade a tearful farewell to his mountain refuge and was escorted by the king's troops to nearby Aquila, where he was crowned Celestine V.

CELESTINE V

The cardinals had hoped that this holy man, devoid of ambition, would lead the reform so badly needed in Christendom by his simple example. Celestine V (1294) turned out to be a weak pope. Duped by Charles II, he became the king's puppet. Charles offered him a castle in Naples in his own territories. This was, in effect, to prevent the elderly pope coming under the influence of the curia in Rome.

Soon the cardinals realised their mistake. They sneered at his poor education, abandoning their elegant Latin to converse with him in simple Italian. They may have made a mistake; now they meant to rectify their error by controlling the papacy. This put them on a collision course with Charles, who had the same idea.

In the event, neither side should have worried. In December, barely five months since he had been elected, Celestine abdicated. The cardinals, unable to dissuade the pope, met 10 days later in conclave at the papal residence in Naples. To their number, Celestine had just added seven new French cardinals and five from Naples. On the first ballot of the opening session, Cardinal Caetani was elected, taking the name Boniface VIII.

BONIFACE VIII

The new pope meant business. Immediately Boniface (1294-1303) ordered the papal court back to Rome, annulled Celestine's acts and dispensed with the officials Celestine had appointed. A few days later he dispatched Celestine to a monastery under armed guard. To his dismay, within a few days he received a message that the former pope had slipped his guards. The wily old man managed to evade his captors for months, taking refuge in the woods of eastern Italy. While fleeing on a ship to Greece, he was betrayed by one of his own supporters, apprehended and handed over to Boniface. The former pontiff was locked into a tower at Fumone, near Boniface's family home outside Naples. Here, in May of 1296, the old man died of an infected abscess. Years later, the poet Dante condemned Celestine for 'the Great Denial'.

The nations of Europe were at this time flexing their muscles. An economic boom in the 11th and 12th centuries, caused by a series of bumper harvests and improved agricultural techniques, had enriched the wealthy classes. The beginning of the 13th century, however, was marked by a series of poor harvests and the economy began to weaken. Famine was reported in many parts of Europe.

Although there was still an emperor in Constantinople, the emerging western kingdoms sought greater independence. The monarchs were particularly determined to exert greater influence over the clergy and the aristocracy. As vernacular languages were formed in the late Middle Ages, Latin became the preserve of the church and royal courts. The wealthy classes commissioned literature in the vernacular, which further marginalised Latin from everyday life.

France and England were engaged in near-permanent conflict over territories. To finance the wars, strict taxes were imposed by the French. In particular, the clergy were levied. The new pope was indignant that the French king, Philip the Fair, should interfere and condemned him roundly. Nobody but the pope, he reminded the sovereign, had permission to impose taxes. The church had long condemned usury, the taking of interest on a loan, in theory if not in practice. Christians had therefore avoided banking activity, which had become the property of the Jews. Rome became the centre of international trading in luxuries. The popes relaxed the restrictions on Christians and commerce, and soon an effort was made to evict Jews from their monopoly. By the end of the 13th century, papal bankers in Florence, such as the Bardi and Peruzzi, had made small fortunes lending money to monarchs to finance the royal armies. The kings were willing to repay interest on a loan as high as 60 per cent.

Boniface had problems nearer home. Ugly rumours were circulating that while still a cardinal he had climbed the roof of the papal palace in Naples. Pretending to be the voice of God, he had called down the chimney urging the bewildered Celestine below to abdicate. Boniface identified the source of the rumours as the Roman Colonna family, which had caused much bloodshed in the search to have a member elected pope.

Boniface was furious and confiscated most of the Colonna cardinals' properties. The Colonna family accused Boniface of murdering the former Celestine. Against those who argued that Celestine's election was invalid, Boniface wrote, 'the Roman pontiff is always free to abdicate'.

It was just the turn of the century. The end of one century and the beginning of another were often accompanied by events and portents in the popular mind. Contemporary accounts record enormous crowds which gathered on the steps of St Peter's Basilica on Christmas Eve, 1299. As much to divert attention from political difficulties as to respond to a spiritual need, Boniface called a Jubilee in 1300.

In February of that year, an elderly man was presented at court. In the presence of the pope he recalled that his father had brought him to Rome as a young boy. Father and son had remained in the city, visiting its churches, until their food ran out and they returned home. The old man claimed that every hundred years those who came to Rome to pray at the tombs of Peter and Paul would have their sins forgiven. This was just what Boniface needed. Indeed, historians wonder if Boniface had not stage-managed the whole thing. He immediately wrote a letter urging pilgrims to come to Rome. The success was undeniable. Up to a million pilgrims came from all over Europe to gain their indulgence, freedom from sins and swell the papal coffers.

In the face of Boniface's success, two of the Colonna cardinals defected to the court of King Philip of France. Boniface rebuked the king for offering shelter to the recalcitrant cardinals and protested at the ruler's levy of tax on the clergy. But to no avail. A year later, on 18 November, Boniface published a bull, *Unam Sanctam*, in which he robustly defended the spiritual power of the papacy over the temporal power of monarchs. With a flourish he closed the document with an uncompromising statement: 'For salvation, it is entirely necessary for all to be subject to the Roman pontiff.'

The following summer, Boniface retired as usual from the torrid heat of Rome to his summer palace at Anagni. In August he prepared a letter in which he intended to excommunicate Philip. By imposing the sentence, he would release all Philip's subjects from their loyalty to the king. An obvious result would also be the freeing of the clergy from their obligation to pay tax.

It was a wild gamble. The day before he was to publish the letter, Guilaume de Nogart, the French king's lieutenant, arrived with an army in Anagni. The pope's palace was poorly guarded and the French troops swarmed through the courtyard and up the flight of steps into the throne room where the pope had taken refuge with his cardinals. The lieutenant was under orders to arrest the pope and bring him to France where he would answer charges, concocted with the help of the Colonna cardinals, that he had assassinated Celestine. The indignant pope managed to face down the French, who withdrew without their prize. The pope was shaken by the events and returned to Rome, his pride badly bruised. Three weeks later he was dead. It was 999 years since Pope Marcellinus had abdicated in the face of the final imperial persecution of Diocletian.

After the brief pontificate of Benedict XI (1303-1304) BENEDICT XI the cardinals met once more in Perugia. The college was divided into two camps. One group was bent on retribution for the humiliation of Boniface, while the other sought compromise with the French king. After 11 months of wrangling, the choice fell on Bertrant de Got, the archbishop of Bordeaux.

The new pope, Clement V (1305-1314), was to spend the CLEMENT V eight years of his pontificate in the shadow of the French king. News travelling across the Alps suggested that a French pope would not be welcome in Rome. King Philip suggested that the papal coronation take place in Lyons. Pope Clement acquiesced. As a temporary measure, the new pope took up residence in the southern town of Avignon. No pope would set foot in Rome again for almost 70 years.

Clement was entirely in King Philip's power, giving in to his desire to hold a church council and even defaming the memory of Boniface VIII in his intemperate bull, *Rex Gloriae*.

The greatest shame for Clement was his suppression of the Knights Templar, established by the first crusaders as a monastic-military order to safeguard the shrines of

Palestine from the Muslim invaders. Little over two centuries had passed since the French knights had been urged by Pope Urban II to drive out the Muslim invaders from the Holy Land. In the process, many of these entrepreneurs had become wealthy landowners and bankers. Their newly-acquired riches had not gone down well in feudal France. Everyone had a predetermined place in society and was expected to stay there. The first-born son was to inherit the father's properties. The church, the army and the law were for those sons born later. Now, thanks to their successes in the crusades, many second-, third- or fourth-born sons had gained riches that even the first born could not imagine.

On the night of 13 October 1307, King Philip moved against the Knights Templar. In swift and vicious raids throughout the kingdom, the knights were rounded up and arrested. No reason was given to the prisoners and months, even years of torture ensued. Philip and his agents used the most sophisticated instruments available to extract confessions from the knights who had risked their lives to fight the fierce Muslims.

Racks, thumbscrews, head-clamps, sizzling charcoal beds, red hot irons gave them what they wanted. From the depths of the dungeons the knights screamed their confessions. Yes, they had committed sodomy, uttered blasphemies, spat on holy images and crosses. They confessed whatever their torturers wanted to hear. Those who failed to do so had their tongues cut out. Philip persuaded the pope to convene a council to judge the guilt of these heretics. Three years after Philip mounted his first attack, his evidence was ready and the council opened, presided over by the French pope. In March 1312, Philip wrote to the pontiff a letter with veiled menace and threats:

Your Beatitude is aware that I have been informed by

trustworthy people of the results of enquiries into the Brethren and Order of Knights Templar. These reveal that they committed such great heresies and other dreadful, detestable crimes that for this reason the orders should justifiably be suppressed.

Clement gave in. Lands, castles, goods, jewellery, all were confiscated and given to the Hospitallers of St John of Jerusalem, a similar monastic-military organisation. In effect, the properties fell to the French crown.

In 1314, the last Grand Master of the Knights Templar, Jacques de Molay, was burned at the stake. As his body was consumed by the flames, he called on God to justify him and avenge his death. Both pope and king were to die within the year.

It is of course of no consolation to those who suffered and died all those centuries ago to know that the charges for which they were persecuted have all been shown to be false by modern historians.

The next six popes were all French. They had little desire to exchange the tranquil surrounding of Avignon for the foul-smelling streets of Rome. At Avignon, under the protection of the French crown, they came to be regarded as monarchs in their own right. In 1338, Pope Benedict XII (1334-1342) built himself a palace worthy for a pope, demanding that all the sycophantic bishops who had made their home at the papal court return to their dioceses. Its stern walls rose in the midst of the town and all around grew up a bureaucracy to service the needs of the Vicar of Christ. A decade later Clement VI (1342-1352) bought the city and the surrounding countryside from Queen Joanna of Naples for 80.000 ducats.

BENEDICT XII

The popes withstood any appeals from the Romans to return to the city. Whatever thoughts they may have harboured were dashed in 1347 with the outbreak of bubonic plague, the Black Death. In October, Italian merchants returning from a trading mission to the Black Sea landed in Sicily. When the ship docked in the port, most of the crew were dead. The corpses were piled high on the harbour walls and burned, their ashes swept into the sea. The plague, transmitted by fleas in the coat of rats, manifested itself in boils and lesions. Within days the plague had spread throughout Italy. During the winter months, the plague seemed to recede, as the fleas were dormant in the cold weather. But when the spring of 1348 arrived, there was a further outbreak of the fatal disease. Within a year, one-third of the population of Europe was dead from the terrible plague. For survivors, the harsh conditions seemed relentless. There were not enough healthy people to tend to the crops, which themselves shrivelled up and died. When labourers demanded higher wages for the extra work they were asked to do, the landlords refused. The peasants revolted against what they saw as unjust punishment. A contemporary account gives us a flavour of the grim conditions all over Europe.

> Realising what a deadly disaster had come to them, the people quickly drove the Italians from their cities. But the disease remained, and soon death was everywhere. Fathers abandoned their sick sons. Lawyers refused to come and make out wills for the dying. Friars and nuns were left to care for the sick, and monasteries and convents were soon deserted, as they too were stricken. Bodies were left in empty houses, and there was no one to give them a Christian burial.

While some people blamed the Jews for the misfortune, Pope Clement wrote letters protecting them and offering them hospitality in the town of Avignon.

In the absence of the pope, a tribune, Cola di Rienzo, had staged a bloodless coup on the steps of the Capitoline Hill in Rome, establishing a short-lived republic.

Clement excommunicated him and the fickle mob soon chased him from the city.

During its time at Avignon, the papal court became both more efficient and more prosperous. Even today there are thousands of documents testifying to the work of long-dead scribes lying unread in the archives of Avignon.

Finally, in the spring of 1366, Pope Urban V (1362-1370) decided to return to Rome. From the city he hoped to launch a new campaign against the Turks and make an overture to reconcile the Greeks.

Astride a white charger, the pope, in full vestments and under the protection of his guard, entered Rome through the Lateran Gate. He was horrified to see the ruins of the Cathedral of St John Lateran which had been burned to the ground six years earlier. The papal palace at the Lateran was uninhabitable. The procession crossed the river and made its way out of the city walls to the Vatican, where the Apostolic Palace lay beside St Peter's. Here, close to St Peter's tomb, he settled and took up residence.

Rome presented a miserable sight. Deprived of papal order and patronage for almost 70 years, brigands and mob rule had both depleted the population and impoverished the remaining citizens. Cows and sheep grazed amidst the ruins of the Forum. In the Colosseum, the Frangipane family had built a fortress, while at the Theatre of Marcellus, the Orsini had taken refuge in the decaying monument of Augustus. The banks of the Tiber were overgrown, and floods regularly destroyed the habitation of those living near the river.

Urban had brought much-needed money from Avignon and he set about restoring the churches and public buildings. From Assisi, the great wooden and iron caskets were brought from the papal treasury.

Urban's time in the city was brief and unhappy. The

French members of his court were unpopular. The Romans were unimpressed with the courtiers and clergy from France, with their troubadours and jesters. Civil disturbances forced him to leave the city and take refuge in nearby Viterbo. However, the pope did have the satisfaction of welcoming the emperor of Constantinople, John V Palaeologus, to Rome. Several of the French cardinals who had bought villas and estates around Avignon put pressure on the pope to return to his French estates. The pontiff finally acquiesced and sailed for Avignon in the summer of 1370. Pope Urban was given a hero's welcome when he returned to Avignon, and he died unexpectedly in December while presiding at High Mass at the cathedral there.

The Great Plague wiped out hundreds of thousands of people. All generations were affected and it was to take a century for Europe to recover from its fatal effects. Central Europe was caught up in hostilities between nations called the Hundred Years' War (1337-1453). The principal belligerents were the French and the English, still fighting over territories. Pope Clements's successor, Gregory XI (1370-78), was also French and was anxious to broker a peace between the nations. Anxious to launch a crusade against the Turks and continue to find a solution to the division between the Greek and the Latin Churches, Gregory decided to return the papacy to Rome. In late 1376, the pope and his courtiers sailed from Marseilles. After spending five months in Rome, city riots obliged the pope to move southwards to Anagni. Gregory's time in Italy was also unexpectedly short and the last of the French popes died the following year.

GREGORY XI

CHAPTER 10

Let the Heavens Rejoice and the Earth Exult

URBAN VI • BONIFACE IX

BENEDICT XIII •INNOCENT VII

ALEXANDER V • MARTIN V

EUGENIUS IV • FELIX V

Of the 16 cardinals meeting in conclave following Gregory's death, 11 of them were French. By electing one of their number, they hoped to leave Rome which had become so loathsome and return to their beloved and more lucrative France. They did not reckon with the unruly mob. The pope had resided in Rome for less than two years and the Romans did not want to see him slip away again. Such an event would be disastrous for business. Carpenters, bakers, innkeepers, cheese makers, textile merchants, chandelers, and even prostitutes surrounded the palace at the Vatican. Business had boomed since the return of the papal court to Rome. The prefect of the city sent a message to the 16 cardinals locked in St Andrew's chapel at the Vatican. It was a thinly veiled threat as to what might happen if another non-Italian were to be elected.

The frightened prelates decided that it would be prudent to elect an Italian. The only name they could agree upon was Bartolomeo Prignano, the archbishop of Bari. The problem was that Prignano was neither a cardinal nor even present at the conclave.

Just as a delegation was about to set off for the southern port to communicate the will of the conclave to Prignano, the Roman mob broke into the chapel where the cardinals were meeting. The terrified cardinals abandoned the chapel and retreated to the sacristy. Dressing an elderly Italian cardinal in the deceased pontiff's robes, they presented the frail old man as the new pope. Contented with their choice, the exhilarated mob left to sack the palace of the successful candidate, by now an honoured tradition.

The archbishop of Bari enthusiastically welcomed his election and set off immediately for Rome. Three days after his arrival in the city he was crowned Urban VI.

From the very beginning Urban (1378-1389) proved to be a disaster. At his first meeting with the cardinals following his coronation, he stripped several of them of their benefices and reduced their salaries. These actions were unlikely to inspire confidence in the pope. Throughout the summer the cardinals tried to reason with the ever-more irascible and irrational pontiff, to no avail. Urban VI

In August, the French cardinals withdrew, one by one, to Anagni south of Rome. Here they conferred about what to do, and finally published a document declaring that the April election of Urban VI had been made under duress and was therefore invalid. They then proceeded to depose the pope, the first time an action of such kind had been taken in history.

The infuriated pontiff excommunicated the cardinals. Fearing for their safety, they moved to nearby Frondi, where they would be under the powerful protection of Queen Joanna of Naples.

Meeting there in conclave once more in mid-September, they elected one of their number, Robert of Geneva, as Pope Clement VII (1378-1394). Clement VII

Pope Urban VI sent out letters to the heads of the European nations and to the emperor at Constantinople denouncing the action. The new pope, or anti-pope as he would be called by his enemies, sent similar letters about Urban. The monarchs had to decide whom they regarded as the validly elected pope, carefully watching the way each other reacted. It was mostly the northern countries which opted to support Clement, while the southern countries remained faithful to Urban.

With their allies lined up, both pontiffs solemnly

excommunicated the other. Urban had lost most of his cardinals and appointed 29 more. He may have been mad but he was shrewd enough to appoint them from the nations which supported him.

Rapidly the situation deteriorated. Cardinals who suggested a reconciliation with Clement were thrown in prison. One cardinal was stripped and publicly flogged on the side of the road for daring to disagree with Urban. When six of the cardinals tried to depose Urban, the pope excommunicated them and sold their possessions. The king and queen of Naples were excommunicated as suspect accomplices. The pope had taken refuge in Nocera, in southern Italy, with the cardinal-prisoners. The royal couple sent an army to besiege the pontiff, who daily called out anathemas from the town's ramparts.

After a siege lasting five months, the pope managed to escape with his prisoners and made for Genoa. Here, some of the cardinals were executed at the pope's command, for daring to challenge his authority.

There was general rejoicing when Urban died, possibly by poisoning, in 1389. Clement sincerely hoped that Urban's cardinals would recognise him as the legitimate pope. These prelates, however, proceeded to elect the 50-year-old Neapolitan, Piero Tomacelli, as Boniface IX (1389-1404).

Genial and generous, Boniface turned out to be popular with the Romans for whom a jubilee year was to be celebrated in 1390. Four years later he received the welcome news that Clement was dead and expectantly prepared to welcome the recalcitrant cardinals of Clement's party. The 21 cardinals, however, were slow to accept the pontiff's overtures. Each swore before the conclave that if one was elected, he would step down if the majority of cardinals so decided. Two days later they chose the Spaniard, Pedro de Luna, who had been a cardinal for almost 20 years. Taking the name Benedict XIII (1417-1423), the following winter he opened negotiations with Boniface, but to no avail. Short of money, Benedict sent a message to Boniface in 1406 that he would abdicate if Boniface would do likewise. Thus the way would be open to a new election. Negotiations were disrupted with the sudden death of Boniface some days later.

His successor, Innocent VII (1404-1406), decided that the only solution to the impasse was to call Benedict's bluff and convene a council. To his surprise, Benedict agreed. The anti-pope set off from Avignon with high hopes. Perhaps it was Benedict's enthusiasm which caused Innocent to falter. Or it may have been a treaty which the wily Innocent had just signed with Ladislas, king of Naples. He had sworn not to sign any agreement with an anti-pope in Avignon which did not recognise Ladislas' claim to the Neapolitan throne. By the time that Innocent died in 1406, no council had taken place.

During the conclave to elect Innocent's successor, each cardinal took the oath made earlier to abdicate if it was the majority decision, or if the stubborn Boniface in Avignon would die or step down.

Things were beginning to look desperate. The 74-year-old anti-pope had seen off three Roman popes and with robust good health, it appeared that he would live for several more years. Unable to decide one way or the other, the cardinals voted for the 81-year-old Angelo Correr from Venice.

The newly-elected Gregory XII (1406-1415) came from an aristocratic family, and was widely respected both for his austerity and his devotion to the church. Having agreed with the cardinals who elected him to abdicate as soon as a reconciliation was achieved, he swiftly entered into a flurry of negotiations with Avignon. With surprising ease, he achieved a promise to meet Benedict. The two pontiffs agreed to travel to Savona in the north of Italy to begin face-to-face discussions. Every convent and monastery along the route was asked to pray for the success of the negotiations. Gregory arrived at the Tuscan town of Lucca with his court, while Benedict and his attendants stopped at Portovenere along the Ligurian coast. They made no further progress. Both men were playing for time as they sent ambassadors back and forth to decide on the minutiae as to where each pontiff would sit, who would sit to the right of the altar, who to the left. In the midst of all this, Gregory made a fatal move. Although he had promised not to create new cardinals, he rashly proceeded to do so. Anxious to bolster his support, he created four new cardinals in May 1408. Two of these were his own nephews. Such blatant nepotism was too much for his cardinals, who deserted him and left for nearby Pisa. Joined by four of Benedict's cardinals, the frustrated prelates called for a general council to be held in the great cathedral of Pisa the following year in an effort to resolve the impasse.

It is not difficult to imagine the reaction of the two contenders to the throne. Benedict and Gregory retorted by calling their own councils.

On the blustery morning of 26 March 1409, lines of cardinals, bishops, chaplains, friars and theologians filed past the famous leaning tower into the cathedral of Pisa. After two months of discussion, the council fathers reached a decision. They realised that neither side was willing to bow to the other. On 5 June, the president of the council read out loud the dramatic decree: 'Gregory and Benedict are obdurate and perjurers. We declare the Holy See to be vacant.'

With great pomp, the cardinals proceeded to elect Pietro Philarghi, archbishop of Milan. The new anti-pope, Alexander V (1409-1410), had been a supporter of

ALEXANDER V

Urban VI. The church now had three rivals to the papal throne. The anti-pope realised that he would have to wrestle Rome from Gregory. Excommunicating Ladislas of Naples, he gave his territories to Louis of Anjou on the understanding that Louis would attack Rome on his behalf. Within a few months Rome had fallen to French troops and the unhappy Romans sent a delegation to Alexander in Bologna urging him to come to the city to take up residence. Shortly before Alexander was to set out for Rome, however, he died unexpectedly.

Scarcely able to believe their bad luck, the cardinals met to elect Boniface's treasurer, who took the name John XXIII (1410-1415). Angelo Roncalli (John XXIII, 1958-1963) took the name John XXIII to prove that Baldassare Cossa was not a legitimate pope. A former pirate with experience of fighting naval skirmishes against Ladislas and Charles of Anjou, Baldassare Cossa was just what the cardinals wanted. Gregory, now in his mid-eighties, had been sheltering in Naples under Ladislas's protection. The elderly pope was double-crossed by Ladislas and was forced to flee northwards and take up residence outside Rimini.

Pope John entered Rome and convened a short-lived council. It achieved little more than the condemnation of the English reformer, John Wycliffe. The shadow of the reformer and his teachings was to cast a shadow over the papacy and was ultimately to undermine its influence for centuries to come.

The years following the Great Plague were marked by religious as much as civil upheaval. People began to doubt a God who would allow such a disaster to happen. In England, where the church owned one-third of the land, many of the clergy were corrupt and immoral. Church offices were sold to the highest bidder. In the 1370s an Oxford priest teaching at the university began to criticise not only the abuses but also the lack of theological content in many ecclesiastical practices. He criticised above all the church's refusal to allow the Bible be translated into the common tongue of the people. Although church authorities fretted that people would not understand the scriptures quoted out of context, Wycliffe showed the shallowness of the argument and prepared the first translation of the Bible into English. Wycliffe ran into difficulties both with the local church and the civil authorities. However, his teaching that the clergy could not hold property won him support from civil authorities who protected him and encouraged his teachings.

When a new council, convened under the patronage of anti-pope John XXIII and the Emperor Sigismund, opened at Constance in 1415, the decision was taken to exhume the body of Wycliffe and burn his bones. Perhaps the council fathers thought they could thus incinerate all his heresies. But the seeds of the reform of the clergy and the education of the laity were sown. Time would be needed before the harvest would come.

The bishops gathered at Constance in southern Germany had, they believed, more pressing matters on their minds. Frustrated at the vision of three popes and perhaps more to come, the bishops called on all three to abdicate. In theory, Gregory and Benedict would retire if only John would do so as well. John, however, managed to slip the city from disguised as a groomsman and to take refuge in nearby Frieburg. The council then took the unprecedented step of declaring itself superior to a pope. John was soon captured and brought before the council. On 29 May, the council fathers declared him deposed.

Gregory also kept his part of the bargain, and abdicated. Benedict, now 87, refused to abdicate, but retired to his castle on the east coast of Spain where he lived on, brooding like an eagle in its nest, for eight more years.

Seizing their opportunity, the 22 cardinals and 30 other bishops at Constance choose a new pope. After centuries of wrangling, the Colonna had their first- and only pope. As fate would have it, Gregory had died just three months before the election of Martin V, Colonna.

Almost three years after his election, in 1417, Martin V (1417-1431) and his entourage entered Rome for the first time. The papal party was horrified to see the state of the city. Churches had been ransacked, houses burned to the ground and rats infested the ruins of Imperial Rome. The people greeted the new pope as a hero. Two years had passed since his election as pope and the people had reason to hope in a restored papacy. Great wooden barrels of wine were placed in the public squares and meat and candied fruits filled the trellis-tables laid outside the churches.

While Martin dispensed lavish gifts to his family and endowed them with enormous properties, he also turned his mind to a promise he had made when he had dissolved the Council of Constance two years earlier. The abuses throughout Christendom called for a true and radical reform. The pope began by a reform of the curia. He entrusted his family members with the improvement of the Papal States, and they took the occasion to enrich themselves even further. This benign attitude extended to a generous treatment of the followers of the Bohemian reformer John Huss, who called for the Bible to be translated into the vernacular.

Concerned about anti-Jewish feeling, the pope composed a document in which he chastised those who tormented the Jewish population:

Whereas the Jews are made in the image of God, and a remnant of them will one day be saved, and whereas they have sought our protection: following in the footsteps of our predecessors, We command that they be

129

not molested in their synagogues; that their laws, rights and customs be not assailed; that they be not baptised by force, constrained to observe Christian festivals, nor to wear new badges, and that they be not hindered in their business relations with Christians.

Against his wishes, but constrained to do so by a promise made prior to his election, Martin convened a council to meet at Pavia to discuss church reform. Due to an outbreak of the plague, the council was postponed, and it was not until 1430 that the bishops met at Basle. The council had only been in session three weeks when Martin unexpectedly died of apoplexy.

The Colonna family had made several enemies amongst the college of cardinals. The majority of the cardinals made a pact to avoid a family member becoming pope. Desiring to find somebody who would show the college more respect than Martin had done, their choice fell on the austere Venetian Gabriele Condulmar.

EUGENE IV   The new pope, Eugene IV (1431-1447), was impatient with the council at Basle and ordered it to close just five months after it had opened. The cardinals were shocked, recalling the events which had followed after the election of Pope Urban VI. The participants at the council were determined to show their steel and ignored the pope's directive. It was an unheard-of move. The bishops and their theologians refused to disband and remained in session for another year. The pope was forced eventually to climb down and acknowledge the decrees of the council.

The enraged Colonna plotted to punish Eugene for his high-handed manner. In the early summer of 1434, they ousted the pope from the Vatican. The pope, vested in the habit of an Augustinian friar, fled down the Tiber to Ostia, where he boarded a ship for Florence. Taking refuge in Florence for the next nine years, Eugene was to come face to face with the extraordinary blooming of the arts and sciences which was taking place in the City of the Flowers. He was lodged in the Dominican friary of Santa Maria Novella. During his stay in the humanist capital, he consecrated Brunelleschi's dome of the cathedral, one of the marvels of the Florentine Renaissance.

None the less, his main preoccupation was with the flouting of his authority on the far side of the Alps. In Switzerland, at Basle, the council fathers continued to sit in session, hour upon hour, day upon day of interminable discussion about the problems besetting the church. Eugene was determined to gain control, refusing to sign many of the decrees. Although he cleverly split the council into factions, on 31 July 1437, the pope was summoned by the council fathers to answer charges of disobedience.

This may indeed have been what Eugene wanted. By his presence at the council, he sought to assert his authority over that of the council. In September of that year, he ordered the council of Basle to dissolve and meet in the city of Ferrara under his presidency.

Most of the cardinals obeyed the pope, but a small number stayed on in Basle, declaring the bull invalid. The following summer the remnant in the Swiss town declared Eugene deposed and in November elected the layman Armand, Duke of Savoy, as Pope Felix V (1439-1449).   FELIX V

Eugene set the Council of Ferrara two tasks. He was chiefly determined to organise a crusade against the Turks. Secondly, he was anxious to find a formula which would unite West and East once more.

The dreaded plague hit the town the year after the council opened at Ferarra. In addition, Eugene's funds were running low and soon he had no money to pay the expenses of his Greek guests. As proof of his earnestness, he sold his family castle at Assisi to fund the entertainment.

Among the friends Eugene had made in Florence was the wealthy banker, politician and patron of the arts, Cosimo de Medici. The shrewd merchant made a generous gesture to the pope. He would give a loan of 1500 gold florins a month if the council would care to transfer its proceedings to Florence. The friendship forged between Cosimo and Eugene was to establish a source of revenue for the Renaissance papacy, and introduce members of the Medici family into the papacy itself.

Eugene was greatly relieved. If he had been unable to organise a council quickly, the bishops at Basle would roar laughing and his deposition would have been a certainty. The Turks were marching on Constantinople. The Eastern emperor, John Palaeologus, sent an urgent message to the pope, wildly promising anything he wanted, even submission, if only the pope would send troops to fight the Muslim troops. As a pledge of his earnestness, the emperor had travelled to Italy and was lodged in the freezing city of Ferarra while all around him dead bodies, victims of the plague, were carried out through the city gates.

For Eugene, the Byzantine emperor was a prize even more tempting. His mind was filled with the idea of being the pope who effected the union of East and West after 400 years. Moreover, the popes would henceforth play a hitherto unimagined role in the development of Europe. They would take their place with emperors and monarchs, and their power and prestige would grow immeasurably. When the huge entourage entered Florence in January 1439, the Byzantine emperor was given the recently-evacuated Pitti palace, the Patriarch of Constantinople was a guest in the Palazzo Ferranti, while the pope returned to the Dominican church of Santa Maria Novella.

There was an air of carnival about the proceedings, the

Greek visitors with their perfumed hair and curled beards strolling arm in arm through the city. The young Greek groomsmen were to be seen chatting in the alleys while they waited for their masters, trying to pronounce new words in their host's tongue. The baptismal registers record a substantial increase in the birth rate over the following months.

Eugene gave orders to make whatever concessions were necessary to gain his prize of unification, as long as they were unobtrusive. Finally, in July, the theologians announced that they had reached a formula acceptable to both sides. The pontiff saw a sweet victory over the stubborn prelates at Basle, while already John Palaeologus could envision the white sails of the battleships full of soldiers sailing from the West to save his beloved city.

Under the dome in the cathedral, the papal and imperial court sat for the last session. In Greek and Latin the formula was proudly pronounced: 'Let the heavens rejoice and the earth exult, for the wall which has divided the Western and Eastern has fallen.'

The much-vaunted reunion was not to last long. Returning to Constantinople, the emperor was unable to gain widespread acceptance for the agreement. Soon an event was to overshadow the proceedings at Florence. On 29 May 1453, the great city of Constantinople, seat of the Eastern empire for over a thousand years, was to fall to the forces of Islam. Over 100,000 soldiers faithful to the teachings of the Prophet Muhammad poured through the gored ramparts. Among the dead lay Constantine X, the last emperor.

Europe now lay open for conquest. Nobody, it was thought, could stop the Muslim onslaught.

CHAPTER 11

Flowers on the Ruins of Rome

NICHOLAS V • SIXTUS IV

As Pope Nicholas V (1447-1455) lay dying, he summoned the cardinals to his bedchamber. The gout-ridden pontiff wished to leave them instructions following his death. After some pious admonitions, the pope modestly enumerated his achievement and urged the cardinals not to neglect the building of imposing churches and the collection of ancient manuscripts.

The pope identified two of the most precious interests of the Renaissance. His death, in 1455, came one year before the publication of the first printed book, the Gutenberg Bible. Nicholas wrote with an elegant hand, and may not have at first admired the new method of copying books. As a young man, he had spent vast sums on acquiring illuminated manuscripts, running into considerable debt. Tommaso Parentucelli had spent his early adult life as a tutor to two Florentine families. His talent was spotted by the bishop of Bologna, who generously sponsored his further education. Appointed to the See of Bologna in 1444, just three years later he succeeded Pope Eugenius IV, as Nicholas V.

The eight years of his pontificate coincided with momentous events in European history. The first notable success came when the anti-pope, Felix V, submitted to him and the Council of Basle capitulated to pontifical authority, putting an end to the last papal schism. From the beginning of his pontificate, Nicholas set about enriching the Papal Library with several thousands of hand-copied manuscripts in Greek and Latin. The pope was immensely proud of the library. In a celebrated letter to Enoch of Ascoli, Nicholas expressed his desire to ensure that 'for the common convenience of the learned we may have a library of all books both in Latin and Greek that is worthy of the dignity of the Pope and the Apostolic See'. The pope was never happier than in his library, arranging the volumes in cabinets, admiring the elaborate binding and leafing through parchment papers. The papal librarians became used to the small figure bent over the table at the centre of the library, his pale face buried in a small book.

The jubilee of 1450 brought hundreds of thousands of pilgrims to Rome, where they admired the churches and works of art commissioned by the pontiff. In this way, the pope established Rome as a vital centre of the Renaissance. The basilica of St Peter's, which had stood for more than a thousand years, was urgently in need of repair. Time and earthquakes had damaged the fabric. The pontiff appointed an architect to design a new, more imposing edifice and began the slow dismantling of Constantine's basilica. Aneas Silvio Piccolomini, later to succeed Nicholas as Pius II, commented that 'what he does not know lies outside the realm of human knowledge'. The jubilee was marred somewhat when plague broke out and later as 200 pilgrims were crushed to death near St Peter's as a bridge across the Tiber collapsed while they were crossing in procession.

The following year, Frederick III was crowned in St Peter's, the last Holy Roman Emperor to celebrate his coronation in Rome. But Nicholas had to deal with serious challenges to his authority. On three occasions the fanatical humanist Stefano Porcaro sought to depose Nicholas and set up a republic in Rome. Twice Nicholas pardoned the Tuscan scholar and provided him with a generous pension. After a foiled assassination attempt in early January of 1453, Nicholas reluctantly signed a warrant for his execution as warning to Porcaro's supporters.

Some weeks later, news arrived that Constantinople was threatened by the Muslims. Nicholas dispatched a legate, who urged the citizens to cancel the Great Schism of 1054. The clergy and people retorted that they would rather live under the Turkish turban than the papal tiara.

Despite the insult, Nicholas sent 10 galleys to aid the defence of Constantinople.

Their arrival was too late, for when they sailed up the Bosporus, the imperial city had fallen. Nicholas was deeply disturbed and issued a bull inditing a crusade. A deep depression descended on him, and two years later he died in Rome. His dreams were to be fulfilled by other Renaissance pontiffs, but not in the way he could have imagined.

For over 500 years, people have crowded into the majestic Sistine Chapel to admire the jewel of the Renaissance papacy and the works of art sponsored by the popes. The chapel takes its name from Pope Sixtus IV (1471-1484) who commissioned it as the court chapel of the Vatican. There can be few places in the world with such an incredible concentration of art. Some of the greatest names worked here, Perugino, Botticelli, Signorelli, Roselli, Pinturicchio, Ghirlandiao and of course, the incomparable Michaelangelo.

Francesco della Rovere came from a small fishing village in the north-west of Italy. Although he joined the Franciscan order as a young man, he had little interest in the vow of poverty that had made the founder, Francis of Assisi, so famous. Nonetheless, he became an admired theologian, publishing an important treatise on the Immaculate Conception. In 1471, at the age of 68, he was elected pope. Surrounded by grudging rivals who had been outbid for the papal throne, della Rovere began his pontificate with an audacious act of nepotism. The new pope appointed a household of family relations to run the government of the church. Pride of place was given to his nephews, Giuliano della Rovere and Pietro Riario. The latter was to die at the relatively young age of 28, worn out, the Romans whispered, by an excess of every vice. A poorly organised papal crusade against the Turks succeeded in capturing no more than two dozen Muslim soldiers who were paraded around the streets of Rome to be jeered and spat upon by the delighted Romans.

The blatant nepotism, as for many popes before him, was almost the cause of his undoing. Sixtus and the young cardinals became important patrons of the finest artists of their day, and were surrounded by sycophants. The pope commissioned churches, widened streets, constructed palaces and employed several of the great artists of the day.

But it all had to be paid for and soon the money ran out. The pope decided to invest in property and bought the town of Imola so that his nephews could earn more revenues by fleecing the unfortunate inhabitants.

The pope asked one of the papal bankers, Lorenzo de Medici, for a loan. Lorenzo was the son of Cosimo, whose friendship with Pope Eugenius IV had gained the family the title of 'Provider to the Apostolic See'. The Florentine banker refused, as he realised well the risk of lending any money to the della Rovere family. He, moreover, had had his eye on the town for quite a while and had recently begun negotiations to buy the *borgo* for his own family. Ignoring Lorenzo's unwillingness to help, Sixtus turned to another Florentine banking family, the Pazzi, for a loan. The Pazzi were delighted to have so prestigious a client as the papacy, as well as scoring against their rivals. The money was lent immediately. The Pazzi savoured the possibility of the collapse of the de Medici power. Going further than they had ever imagined, they devised an audacious coup. They would assassinate the male members of the de Medici family while they attended Mass at the cathedral. The motives may have been mixed, for the Pazzi family suspected that the de Medici were plotting against them.

The date was set. Giuliano and Lorenzo were to be

struck down as they attended Mass on Easter Sunday morning, 26 April 1478. The pope's nephews were implicated in the plot.

While the archbishop of Florence, who also happened to be a member of the Pazzi family, was celebrating Mass at the high altar, the assassins struck. Giuliano was killed instantly, while Lorenzo managed to escape to safety with minor cuts through the sacristy. Uproar ensued. Blame immediately focused on the Pazzi family. The archbishop, still in his cloth-of-gold damask vestments, was dragged by the mob to the Palazzo Vecchio. Here he was stripped and hoisted to the balcony, where he was hanged and a wooden stake was driven through his genitals. Within a few hours, all the assassins hired by the Pazzi family were arrested and also hanged. From below, Leonardo Da Vinci sketched the bodies of the assassins as they writhed and choked to death. The 10-year-old Nicolò Machiavelli was also a shocked witness. One of the assassins, Montesecco, betrayed the involvement of the pope. He claimed that the pontiff had known all along of the plot and indeed had even approved the assassination. It is not difficult to imagine how quickly popular opinion turned against the pontiff. Cornered, the pope blamed the de Medici and excommunicated them. Pointing out that Montesecco was a murderer, Sixtus flatly denied any involvement in the plot or knowledge of an assassination. The indignant pontiff laid Florence under interdict and excommunicated Lorenzo the Magnificent.

Hostilities broke out between Florence and Naples, a series of incursions that would soon involve the whole Italian peninsula. The behaviour of the pope and his family ensured that the papacy would remain entwined with the secular fate of the Italian states for generations.

Shortly afterwards, Sixtus agreed to a request from the

monarchs of Spain, their Most Catholic Majesties, Ferdinand and Isabella. Worried about the continued Moorish and Jewish presence in the predominantly Christian Spain, the king and queen asked the pope for permission to institute the Inquisition in the Kingdom of Castile and Aragon. The intent was to purify Catholic Spain from heretics, real or imagined. Thus the pope placed an important political tool in the hands of the Spanish rulers. Moreover, the appropriation of money and property of the accused enriched the Spanish crown immeasurably.

In 1483, the year before Pope Sixtus' death, the Spanish Dominican, Tomás de Torquemada, was appointed Grand Inquisitor of Castile and Aragon. To the crown was given the task of extracting the confessions, to the church the power of sentence and punishment. The tortures employed to extract the confessions were hideous. Victims were stretched by pulleys or their stomachs filled to bursting point with water. Torquemada retained his post until 1498. During that time, as many as 2,000 people, many of them Jews, were burned at the stake and the lives of countless thousands of victims were destroyed. The contemporary Spanish chronicler, Sebastian de Olmedo, called Torquemada, with evident pride, 'the hammer of heretics, the light of Spain, the saviour of his country, the honour of his order'.

For all the beautiful artefacts commissioned by Sixtus, the price was impossible to pay in terms of suffering and abuse of rights.

CHAPTER 12

The Pope Divides the World

ALEXANDER VI • CALLISTUS III

PIUS II • INNOCENT VIII

Pope Alexander VI drew a line and changed the world. It was that simple. In August 1492, Christopher Columbus set sail from the Andalucian port of Palos in Spain intent on discovering a shorter route to the Spice Islands. In the early morning of 12 October, Columbus landed on an island in the Bahamas. After several months of circumnavigation of the area, and the discovery of further islands, he returned to Europe, landing in Portugal on 4 March 1493. He was immediately invited to meet King John II at the court in Lisbon, and give a report of his adventures. Under a papal treaty signed by Pope Sixtus in 1479, the monarch claimed the new lands for Portugal. Columbus explained that his commission had come from the king and queen of Castile and Aragon and therefore he was bound to offer the news of his discoveries to the Spanish rulers.

On 15 March, Columbus sailed up the coast where he landed at Palos, from whence he had sailed eight months earlier. After a brief pause to dispatch a report, Columbus travelled to Barcelona, to the court of Ferdinand and Isabella, the Most Catholic Monarchs of Spain. The court listened mesmerised to the swarthy mariner as he recounted the details of his exotic journey. As a reward for his work, Columbus was granted a coat of arms and made Admiral of the Ocean Seas.

King John II of Portugal was deeply concerned that the newly-discovered territories might be appropriated by the Spanish monarchs. He appealed to a Bull, *Romanus Pontifex*, which had been published on 8 January 1455 by Pope Nicholas V. In that document, Nicholas had urged the Portuguese King Alfonso 'to invade, search out, capture, vanquish, and subdue all Saracens and pagans whatsoever, and other enemies of Christ wheresoever placed, and the kingdoms, dukedoms, principalities, dominions, possessions, and all movable and immovable goods whatsoever held and possessed by them and to reduce their persons to perpetual slavery, and to apply and appropriate to himself and his successors the kingdoms, dukedoms, counties, principalities, dominions, possessions, and goods, and to convert them to his and their use and profit.'

The king argued that all new territories should therefore become part of the realm of Portugal. The Spanish monarchs retorted that they had financed the expedition. It was now only just that the enterprising zeal of the Spanish royal couple should be rewarded.

Months of arguing failed to resolve the issue, so the three monarchs appealed to Pope Alexander, as the highest authority in the world, to arbitrate.

With the Bull *Inter Caetera*, dated 4 May 1493, Pope Alexander VI drew a line down the map of the New World. The line of demarcation ran due north to due south, about 100 leagues (480 km) west of the Azores and Cape Verde Islands. Everything to the west of the line was to belong to Spain, everything to the east pertained to Portugal. The Spanish were granted the privilege of acquiring territory or trading in the newly-discovered lands.

Should any of said islands have been found by your envoys and captains, We give, grant, and assign to you and your heirs and successors, kings of Castile and Leon, forever, together with all their dominions, cities, camps, places, and villages, and all rights, jurisdictions, and appurtenances, all islands and mainland found and to be found, discovered and to be discovered towards the west and south, by drawing and establishing a line from the Arctic pole, namely the north, to the Antarctic pole, namely the south, no matter whether the said mainland and islands are found and to be found in the direction of India or towards any other quarter, the said line to be distant one hundred leagues towards the west and south from any of the islands commonly known as the Azores and Cape Verde.

The Portuguese objected to the papal ruling. After all, the pope was Spanish, and perhaps swayed by patriotic sentiments. Added to that was the knowledge that some of the first gold from the New World had been sent to the pope, with which he was to gild the roof of the ancient basilica of St Mary Major in Rome. Months of diplomatic negotiation between the Spanish, Portuguese and Vatican ambassadors sought to resolve the impasse.

The two sides agreed a year later to realign the boundary with the Treaty of Tordesillas, signed the following summer, setting it 370 leagues (about 1770 km) west of the Cape Verde Islands. Portugal was given possession of large swaths of West Africa. The treaty received papal approval in 1503, shortly after the death of Pope Alexander. In effect, Brazil was given to Portugal, while the rest of Latin America was given to the Spanish crown. It is for this reason that Portuguese is spoken to this day in Brazil, and Spanish in the rest of Latin America.

So was launched, by papal approval, centuries of trade which would see the near-extermination of the native Indians, and the selling of countless millions into slavery, both from Latin America and Africa.

Alexander is one of the most colourful and fascinating of the popes. A native of Valencia, Rodrigo Borgia was a favourite nephew of Pope Callistus III (1455-1458), the pope who had led an ill-fated attack on Constantinople to

CALLISTUS III

recover it from the Turks. Rodrigo was made a cardinal at the age of 25 and rose rapidly in the papal court. In June 1460, Pope Pius II (1458-1464) had written a severe letter concerning the 29-year-old cardinal's behaviour:

Beloved son,

We have heard that, four days ago, several ladies of Siena – ladies entirely given over to worldly frivolities – were assembled in the garden of Giovanni di Bichis and that you, quite forgetful of the high office with which you are invested, were with them from the seventeenth hour to the twenty-second hour. With you was one of your colleagues whose age alone, if not the dignity of his office, ought to have recalled him to his duty. We have heard that most licentious dances were indulged in, none of the allurements of love were lacking and that you conducted yourself in a wholly worldly manner. Shame forbids mention of all that took place – not only in the acts themselves, but their very names are unworthy of your position. In order that your lusts might be given free rein, the husbands, fathers, brothers and kinsmen of the young women were not admitted. All Siena is talking about this orgy. Our displeasure is beyond words, for a cardinal should be beyond such reproach.

Although he almost fell out of favour with Pope Sixtus IV, he managed to retain and increase his influence throughout the pontificate of Innocent VIII (1484-1492). On the latter's death in 1492, Rodrigo succeeded as pope. The choice of the name Alexander was as much in deference to his predecessors as in admiration of Alexander the Great, the conqueror of the ancient world. It was widely believed that he paid so many bribes to cardinals at the conclave that he virtually bought the papacy. To the Milanese cardinal, Ascanio Sforza, Borgia give four mule-loads of silver. The deciding vote was made with the agreement of the 96-year-old Patriarch of Venice, who did not live long to enjoy the fruits of his simony.

Alexander had a number of illegitimate children, nine by some counts, by different women. The best-known of his sons was Caesare Borgia.

The year after his father' election, the 18-year-old Caesare was created a cardinal as well as receiving the titular archbishopric of Valencia and numerous Spanish abbeys. These were mere sinecures, which brought him several lucrative stipends, as he was never ordained. This was a happy chance, because the young man had a vile reputation. The new pope's son was loathed for his underhand and often violent scheming. Indeed, it is no credit to his memory that Nicolò Machiavelli used him as the model for his book, *The Prince*. This work described how corrupt politicians work successfully on the principle that the end justifies the means.

Alexander VI was determined to use his position as pope to further his own family, and marry them into rich and influential families. He believed that this would also protect the Papal States from invasions in the future. Indeed, in 1494 the king of France, Charles VIII, marched through Italy on his way to claim the throne of Naples. As he passed through Rome, the pope was forced to take refuge in Castel Sant' Angelo for his own safety.

In 1493, Alexander arranged for the betrothal of his 13-year-old daughter, Lucrezia, but he later annulled the contract in favour of a marriage to a nephew of the king of Naples. This young man, however, was murdered by his own bodyguard whom the courtiers of the Papal Palace claimed had been bribed by Caesare. Although the pope denied any knowledge of the plot, Lucrezia was married once more, the following year, to Alfonso I, duke of Este, and later of Ferrara. The pope suffered a personal tragedy in 1497. In June of that year his youngest and possibly favourite son, Juan duke of Gandia, was murdered. Returning from a dinner party at his mother's house, he failed to come to his apartments by dawn. The pope was not unduly worried, as he knew his son may have stayed with friends overnight. After a day had passed, his horse was found near the Vatican. Of the young Duke there was no sign. Days later, his body, perforated with stab wounds, was dragged out of the Tiber. An eyewitness recounted how he had seen a cloaked stranger throw the corpse into the murky waters of the river by night. The finger pointed at Caesere.

The father of the young victim was inconsolable. He locked himself up in his apartment for nine days, refusing to wash, shave, dress or eat. When he emerged, the corpulent Alexander promised to reform his life and, indeed, reform the papacy. His resolve did not last too long. Alexander seems to have been a carnal, jovial man who combined genuine piety and religious devotion with blind nepotism. For years he had been verbally abused by the Dominican friar, Girolamo Savonarola of Florence, who upbraided him for his lecherous lifestyle. Alexander excommunicated the troublesome friar and was secretly relieved when the Florentines burned Savonarola at the stake in May 1498.

After a rewarding jubilee in 1500, Alexander and Caesare devoted themselves to the forging of ever-stronger ties with Italian and Spanish states. In August 1503, Alexander and Caesare returned from a dinner hosted by Cardinal Antonio Corneto. Both fell ill, and on 18 August, Alexander died in his 73rd year. Rumour had it that father and son had been poisoned by their host.

Terrified that the mob would break into the Vatican palace before he had time to transfer the papal treasures to his own villa, the weakened Caesare struggled to oversee the arrangements for his father's funeral. When Johannes Buchard, the Master of Ceremonies, arrived to prepare the body for burial, he found it swollen beyond belief. To his diary he confided, 'the face was mulberry-coloured and thickly covered with blue-black spots. The nose swollen, the mouth distorted, the tongue doubled over, the lips puffed out so that they seemed to cover the whole lower face.' The coffin was too small for the body. In the sweltering heat, the assistants shoved the corpse into the coffin. A servant had to sit on the lid as the nails were driven home.

Alexander may have been able to change the map of the world by a single line. But he was not able to change the papacy that continued to be governed alternately by overpowering or weak men.

CHAPTER 13

A New Era

Julius II • Innocent VIII

Leo X • Clement VII

Paul III • Marcellus II

Paul IV • Pius IV

Pius V • Gregory XIII

On 1 November 1503, the cardinals filed into the Sistine Chapel in the Vatican Palace to begin voting. The papal choir sang the *Veni Creator Spiritus*, invoking the guidance of the Holy Spirit on their assembly. By sunset, they had chosen Giuliano della Rovere, nephew of Pope Sixtus IV, who had built the chapel. It was the shortest conclave in history. The new pope announced that he would be known as Julius II (1503-1513).

During the conclave, the cardinals struck a deal with whomsoever would emerge as the successful candidate. The new pope was to launch a crusade to drive the Turks back into the East and agree to convene a council to deal with abuses within the Roman curia and the church.

Julius II had had long experience of Vatican politics and had no intention of allowing the cardinals bind his hands in such a manner. Stubborn and resolute, the newly-elected pontiff turned his attention to the Papal States. Venice had encroached on the territories of the pope and Julius was determined to vanquish their attempts. A temporary truce was arranged but Julius was infuriated when Perugia and Bologna rose against his authority. A delegation was dispatched to strike negotiation with the rebellious cities. Contemporaries soon began to compare the new pontiff with Julius Caesar.

When the deliberations had failed, Julius set out at the head of the papal army in August 1506. Clad in an elaborate silver breastplate, the warlike pontiff personally led the troops in the attack on the two cities. Without any bloodshed, Perugia capitulated, whereupon Julius rode on to Bologna. The elderly cardinals who accompanied the resolute pontiff must have had occasion to regret their hasty election of della Rovere. They were greatly relieved when a long winter siege outside the city came to an end and they returned to Rome. Julius' main concern was to prevent the French king entering and expropriating Italian territories.

Julius had been an implacable enemy of Alexander VI and his family, refusing to set foot in the Vatican during the Borgia pontificate. The objections were not likely to have anything to do with his predecessor's morals. He himself had fathered three illegitimate daughters prior to attaining the papal throne.

Within weeks of his election, he ordered the arrest of Caesare Borgia. The pontiff refused to live in the apartments which Alexander and his family had inhabited at the Vatican. Imperiously he ordered a whole new set of apartments designed for his use, commissioning Raphael to decorate the walls. The frescos were designed to recount the great episodes of his pontificate. The Expulsion of Heliodorus from the Temple depicts a scene related in the Book of Machabees, where the Greek commander was expelled having profaned the sacred precincts. The artist shows Julius observing the event from the side of the fresco. The seated pontiff wears a short white beard, which he had grown following a defeat at Bologna two years before he died. The parallel cannot be missed. Here is Julius expelling the French allies for profaning the soil of the Papal States. The last of the frescos was still being painted when he succumbed to a fatal fever. The decorative plan was to show Pope Leo the Great with Attila the Hun, when the pontiff travelled north of Rome to meet the invader. The figures of St Peter and St Paul appear above the the pontiff brandishing swords. Pope Julius in fact died prior to the completion of the cycle and a portrait of his successor, Leo X, was substituted instead.

No pope had ever been such a magnificent sponsor of the arts as Julius. Shortly after his election, the pontiff examined plans by the Florentine artist Bernardo Rosellino to rebuild St Peter's Basilica, which Nicholas V had commissioned in 1453. The plans, Julius decided, were not sufficiently grandiose. Accordingly he commissioned Bramante, who had recently completed the Tempietto on the spot where St Peter was thought to have been martyred, to undertake the replacement of the millennium-old basilica of Constantine.

On Low Sunday, 18 April 1506, Pope Julius laid the foundation stone of the new basilica. In glittering vestments of gold-embroidered cloth, the pontiff blessed the cornerstone close to the high altar. 120 years and seven architects later, the new basilica was finally dedicated.

The scale of the new edifice called for enormous resources. Gold and other goods from the New World continued to pour in as gifts from the grateful Spanish *conquistadores*. Loans were raised from the great banking families of Europe and soon indulgences were sold to pay for the army of two-and-a-half thousand workmen who laboured to raise the finest church in Christendom. This unusual arrangement was shortly to spark the fuse for the Reformation in Germany.

By the 16th century, the Renaissance was in full flower. Masterpieces from the ancient Roman world unearthed by eager antiquarians drew crowds who admired the impressive finds. In January 1506, the ancient statue of the Laocoon was discovered on the site of the palace of the emperor Titus. Michaelangelo, recently summoned from Florence by the pope to sculpt his tomb, hurried to see the statue which had been buried for a thousand years. As the workmen cleaned the earth from the statue, the 30-year-old artist stood in amazement as the marble representation of the priest and his sons emerged from the earth. The pope had the statue transported to the Vatican galleries amid scenes of delight, petals being thrown in its path and all the church bells of Rome pealing the joyful news of its rediscovery.

In 1508, Julius turned his attention to the redecoration of the Sistine Chapel, built by his uncle some 40 years earlier. The vault of the church had been painted a pale blue, with golden stars to represent the sky. Julius decided that a great fresco would be more in keeping with the spirit of the times. With pride and confidence, he commissioned his favourite artist, Michaelangelo, to cover the vault with bright fresco.

Michaelangelo objected that he was a sculptor rather than a painter. The pope charmed his vanity and offered him generous gifts of money as well as some taxes levied by the papacy on the towns within the Papal States. The work was to drag on for four years, longer by far than Julius had anticipated. He regularly came to the foot of the scaffold to berate Michaelangelo for his tardy work. Covered with dust and paint, the artist became frustrated with the constant surveillance. 'I cannot live under pressure from patrons, let alone paint,' he complained. The pope hounded him. 'When will you make an end of it?' he asked repetitively. 'When I am content with it as an artist,' snapped Michaelangelo, his face covered with a mosaic of paint dripping from the ceiling.

Julius had good reason to fear both the French king and indeed some of his own cardinals. In 1511, a number of them banded together with Louis XII of France, who sought to depose him. The wily pontiff, however, outwitted them by calling a council to reform the alleged abuses of the papacy.

The death of the irascible old man in February 1513 left

the papacy stronger in political terms and the undoubted chief patron of the arts of the Renaissance. The cardinals searched carefully for a member of their college as different from the headstrong Julius as possible. Their choice fell on the son of one of the richest men in Italy.

Leo X Giovanni de Medici was the second son of Lorenzo the Magnificent. Shortly after his election as Leo X (1513-1521), the 37-year-old allegedly confided in his brother Giuliano, 'Since God has given Us the papacy, let Us enjoy it!'

The excesses of papal corruption were evident in the life of Giovanni from his earliest youth. At the age of eight he was made abbot of Font Douce in France and by the age of 11, he was abbot of Montecassino. Three years Innocent VIII later, he was created a cardinal by Pope Innocent VIII (1484-1492). Nonetheless, Giovanni received an excellent education at his father's humanistic court under such men as Angelo Poliziano, the classical scholar, Pico della Mirandola, the philosopher and theologian and Marsilio Ficino who sought to unite the Platonic philosophy with Christian theology. As pope, Leo liked to recall his happy childhood with Michaelangelo who was educated along with him at the Medici palace, although he had little patience for Michaelangelo's tempestuous nature. Refusing to vote for Cardinal Borgia in the conclave of 1492, the Medici cardinal was nevertheless astute enough to curry favour firstly with Pope Alexander VI and later Pope Julius II.

After the latter's death in 1513, Giovanni de Medici entered the conclave carried on a litter. He was suffering from ulcers and while in the precincts of the conclave underwent an operation. After seven stormy days, he was elected pope to the delight of the people of Florence. Still in minor orders, he was ordained a priest on 17 March and a bishop two days later. His coronation as pope was one of the most spectacular events seen for decades, and over the three-day celebration, all the money in the papal safe was spent on a spectacular party. A wit later remarked that 'Leo X had consumed three pontificates: the treasure of Julius II, the revenues of his own reign, and those of his successor.' Cardinal Andrea della Valle built a triumphal arch under which the papal procession was to pass, placing on it statues of Apollo, Bacchus, Mercury, Hercules and Venus.

The newly-elected Leo X's childlike determination to make the most of his papacy was the indirect cause of the greatest rift in Christianity in Europe, the Reformation. Moreover, it was to lead to violent wars which carved up the map of Europe a century later.

Delighting in the achievements of artists such as Raphael, Michaelangelo and others, Leo blissfully ignored the calls for reform within the church. Vast sums of money were spent in lavish entertainment at the papal court. The Venetian ambassador, Marino Giorgi, described the pope as 'a good-natured and extremely free-hearted man, who avoids every difficult situation and above all wants peace; he would not undertake a war himself unless his own personal interests were involved; he loves learning; of canon law and literature he possesses remarkable knowledge; he is, moreover, a very excellent musician.'

Leo summoned the humanist Theodore Lascaris to Rome to give instruction in Greek to the papal court and established a printing-press from which the first book printed in Greek appeared in 1515. Moreover, he gave permission to the Jews of the city, the oldest Jewish colony in Europe, to print their own books in Hebrew.

Never happier than hunting boar in the countryside – the boars were in wooden pens – Leo viewed the government of the church as toilsome. Overweight and physically lazy, the Florentine pontiff was so short-sighted that he had to read every document with a thick eyeglass.

In political terms, the pope was equally myopic. In order to limit French influence in Italy, Leo entered into a political alliance with the emperor Maximilian, Henry VIII of England and Ferdinand of Spain. After a momentous victory by the French near Milan in 1515, the duplicitous Leo struck an agreement with the new French king, Francis I. The death of the emperor Maximilian four years later tested Leo's political skills to the utmost. The pope entered into secret negotiations with all the crowned heads of Europe who were competing for the imperial laurels. More by good fortune than political skill, Leo managed to make a favourable alliance with Maximilian's grandson, who eventually succeeded to the throne as Charles V.

In 1517, the papal court was thrown into confusion by a plot on the pope's life by a group of cardinals. The ringleader of the plot was the vain Cardinal Petrucci of Siena, disgruntled because the pontiff had removed from his brother the governance of the Tuscan town. The cardinal had bribed the pope's personal physician to administer poison during the treatment of piles. The plot was discovered and both the cardinal and physician were strangled to death in the dungeon of Castel Sant' Angelo. The other cardinals implicated were obliged to pay exorbitant fines to expiate their crime. To further ensure loyalty within the college and to provide himself with more funds, the pope created 31 new cardinals. The following year, he launched a crusade against the advance of Islam, but to little avail. Little could the pope know, but the greatest threat to the political and religious stability of Europe was festering at its centre. Consumed by the political complexities with which he was forced to deal, Leo paid little attention to the complaints from Germany concerning the activities of an Augustinian friar called Martin Luther.

In order to pay for some of the debts of Albert, the archbishop of Magdeburg and Mainz, and to finance the spiralling costs of St Peter's, Leo had continued to sanction Julius' practice of selling indulgences to benefit the dead. An indulgence was a pardon obtained by the living to release the souls of the dead from Purgatory. Traditionally, these indulgences had been acquired by fasting, alms-giving and other good works in favour of the deceased. Over the centuries, however, the living were happier to pay a small donation to church authorities. While the idea may have had some merit, it led to abuses so grave as to threaten the future of Christendom. Pope Leo gave permission to Albert to allow the indulgence be preached in his territories. Half the money obtained was to be sent to Rome, while the archbishop was allowed keep the rest.

In 1517, Martin Luther, an Augustinian friar and a university lecturer, made public his criticisms in a tract known as the 95 Theses. On 31 October, he nailed the criticisms to the door of Wittenberg Church. Relentlessly, Luther attacked and exposed the hypocrisy of the practice whereby papal-approved 'indulgence-sellers' travelled through the towns of Germany exchanging pardons for money. As the people gathered in the markets, indulgence hawkers set up stalls, selling the benefits for the dead. 'As soon as the coin into the coffer rings, the soul from Purgatory springs,' ran one popular ditty.

Martin Luther was the eldest son of a German miner. Born in Eisleben in 1483, young Martin entered the Augustinian order in 1505, being ordained a priest some years later. During a visit to Rome, Luther was shocked by the corruption of the papal court. Returning to Germany, Luther taught theology in Wittenberg combined with hectic pastoral activity for the area of Saxony. The pinning of the 95 theses was designed to create a climate of discussion and debate. The university authorities, however, decided that the theses were heretical. The following year a report was sent to the pope, who summoned the Augustinian friar to Rome within 60 days. Claiming ill health, Luther declined to travel and instead a papal legate was dispatched to Germany. Cardinal Cajetan was a respected theologian of blameless life. In March 1519, Luther wrote to Pope Leo, 'Before God and all his creatures, I bear testimony that I neither did desire, nor do desire to touch or by intrigue to undermine the authority of the Roman Church and that of Your Holiness.'

Leo indignantly condemned Luther in a bull sent in the summer of 1520 as a 'wolf in the vineyard of the Lord'. Many realised that Luther's criticisms were valid. Arguing that most people could not understand the Latin in which the Bible was read in churches, Luther set himself the task of translating the text into German. The great humanist Erasmus had tried to call for reform through satire, but Luther set in motion a whirlwind, the results of which he could not have foreseen.

The German rulers sensed political benefit from the upheaval. For centuries, the church had been a major landowner and many looked forward to enriching themselves when ecclesiastical property was sold.

Failing to understand Luther's criticisms, Leo excommunicated Luther on 3 January 1521. In April of that year, Luther was summoned to Worms by the emperor Charles V. The emperor was determined to stamp out the cause of religious turbulence in his territories. Times had changed since Alexander had excommunicated Savonarola two decades earlier. As Christians broke into factions, some following the reform movement, others remaining with the papal party, the war of religion soon turned to bloody encounters.

Even with Pope Leo's sudden death of malaria in 1521, the papacy found itself without the energy or determination to resolve the dramatic developments in the German territories. With horror, the pope realised that the Reformation was not to be long contained solely in Germany. Already in 1520, there had been a popular uprising against Charles V. In 1524, the peasants rose against the landed rulers and the abbeys and convents of Germany. Luther himself condemned their action. Up to 100,000 peasants lost their lives in the failed uprising.

Leo was succeeded almost immediately by his cousin, who took the name Clement VII (1523-1534). The new pope CLEMENT VII had spent years at the papal court, yet his personality was unmatched to the political and religious needs of the day. At his coronation, Francis I of France and Charles V of Spain were at war. Anxious to ingratiate himself with both sides, the pontiff succeeded only in alienating both rulers who were vying for possession of Italy. Clement vacillated between the two, switching allegiance regularly. In 1527, Charles tired of the pope's machinations. He dispatched his troops to lay siege to Rome. On 6 May, the guards surrounding the city made their move. An early morning mist prevented the Romans from seeing their assailants who emerged from the dawn brandishing bayonets and muskets. The canon at the fortress of Castel Sant' Angelo fired blindly into the gloom. As German mercenary soldiers swarmed into the city, they ransacked and plundered the wealth of the churches and cardinals' palaces. Pope Clement VII was obliged to flee from the Vatican and take refuge in the fortified Castel Sant' Angelo, a cloak thrown over his white robes. The soldiers stabled their horses in St Peter's and to this day it is still possible to read on frescos in Roman palaces the graffiti, *Viva Martin Luther!*

The pope remained a prisoner of Emperor Charles V until he managed to pay his ransom on 6 December of the same year. The papal jeweller, Benvenuto Cellini, was charged with pawning the gems from the papal tiaras and melting gold utensils into slabs. For a year and a half Clement lived at Orvieto and Viterbo unable to return to the papal city.

In 1527, King Henry VIII of England petitioned Pope Clement for permission to divorce Queen Catherine of Aragon. The king's lawyers argued that Henry had erred in marrying his brother's widow. Citing texts from the Bible, the royal party maintained that the marriage of Henry to Catherine was therefore invalid.

Clement was favourably disposed to Henry. In 1521, Pope Leo X had awarded the king of England the title *Fidei Defensor*, defender of the Faith, for a treatise the king had composed on the seven sacraments in the face of Luther's criticisms. Moreover, Henry VIII had briefly been Clement's political ally. The chancellor of England, Cardinal Wolsey, almost succeeded in convincing the pope to annul the marriage. A draft of the document was drawn up, but it was never published. The draft remains in the Vatican archives to this day.

As Catherine of Aragon was the favourite aunt of the emperor, Charles V, Clement procrastinated on the case of the king of England's request for an annulment. In 1530, Clement crowned Charles Holy Roman Emperor – the last pope to do so. In 1533, he finally placed Henry under a suspended sentence of excommunication. The offended king responded by embracing the Reformation in his territories and appropriating church properties to the crown. The fate and culture of Britain was to be changed irreversibly.

Any hope for reform of church abuse seemed dashed with the election of Alessandro Farnese as Pope Paul III (1534-1549). The pope owed his fortune to the fact that his sister, Giulia was mistress to Pope Alexander VI – his nickname was Cardinal Petticoat. The new pope acknowledged three boys and a girl as his legitimate children. With his election the carnival was restored, as were bullfights and horse races. Although a *bon viveur*, Paul agreed with Emperor Charles V on the need for reform within the church. A document which he commissioned was leaked to the public in 1537. The result of the survey firmly laid the blame for the Reformation at the door of the corrupt papacy. Luther obtained a copy of the Latin document and translated it into German, gleefully vindicating his stand against the papacy.

War between France and the empire frustrated Paul's attempts to hold a council to confront the issues. The spiritual reform initiated by Luther had developed into political upheaval in the heart of the Holy Roman Empire. Finally, after years of delay, in 1545, a general council was convened at Trent, close to the foot of the Italian Alps. The small town had the advantage of being in German territory, and just eight miles from Tyrol, of which Charles V was count. The sessions met on and off until the autumn of 1548, and with the pope's death the following year, it seemed that the council would come to an abrupt halt.

After a conclave of 10 weeks, a new pope was elected, despite the fact that the emperor had excluded his name from the list of candidates. Pope Julius III (1550-1555) convened the Council at Trent a year later. After only a few months, the council was suspended as the French bishops refused to attend the sessions.

Julius III did not appear to be the type of pope anxious for reform. He had set the gossips of Rome chattering when he appointed a handsome 17-year-old street boy from Parma as keeper of the apes and named him a cardinal. The pope ordered his brother to adopt him as Inocenzo del Monte, although the youth lived with the pontiff in his villa close to the Piazza del Popolo. Julius supported the recently-formed Society of Jesus and its founder, Ignatius of Loyola. These enthusiastic members took a special oath of loyalty to the pope and dedicated themselves to missionary work and education. The pope entrusted to these Jesuits a college for the purpose of training priests to work in the Protestant lands of Germany. Rejoicing at the succession of Mary I of England, he absolved the kingdom of its interdict.

MARCELLUS II

PAUL IV

After the 22-day reign of Marcellus II, the Neapolitan Giampietro Carafa succeeded to the papacy as Paul IV (1555-1559). Elected at the age of seventy-nine, Carafa had a reputation for harshness. The principal object of his dislike were the Lutherans. Paul rejected the Treaty of Augsburg, agreed in 1530, which had allowed Catholics and Protestants live in peace with each other. A Latin tag summed up the political compromise: *Cuius regio eius religio*, whoever the king, so his religion. This agreement allowed whole populations follow the religion of their ruler, but prevented the monarchs from changing their faith.

The Council of Trent, Paul argued, only gave further credence to the cause of the reformers. Accordingly, the pope instituted his own ways of reform. The Congregation of the Inquisition provided him with information regarding anyone suspected of heresy. Realising that the reformers had made capital with inexpensive pamphlets and books, the pope created an Index of Forbidden Books. When the Index was abolished in 1966, it listed over 4,000 titles which Catholics were forbidden to read.

Distrust of the Jews in Rome was behind Pope Paul's

decision to confine them to a specially reserved area near the river, called the ghetto. Already in 1516, the Venetian authorities had enclosed the Jews in a small area, the gates of which were locked at night. Paul approved the introduction of the practice in Rome. Although Jews could work anywhere in the city during the day, they were obliged to sleep within the ghetto walls. Moreover, when they left the confined space, they had to wear a special yellow hat. On Sundays, the Jews attended prayer services, where they listened to lengthy sermons delivered in the hopes of converting them to Christianity. The ghetto was to survive until the abolition of the papal states in 1870.

The Council of Trent was revived by Pope Pius IV (1559-1565) and brought to a successful conclusion in 1563. Its decrees were executed by the Dominican Pius V (1566-1572). Romans lamented that the pope wanted to turn Rome into a convent. Prostitutes were banned from the city, bullfights outlawed and those killed in the ring were denied Christian burial. The sniff of heresy in Italy was to be stamped out mercilessly. Pius's excommunication of Queen Elizabeth I of England was foolhardy, and made the lot of Catholics more difficult in her realm. The threat of Turkish advances into Europe continued to be repulsed. The formation of a naval alliance between the papacy, Venice and Spain was responsible for the victory over the Turks at the battle of Lepanto in October 1571, when the Turks were vanquished from the Mediterranean.

Britain continued to trouble the papacy. Elected in 1572 at the age of 70, Pope Gregory XIII (1572-1585) was still full of energy and ambition. He prodded Philip II of Spain to launch an Armada against England, enlisting the help of the oppressed Catholic majority of Ireland. He also gave China and Japan as the exclusive mission-

Pius IV

Pius V

Gregory XIII

ary territories to the Jesuits. Gregory had a simple view of the papacy. Willed by Christ, all civil powers ought to support the pope in his efforts to oust the enemies of Christianity, heretics, Protestants and Turks from Christian territories. In 1572, after the slaughter of between six and ten thousand Huguenots, Pope Gregory presided over a solemn *Te Deum* in thanksgiving for the victory of the Catholic side. Such acts were hardly likely to inspire confidence in countries led by Protestant rulers, and displayed narrow bigotry on the part of the papal court. However, the monarchs of Europe paid less and less attention to the dictates of the popes as they enjoyed their hard-won independence .

One of Pope Gregory's acts was a prime example of the influence of the papacy on history. In the face of stiff opposition, the pontiff ordered the reform of the calendar.

From ancient times, societies have used calendars to regulate the solar year. The Romans traditionally dated their calendar *ab urbe condita*, from the mythical foundation of the city by Romulus and Remus. During an expedition to Egypt in 48 BC, Julius Caesar enlisted the help of the Alexandrian astronomer, Sosigenes, to help him reform the calendar. Within two years, Sosigenes presented Caesar with a new calendar of 12 months, comprising 365 days. The months were calculated between 28 and 31 days. Every fourth year possessed one extra day. The first day of the year was set on 1 January, the day on which the Senate took office. The designation of the rogue day was established in AD 4.

The length of the Julian year and the solar year was out of balance one day every 131 years. By the 16th century, this amounted to just short of 11 days. In 1582, Pope Gregory accepted the calculations of the Jesuit astronomer, Christopher Clavius (1537-1612), and reformed the Julian calendar. In order to resolve the discrepancies, Gregory published a bull, *Inter Gravissimas*, on 24 February 1582. To bring the calculations up to date, 10 days were omitted from the calendar. The changes were to take effect in the autumn. The day following Thursday, 4 October 1582, was therefore to be Friday, 15 October 1582.

The papal promulgation was immediately accepted by Italy, Spain, Poland and Portugal. Shortly afterwards Luxembourg and France adopted the new calandar. The Catholic regions of Belgium, Switzerland, Germany, Hungary and the Netherlands followed within a few years. Several of the Protestant countries refused to take part. Not until 1752 did Russia, Britain and her colonies adopt the Gregorian Calendar decreeing that Wednesday, 2 September was followed the next day by Thursday, 14 September 1752.

To this day, however, the Orthodox Churches continue to use the calendar of Julius Caesar.

Chapter 14

From the Rising of the Sun

Urban VIII

I f the papacy had managed to change the annual calculation of the world, soon it was to be at the centre
of a more momentous event, the Galileo Affair.

Having achieved 50 of the 55 votes available, Maffeo
Barberini emerged from the sweltering conclave at the
Vatican on 6 August 1623, as Pope Urban VIII (1623-
1644). The pontiff was described by a contemporary,
Andrea Nicoletti, in a vivid pen-picture: 'His stature was
rather tall, with olive complexion. His head was large,
giving evidence of a wonderful intellect and a most
tenacious memory. The colour of his eyes was light blue,
the cheeks round, his voice sonorous. He wore his beard
of moderate length and square in form.'

The new pope had spent most of his life in diplomacy
and he had supreme confidence in his own powers of
administration. Excessive nepotism soon made the Barberini family one of the richest in Rome. Urban set himself an ambitious programme of fortifications and building projects on which were emblazoned the escutcheon
of the Barberini family with its three bees. During the 21
years of his pontificate, classical Rome was reduced to
rubble as Urban's architects stripped the abandoned
ruins to erect magnificent Baroque churches. On 18
November 1626, Urban formally consecrated the new
basilica of St Peter's which had risen over the preceding
120 years. It was 1,300 years to the day since Pope
Sylvester had consecrated the first basilica in the presence of the emperor Constantine.

Some years later he ripped the bronze rafters of the
second-century Pantheon temple in Rome to provide

bronze for cannons and a canopy over the altar of St Peter's. The work, which occupied the sculptor Gian Lorenzo Bernini for nine years, was an imitation of the white marble columns placed by Constantine over the tomb of St Peter over a thousand years earlier. One wag coined the Latin phrase, '*Quod non fecerunt barbari, fecerunt Barberini*' – what the barbarians did not do, the Barberini did.

Already at the time of his election, Europe was engulfed in the 30 Years War (1618-1648). The hostilities began in May 1618 when some Protestant noblemen hurled two Catholic aristocrats out a window as they met in a castle in Prague. The event, the 'defenestration of Prague', was to cause delight to generations of school-children as they learned that adults could enjoy themselves too.

Soon all of Europe was engulfed in violent clashes which set Catholics against Protestants in religious as much as territorial wars. In France the architect of the French expansion was Armand du Plessis de Richelieu. A soldier-turned-priest for family reasons, Cardinal Richelieu insinuated himself into royal circles, where he was appointed Minister of State in 1624. Four years later, he destroyed Protestant power in France at the Siege of La Rochelle, and subdued the nobility. Of his self-aggrandisement, Pope Urban VIII observed, 'If God exists, Cardinal Richelieu has much to fear. If he does not, the Cardinal has done well for himself.'

The pope sought to maintain a much-needed neutrality, which his predecessors had shunned. 'It is impossible for me,' he wrote to Nagni, the French nuncio, on 2 April 1629, 'to put in jeopardy the common fatherhood and, in consequence, to be no longer able to heal and pacify, which is the proper business of the pope as vicar of Christ.'

But it is with the name of Galileo Galilei that Urban is best remembered.

Galileo was born in the Italian city of Pisa in 1564, the same year in which William Shakespeare was born and Michaelangelo died. As a young man he became fascinated with the movement of the stars. His study of astrology convinced him of the veracity of the claim made by the Polish astronomer, Nicholas Copernicus, in 1514 that the earth revolved around the sun. Already by the age of 20, he had carried out experiments from the leaning tower of Pisa which satisfactorily proved the theory of the oscillating pendulum. Further experiments allowed him to disprove the theory that falling objects are pulled by gravity in proportion to their weight.

Skilled with his hands, Galileo had learned how to construct a 'spy-glass' and study the movement of the stars and planets. By 1610, he began to publish some of his findings. The moon was not a flat disc, he argued, but rather a planet like the earth on which were found craters and mountains. The planets had rings and moons which circled them, enhancing their fascination for those who looked up Galileo's telescope into the dark night sky.

The following year, on a visit to Rome, he was acclaimed by the learned men of the city and feted as a genius. The aristocracy and clergy of Rome flocked to see him at the Quirinal Gardens, where he allowed the admiring throng admire a number of his optical instruments. Further studies convinced Galileo that Copernicus was correct and that the earth indeed revolved around the sun. Soon, however, the Pisan astronomer ran foul of church authorities. The principal difficulty lay in biblical texts. In the Book of Psalms it was written, 'From the rising of the sun to its setting, great is the name of the Lord.'

Already the opponents of Copernicus had quoted the

Book of Ecclesiasticus to refute the Polish astronomer. 'The sun rises and sets and hastens to the place where it rises.' (Eccl 15) Copernicus argued that this was only a figurative use of language. The biblical experts quoted from the Book of Joshua to vanquish Galileo's arguments: 'O Sun, stand still over Gideon and moon in the valley of Aijalon. And the sun stood still and the moon stayed. And the sun stayed in the midst of the heavens and did not go down for a whole day.' (Jos 10:12-14)

Galileo was summoned to appear before the Inquisition in Rome in late December 1615, to answer charges that he had rashly challenged the Holy Scriptures. In the following spring, the Inquisition published a decree forbidding the dissemination of 'improvable theories'. The aim of the document, although it did not mention Galileo by name, was clearly to silence the astronomer.

Cardinal Maffeo Barberini had known Galileo for more than a decade prior to his election as pope. Urban was fascinated by astronomy, and often consulted astrologers before taking important decisions. Among his personal effects were crystal balls and astrological charts used by fortune-tellers. In 1628, the pope summoned the Dominican friar, Tommaso Campanella, renowned for his skills in astrology. The pope expressed his concern about an imminent lunar eclipse. In a rather bizarre ceremony, the room was hung with white silk sheets and illuminated by scented candles. Lanterns representing the sun and the moon were moved around the virtual 'sky', while incantations to protect the pope were sung.

The pontiff's admiration for Galileo was unlimited but he feared that Galileo might go too far for his own good. The year after his election to the papacy, Urban VIII had received Galileo in six audiences and settled him with an annual pension from the papal coffers. The pope continued to be impressed by Galileo's views but cautioned him to treat them always as hypotheses. Otherwise, he warned Galileo, the Tuscan astronomer could fall foul of the Inquisition.

Galileo failed to heed Urban's friendly advice and in 1632 he published the *Dialogue of the Two Chief Systems of the World*. In September of that year, the pope referred Galileo to the Roman Inquisition. Throughout the spring of the following year, Galileo was forced to attend sessions of the Inquisition. The cardinals argued that the church could not give in on this issue as, by contradicting their interpretation of the Bible, they would scandalise the faithful. In June 1633, sentence was passed. Galileo was forced the deny the Copernican system or face severe penalties. The pope was unwilling to intervene and abandoned Galileo to the Inquisition. Galileo submitted, and spent the rest of his life confined to his home in Florence or the villas of some friends. As part of his deferred punishment, he was obliged to recite the Seven Penitential Psalms once a week for three years. Now almost blind, forbidden to publish or teach, Galileo lived out the last nine years of his life working on the mechanics of clocks and pendulums. The great years of his astrological discoveries were behind him. On his deathbed, a legate from Urban VIII brought the pontiff's blessing to the man who changed the universe.

It was not until 1992 that a commission appointed by Pope John Paul II re-examined the proceedings of the trial of 1633, and concluded that the cardinals were subjectively wrong in their judgement and Galileo's views on the universe were vindicated by the church. It was centuries late, as science had long since proved the case.

CHAPTER 15

I Have no Money to Bury the Pope

INNOCENT X • ALEXANDER VII

INNOCENT XI • CLEMENT XI

I n its quieter moments, Rome is a city of graceful buildings and stately ruins. The sky is punctuated by cupolas and domes and ample gardens provide perfumed oases in which one may retreat from the pressures of life. The piazzas are adorned with fountains, which bring refreshment and delight to the eye.

Much of the architecture of present-day Rome is a direct result of the patronage of the popes. If the Renaissance had its heart in Florence, the Baroque found its unique expression in Rome.

Thanks to the division of the world by Pope Alexander VI in 1493, Africa and America supplied precious materials and slaves to enrich the Old Continent. As the influence of the papacy began to wane on the political scene of Europe, the power of the popes became evermore important in the mission territories. European civilisation and Christianity advanced into the New World hand in hand.

The papacy, nonetheless, through overspending and bad management, spiralled several times close to bankruptcy. Successive popes indulged in patronage of arts they could no longer afford. Much of the monies accruing to the papacy wound up in their family coffers.

In September 1644, Cardinal Giammbattista Pamfili emerged as a compromise candidate among the warring French and Spanish cardinals. The election was precipitate on the 37th day of the conclave with the outbreak of malaria among the electors. Assuming the papacy, the elderly Innocent X (1644-1655) ordered an investigation into the manner in which the Barbarini relatives had squandered the papal treasury.

The papacy was deeply in debt but this did not deter the pope from building a fine palace at Piazza Navona, and decorating the enormous church of St Agnes as the private family chapel.

Elected at the age of 70, Giacinto Gigli vividly described Innocent's features: 'He was tall in stature, thin, choleric, splenetic, with a red face, bald in front with thick eyebrows bent above the nose, that revealed his severity and harshness. His face was the most deformed ever born among men.' The pope was not popular at court, where his sullen countenance surveyed the courtiers with suspicion, and perhaps with good reason.

Innocent's rapacious sister-in-law, the Donna Olympia Maidalchini-Pamfili, moved into the Vatican with the pope. Her daily access to the elderly pontiff, and the jealous way in which she guarded him, made her the object of suspicion and malicious gossip. A woman of few attractions, she sold church benefices on behalf of the pope, as well as herself.

Innocent was universally disliked. Shortly before his death, his cardinals finally convinced Innocent that the influence of Donna Olympia was detrimental to the papacy. To her enduring rage, he banished her from the papal apartments. When, some years later, Innocent died, the papal chamberlains went to inform the venerable lady of her bereavement. Delicately they pressed her for money to pay for the funeral expenses for the deceased pontiff. 'I am a poor widow,' came the reproachful reply, 'I have no money to bury the pope.' The decomposing corpse of the old man remained for several days in the sacristy of the Quirinal Palace until an elderly canon of St Peter's Basilica paid the cost of the funeral.

It is in the political sphere, however, that the papacy changed so dramatically under Innocent. When the 30 Years War finally ended with the Treaty of Westphalia in

1648, the pope was shocked to find that he was not invited to play any part in the final deliberations. His delegate, Cardinal Fabio Chigi, watched almost helplessly as the powers of Europe drew up concordats that excluded the church from playing any part in the division of the new Europe. The empire was reduced to over 300 semi-autonomous states, under the nominal authority of the Holy Roman Emperor. France, under Louis XIV, was to emerge as the major power of Europe, while Habsburg Spain disintegrated, consumed by squabbling aristocrats. In Germany, where the population had been halved during the war, poverty was fed by plague. The fields lay barren as crops failed and few had the strength to harvest the miserable growth. Starving people roamed through the deserted towns and villages, scavenging for what food they could find. A general sense of hopelessness and despair marks the collapse of the empire in the centre of Europe.

On the religious front, the Catholic Church had to face a new reality. Lutheranism and Calvinism were officially sanctioned. Catholicism was finally vanquished as the major force of Christian Europe. Hoping that the European monarchs would come to their senses, the pope delayed publishing a condemnation of the treaty. It was obvious that the powers had firmly rejected the perceived interference by the church in state matters, and the elderly pontiff nursed a particular grudge against the French, whom he had hoped would defend church interests. A year before the pontiff's death at the age of 80, Queen Christina of Sweden abdicated the throne in favour of the Catholic faith. There was an unrealistic expectation that other crowned heads might follow her example. But that was not to be. Soon, with her ambiguous sexual behaviour and outrageous parties, she became both the scandal and delight of Rome.

It was Cardinal Fabio Chigi who emerged from the three-month conclave held at the Vatican as Alexander VII (1655-1667), despite the French Cardinal Mazzarin's veto, which arrived too late. Alexander was suave and urbane, a member of the wealthy banking family, the Chigi of Siena. As a competent diplomat, he took part in the Conference of Münster, which led to the Treaty of Westphalia. Pleased with the manner in which he defended papal interests in the face of French opposition, Innocent called Chigi to Rome in 1651 and appointed him Secretary of State. The pope was particularly impressed by the manner in which Chigi had opposed Cardinal Mazzarin, the Prime Minister of France. The prime minister was not to forgive the new pope his victory.

Alexander was as anti-French as his predecessor and suffered the indignation of a French occupation of the papal estates of Avignon and Venaissin. The young king, Louis XIV, continued to irritate the pope as did his cardinal prime minister. Diplomacy succeeded in recovering the French estates but relations cooled between the pope and monarch soon afterwards.

Having been snubbed by the rulers of Europe, Alexander turned his attention to China, where he gave permission for Jesuit clergy to adapt rites into the Chinese language. A poorly organised crusade against the Turks did little to hinder their westward advance. He could scarcely conceal his delight when Queen Christina abdicated the throne to become a Catholic. He gave her an enthusiastic welcome, allowing her the rare honour of sleeping at the Vatican on her first night in Rome. On Christmas Day, 1655, in an action reminiscent of Charlemagne's coronation, the ex-queen was confirmed by Alexander, who became her trusted friend and benefactor.

When Alexander died of perforated kidneys in May 1667, Bernini, who had already laid out St Peter's Square for the pope, designed a monumental tomb. In a pointed political gesture, Bernini sculpted a statue of Truth as a female figure resting a foot on the globe. The artist shows Italy as the centre of the world, while Truth stubs her toe on England, so lately apostate from the Catholic faith. A canopy, made up of almost 100 pieces of red Porta Sancta marble lies over the tomb. A bronze skeleton of the angel of death rises from the vault. In his bony hand, an hourglass reminds us that all must die. His covered skull, however, indicates that we know not the day nor the hour.

A glance over the popes of the late 17th and 18th centuries does not reveal more than one or two fine pontiffs. Most of them were elderly men; the younger ones, in their sixties, often suffered poor health. Uneasy relations between different European rulers marked their pontificates.

Louis XIV, who reigned over France for more than 46 years, married Madame de Maintenon in 1683 in a secret ceremony. Spurred on by his pious wife, Louis revoked the religious freedom that had been granted to the Calvinists by the Edict of Nantes two years later. It was a fateful change that was to backfire with mortal consequence for France. Upwards of 200,000 French Huguenots fled France, taking refuge in Germany, Holland, Ireland and England. Their departure weakened France immeasurably as it strengthened greatly its neighbours.

A year earlier, the king had published the Galician Articles, which sought to limit the power of the papacy in INNOCENT XI secular affairs. Pope Innocent XI (1676-1689) retorted by rejecting the attack on papal authority. However, political developments diverted the pope from affairs in France. The Turks were making headway in their advance into Europe. The pontiff encouraged a Capuchin friar, Marco

D'Aviano, to use his considerable preaching talents to stir up opposition to the advance. The diminutive friar, under the pope's direct command, travelled throughout the north of Italy, Germany, Switzerland and Austria. The friar soon became a welcome visitor at the Christian royal courts, and struck up a strong friendship with the Emperor Leopold and his empress Leonora. The visits of D'Aviano helped a successful alliance between the empire and Poland. The Turks made no secret of their intent, as is recorded in a contemporary Muslim prayer for victory over the Christians:

> Break all their bones in pieces, and consume the flesh and blood of those who defile Your sacrifice, and hang the sacred light of circumcision on their cross. Wash them with showers of many waters, who are so stupid to worship gods they know not: and make their Christ a son to that God who never begot him. Hasten therefore their destruction we humbly entreat You, and blot out their name and religion, which they glory so much in, from off the face of the earth, that they may be no more, who condemn and mock at Your law.

For two months, the city of Vienna was laid under siege by an army of upwards of 100,000 Turkish soldiers. Marco scaled the battlements of the city, urging the troops to resist the attack of the Muslims. On 13 September, the siege was broken with the arrival of 30,000 Polish troops, led by King Jan Sobieski. The king's cavalry thundered down the hill, slaughtering everything in sight. As the infantry of 20,000 men slammed into the lines of the surprised Turkish warriors, the garrison in the city burst out of the city gates, massacring the Turks fleeing towards the city walls. At five-thirty in the evening, the siege was over. The Polish king entered the tent of the Grand Vizor. In a letter the king recalled with pride the booty of war:

I have presented the Turkish standard to His Holiness, who was instrumental no less by his money, than his prayers, to their overthrow. The Prime Vizor's horse with all his trappings, I reserved for myself.

It is sobering to think how different European history may have been had the siege not been lifted, and the Turkish advance not repulsed. The Turks retreated back eastwards, where they consolidated the Ottoman Empire.

Friar Marco D'Aviano took the sacks of coffee which had been abandoned by the Turks and brewed it, mixing it with sugar and milk. It may be a surprise that this act has given the world the beverage known universally after this Capuchin friar. In 2003 he was beatified by Pope John Paul II.

As Pope Innocent rejoiced at the withdrawal of the Turks from their westward advance, Austria was immeasurably strengthened. In France, however, relations between monarch and pope deteriorated. The king rallied the Assembly of the Clergy against the pontiff, with the veiled threat of a council. The pontiff replied by revoking the licences of a number of French clergy living in Rome and refused to accept a new French ambassador.

In 1688, a revolution in England brought William of Orange, Louis's mortal enemy, to the throne. Innocent had written to King James II (1685-1688) urging him not to make too much of his Catholic faith. The pope knew the incendiary power of religion in 17th-century Britain and cautioned that too rapid a restoration of the faith in England would serve only to exasperate the Protestants. The king rejected the papal advice and Catholic rituals soon appeared in Catholic and Protestant churches throughout the kingdom. English Protestants prayed for the day when Mary, the Anglican daughter of King James, would succeed her father to the throne. Their hopes were dashed with the birth of a son to James in June 1688. The king had the infant prince baptised a Catholic.

The English Protestants were dismayed when they realised that the Catholic line would continue in England unless challenged. In November of that year, William crossed the English Channel at Dover and from there marched to Whitehall. In the face of his unopposed advance, James fled to seek refuge in France.

When Innocent died in 1689, his tomb was constructed in the side aisle of St Peter's. Flanking the bronze statue of the seated pope were the personifications of War and Peace. The pope's gaze turns towards the figure of peace. Below is a marble panel showing the proudest moment of his pontificate, the Siege of Vienna. If the pope was unable to halt the disintegration of Catholic Europe, he was comforted in the thought that he had at least kept the Turks from their cherished conquest.

The long-lived Louis was to continue to be a thorn in the side of successive popes. When the Spanish throne became vacant at the beginning of the 18th century, Pope Clement XI (1700-1721) supported the French king in his CLEMENT XI claim to the throne. It was a poorly-judged choice. In retaliation for such support, an Austrian Habsburg army invaded Italy and defeated the papal troops, while Spain broke off relations with the Holy See for six years.

A glance over the list of popes in the 18th century reveals a line of predominantly elderly men whose moral authority waned gradually in the face of a rapidly changing world. From the Peace of Westphalia in 1648, the papacy was increasingly marginalised from the courts and centres of political power. Pope Clement XI initially supported the claim of Philip V as king of Spain, but turned against the king in favour of King Charles VI in a political reverse manoeuvre. War was declared between the Spanish and the British over succession to the Spanish throne. When the hostilities ceased in 1713 with the Peace of Utrecht, the papal party was barred from the negotiations. Some two years later, a simmering conflict between the Dominicans and the Jesuit missionaries in China came to a head. For over a century, the Jesuits had developed successful missions to the native Chinese, adapting rites and ceremonies to the culture. Some Jesuits had even become respected members of the Imperial Court.

In a decree of the emperor K'ang-his, dated 1692, we read that:

> the Europeans are very quiet; they do not excite any disturbances in the provinces, they do no harm to anyone, they commit no crimes, and their doctrine has nothing in common with that of the false sects in the empire, nor has it any tendency to excite sedition ... We decide therefore that all temples dedicated to the Lord of heaven, in whatever place they may be found, ought to be preserved, and that it may be permitted to all who wish to worship this God to enter these temples, offer him incense, and perform the ceremonies practised according to ancient custom by the Christians. Therefore let no one henceforth offer them any opposition.

Jealous of their success, the Dominicans reported their unconventional tactics to the Vatican. The Jesuits, argued the Dominicans to the pope, encouraged ancestor worship. Clement eventually published a bull prohibiting any further cross-fertilisation of the two religions.

'No Chinese Catholics,' wrote the pope 'are allowed to worship ancestors in their familial temples. Whether at home, in the cemetery, or during the time of a funeral, a

Chinese Catholic is not allowed to perform the ritual of ancestor worship.'

The emperor was dismayed by Clement's reaction and decreed: 'Reading this proclamation, I have concluded that the Westerners are petty indeed. It is impossible to reason with them because they do not understand larger issues as we understand them in China. There is not a single Westerner versed in Chinese works, and their remarks are often incredible and ridiculous. To judge from this proclamation, their religion is no different from the other small, bigoted sects of Buddhism or Taoism. I have never seen a document which contains so much non-sense. From now on, Westerners should not be allowed to preach in China, to avoid further trouble.'

Thus the missionaries were expelled from China and Christianity lost for more than a century an important foothold in Asia.

CHAPTER 16

If You Want an Honest Man, Elect Me

INNOCENT XIII • BENEDICT XIV

CLEMENT XIV

Politics played an important part in the papal elections of the 18th century, even though the papal office continued to be debased. During the conclave of 1721, the French and pro-imperial factions fought furiously to prevent either side electing a pontiff.

INNOCENT XIII In 1722, shortly after his election, Pope Innocent XIII (1721-1724) was obliged to give Naples and Sicily to the emperor, Charles VI. When the emperor in turn gave Don Carlos the duchies of Parma and Piacenza the following year, Charles ignored the whimpering lamentations coming from the papal court.

In the second year of his pontificate, in 1731, the 79-year-
CLEMENT XII old Pope Clement XII (1730-1740) became totally blind, and for the remaining eight years of his life, he conducted most of his audiences from his bed. Through his nephew, Cardinal Neri Corsini, Clement held a tight rein on papal government, issuing the first condemnation of Freemasonry. The church feared Freemasonry both for its secrecy and for its religious toleration. When Clement died in 1740, the French scholar, Charles de Brosses, went to pay his respects at the Apostolic Palace. He recalled following the abandoned corridors before coming to the pope's bedchamber. The pope's corpse had been laid out in the pontifical vestments, with his cheeks tinged with rouge to disguise his ivory pallor. De Brosses found 'a sad image of human grandeur, who certainly looked better in death than when he was alive'.

Each time they throw a coin into the Trevi Fountain, modern visitors to Rome unwittingly salute the memory of the pontiff who ordered the construction of the grandiose monument at the terminal of the Aqua Vergine aqueduct.

Throughout the 18th century, young noblemen of sufficient means and leisure from the British Isles made a visit to Italy. Imbibing at the very fountain of classicism, here they could gaze on Latin inscriptions in their original setting and inspect the treasures of the ancient world. Such a visit could last from months to years. Strolling through the valley of the Forum, the young men could pause and listen to their tutor recount the deeds of the Roman ancestors who built the empire. Perched on a broken column, they could sketch the remains of the great temples and triumphal arches. In the winter, they could buy roasted chestnuts from street vendors or drink coffee in the crowded cafes. After a fine meal with plenty of wine in their local hostelry, they could venture out to visit the brothels which were licensed by the Cardinal Vicar of Rome.

Horse races were held in the Corso, where Arabian stallions lunged along the ancient street, goaded on by the excited crowd. Pickpockets mingled among the visitors and pilgrims, relieving them of their purses and other goods.

Throughout the century, the popes founded galleries and museums where the unearthed treasures of ancient Rome could be displayed for the admiration of all. The Capitoline Museums were as much intended to display the glories of papal patronage as to preserve the patrimony of the past. The taste for archaeology was undiminished. As the villa of the emperor Trajan was excavated and the city of Pompeii unearthed, statues of marble and bronze were carried off to the papal and royal collections.

For the feast days, there was the spectacle of a ceremony at the Vatican to hear the papal choir sing at the pontifical ceremonies. Since 1589 at least, if not earlier, *castrati* had been employed at the Sistine Chapel, the private chapel of the pope. These men, who had been emasculated before the age of nine, delighted listeners with their high sweet voices, soaring through the vaults of the gilded churches. At other times, they could be found on the stage where they sang in the opera. Such was the public appetite for these choristers that the pope prohibited them from singing elsewhere and, at times, from leaving the Papal States.

BENEDICT XIV

The finest pope of the 18th century was Prospero Lambertini, who was elected after a six-month conclave as Benedict XIV (1740-1759). In the torrid heat of August, the cardinals had come to the end of their patience as they fought over who should ascend the papal throne. According to one account, Lambertini proposed himself as the most sensible compromise. 'If you wish to elect a saint,' he is reported to have said, 'choose Gotti; a statesman, Aldobrandini; an honest man, elect me!'

Urbane and witty, the genial pontiff fostered good relations with most of the monarchs of Europe, both Protestant and Catholic. The concordats that he drafted served to protect church interests throughout Europe. However, his procrastination in confirming relations with Austria damaged the church's interests in those territories. Moreover, by condemning the efforts of the Jesuits in China, Benedict lost the possibility of resuming missionary activity in Asia.

Benedict delighted in a vast building project for the jubilee of 1750. The façade of St Mary Major's Basilica was entirely redesigned, and a fine staircase at the Spanish Steps was commissioned in the English Quarter. As thousands of pilgrims filled Rome during the Holy Year, Benedict himself led the torchlight processions at the Colosseum, commemorating the witness of the early

Christian martyrs. One visitor to Rome made the extraordinary claim that Benedict stooped down to pick up a handful of sand from the Colosseum. As he sqeezed his fist closed, blood dripped to the ground. 'This is the blood of the martyrs,' the pope benignly remarked.

A scholar, Benedict founded several academies in Rome and had the satisfaction of having one of Voltaire's plays, *Mahomout*, dedicated to him. In a warm reply to Voltaire's letter of dedication, Benedict wrote: 'Doubt not the esteem we feel for your much and deservedly applauded merits.' Each Monday he received scholars in his private apartments to discuss issues of learning. Confessedly not a keen walker, the pope often took his carriage from the Vatican or the Quirinal Palace to inspect the museums which he filled with antiquities.

The pope was always ready to chat with those he met on the street. During an afternoon stroll, a madman approached the pontiff to inform him that the Antichrist had been born. 'And when did the birth take place?' the pontiff inquired politely. 'He is but an infant,' came the reply. 'In that case,' responded the pontiff, 'I can leave the problem to my successor!'

One of Benedict's curious appointments as cardinal was Henry, Duke of York, who was the son of exiled King James III of England. The pope wrote to Henry, informing him of his intention to create him a cardinal. The pope admitted that he himself had reservations about the promotion lest this should interfere with a possible restoration of the Stuarts to the English throne. None the less, he cheerfully anticipated an acceptable resolution to such an eventual impasse. 'If hereafter,' he observed, 'circumstances should make it advisable, you can resign the hat, marry, and thus avoid destroying the hopes of Ireland, that firm friend of the Stuarts and of that portion of Scotland which has remained pious and faithful.'

Two years before Benedict's death, the Seven Years War broke out, hostilities which involved France, Saxony, Austria, Prussia, Great Britain and Spain. Yet on his death, the English politician Horace Walpole wrote of Benedict:

He restored the lustre to the tiara. By what art did he achieve that glory? Solely by his virtues. Honoured by the friends of the papacy and esteemed by Protestants, he was an ecclesiastic free from interestedness and insolence; a prince without a favourite; a pope without nepotism; an author without vanity; a man whom neither intellect nor power could corrupt. Such is the deserved homage that the favourite son of a minister who never courted any prince, or venerated any churchman, presents to the excellent Roman pontiff.

Europe was also changing dramatically on the industrial front. A rapidly developing series of inventions improved techniques of production, often at the expense of human labour. The 'spinning jenny' invented in 1764 revolutionised the production of textiles. Coke increased the output from the iron-smelting furnaces. The invention of the steam engine by James Watt radically altered the transport of peoples. With increased production, roads, railways and canals were improved and prices were lowered. Banks were set up to accommodate the new middle classes who began to amass considerable fortunes. The advances in agricultural implements eased the lot of farmers and increased their harvests. Yet this was a period when people began to flock to the towns, gradually turning them into overcrowded and poorly-serviced cities.

Aided by the importation of precious materials and stones from the New World, Europe's expanding population greatly benefited from the new found prosperity. In all these endeavours, Protestant England led the field.

CLEMENT XIV   On 16 August 1773, Pope Clement XIV (1769-1774) issued a bull suppressing the Society of Jesus, known as the Jesuits. In the document, the pope gave two reasons. The first, argued the pontiff, was that the Society founded by St Ignatius of Loyola in 1540 had outlived its usefulness. The second and more important reason was that as long as the Jesuits were in existence, it was 'hardly, if at all, possible for peace to be established in the church'. The Jesuits had, within two centuries, established schools and universities throughout Europe and in the mission territories. Moreover, they had gained the ear of the powerful aristocrats of the royal courts. It was from these rulers that the request for the dissolution of the Society came.

Shortly before his death in 1758, Benedict XIV appointed the Portuguese Cardinal Saldanha to investigate complaints against the Jesuits. Encouraged by the Marquis de Pombal, the cardinal condemned the Jesuits as scandalous merchants and the following year the Jesuits were civilly suppressed. In 1761, the Jesuit Father Malagrida was burned at the stake for heresy, even though all acknowledged the torture as the work of de Pombal. Relations between the Portuguese crown and the papacy were severed until 1770.

In France, the Jesuits had earned the envy of the aristocracy by their shrewd and successful farming techniques, the profits of which favoured the Indians of the missions. In 1764, the king signed an edict dissolving the Society within his dominions. Three years later, Spain followed suit, and the Jesuits fled first to the Papal States, and from thence to Corsica.

The pope confided in a friend his worries that, if he signed the order of suppression, he might be poisoned. Pressure from France, Spain and Portugal mounted on the elderly pontiff. On 21 July 1773, the Society of Jesus was abolished in a brief which bore the pope's signature.

In the letter, the pope claimed 'that the Society from its earliest days bore the germs of dissensions and jealousies which tore its own members asunder, led them to rise against other religious orders, against the secular clergy and the universities, nay even against the sovereigns who had received them in their states'. Two non-Catholic sovereigns, Frederick of Prussia and Catherine of Russia, took the Jesuits under their protection and thus kept the order alive until its full restoration in 1804. On the horizon, the papacy had far greater threats to face, even to its continued existence.

CHAPTER 17

'I am Nothing but Dust and Ashes'

Pius VI • Pius VII

On a pleasant spring day, 5 May 1789, King Louis XVI of France took his seat in the Great Hall of the Palace of Versailles. The orchestra in the loft of the hall played a royal fanfare as the Estates General commenced the opening session. Not since 1614 had the Estates General been convened and there was an air of excitement about the historic proceedings. The Third Estate, in their black coats and stockings, sat near the door. The nobility with their silk embroidered cloaks faced the sumptuously robed bishops and cardinals close to the royal throne

The debates over the next few days were to present a précis of the changes wrought in Europe over the past century. The Declaration of Independence of the Americas, published in 1776, had greatly influenced the delegates at the assembly.

The Third Estate comprised everyone who was not a cleric or a noble. This amounted to about 95 per cent of the population. Declaring themselves to be the rightful majority, they decreed that only taxes to which they would agree should be paid. The startled king had not expected this kind of impudence and forbade them to meet in the hall allotted to them. The deputies of the Third Estate adjourned to a nearby tennis court, where some days later they were joined by several clerics and nobles.

Louis had lost the initiative for leading so necessary a reform. Rather than lose face, the king ordered a meeting of the three Estates on 27 June. In a foolish move, he placed his troops all around the palace to cow the members into submission. At Paris, the mob heard rumours that the delegates of the Third Estate had been arrested on the king's orders. Impoverished by the recent changes in agricultural policies, the Parisians began to riot, culminating in the storm of the Bastille prison. The uprising spread throughout the county. The attack was on the privileges of the upper classes, which served in effect to keep the Third Estate subject to their considerable power. On 11 August, the payment of tithes was abolished and three months later, the enormous lands of the church in France became public property.

On 22 July 1790, the king was forced to accept a new constitution which had been drawn up by the federation meeting at Versailles. Pope Pius VI had been 15 years on PIUS VI the papal throne and watched these events unroll with growing dismay. Prior to entering the church, Pius had studied law and had made rapid progress in his career. He had a finely tuned mind and, claimed his enemies, a deep-seated sense of pride. He enriched his family, building the last great pontifical palace in Rome to be inhabited by his relatives. With his pontificate, the era of the monarchical popes seemed to come to an end. Pius insisted on preserving the rights of the papacy which he saw threatened on all sides. Upon hearing of the publication of the French Constitution, Pope Pius VI dispatched a letter through his ambassador, urging the king to reject the terms of the constitution.

Several years earlier the pope and the emperor Joseph had engaged in a battle of minds and wills. The Austrian ruler was determined to have the church directed by his government. Pius would not countenance the imperial interference and travelled to Vienna to dissuade Joseph. The pontiff's efforts were to no avail. The emperor had been greatly impressed by an auxiliary bishop of Trier, who proposed that the contemporary papacy, with its pomp and prestige, was not that which was wished by

Christ. Moreover, argued the bishop, the pope was to be neither more nor less important than any other bishop. Pius had been startled by the proposals but found himself unable to counter the edicts of Joseph which the emperor began to impose on the bishops.

King Louis XVI was both obdurate and a procrastinator. In early 1791, the religious orders were abolished in France and their properties were appropriated to the new authority. Pius hoped that a swift rebuke would stir the king's resolve and that the royal court would help defend the interests of the church. But events were rapidly spiralling out of the control of both king and pontiff.

In 1791, a new constitution was drawn up, in which the king was described merely as the 'first public servant'. The feudal system was dismantled, the nobility was abolished, and the last of the religious houses were suppressed. The revolution in France continued apace. On 10 August 1792, the royal palace in Paris was stormed by the mob. Taking refuge with his family at the Legislative Hall, the monarch was deposed. A new assembly, the Convention, took control of the government. After a long trial, King Louis XVI was beheaded at the guillotine, the sentence of death being passed by a majority of one.

Over the following two years, Christianity itself was attacked in a violent purge. Over 30,000 clergy fled France, while a further 22,000 abandoned their religious vows. The guillotine and executioner's axe provided more martyrs to the Christian faith. Cathedrals, churches, abbeys and convents were confiscated by the new regime. The elaborate marble altars and gilded sanctuaries were destroyed, while richly-embroidered liturgical vestments were dragged through the streets. At Notre Dame in Paris, a prostitute was enthroned on the high altar, and the goddess of reason worshipped by anti-Christian zealots.

Pope Pius was not alone in his horror and opposition to what was happening in France. The crowned heads of Europe came to the defence of the deposed monarch. The pope, anxious not to provoke a French attack in Italy, avoided taking sides. Appealing to a rather vague tradition whereby the pope remained neutral when the belligerents were Catholic, Pius tried to secure the fate of the persecuted clergy and religious.

The third and final challenge to the 18th-century papacy presented itself in the person of a Corsican soldier, Napoleon Bonaparte.

Born on 15 August 1769 at Ajaccio, Napoleon Bonaparte was one of eight children. Through a royal bursary, the young Napoleon studied at a military academy, and at the age of 15 was enrolled at the Royal Military School at Paris. His competence at mathematics and regimental formation translated itself onto the battlefield, where he showed considerable skill in the placement of troops. As a young man, Napoleon became deeply attached to the ideals of the revolution, which he watched unfold around him. His ambition, combined with energy and skill, ensured his rapid advancement in the army. In 1796, at the age of 28, Bonaparte led a brilliant campaign in Italy, either conquering states or agreeing beneficial armistices.

The government in Paris recognised in Napoleon a soldier who would not hesitate to enrich France at the expense of his enemies. Arriving in Rome, he made a bargain with Pope Pius, exacting in exchange for peace priceless treasures from the Vatican museums. The pope could keep his throne, but the price was high. Churches, convents and monasteries were stripped, and the treasures loaded onto wagons which brought them over the Alps to Paris. Napoleon, who deeply admired the ancient

Roman Empire, dreamt of ridding Rome of its papal accretions, and restoring the capital of the Caesars.

In December of the following year, the French representative, General Duphot, was killed during riots in Rome. This provided the perfect pretext for invading the Papal States, allegedly to subdue anti-French sentiments. A French regiment was dispatched to Rome, entering the city on 15 February, the 23rd anniversary of the pope's coronation.

The States were appropriated to France and the pope was deposed as the reigning monarch. Napoleon decided that it would no longer be prudent for the pope to remain in Rome, a focus for pro-Catholic sentiment. Accordingly, four days later, the elderly pontiff was placed under arrest and deported from Rome. The cardinals protested to the French authorities that the pope was seriously ill, and thus not in any fit condition to enter exile. The plea for clemency was rejected.

The sombre crowds knelt in the rain to receive the pope's blessing as his carriage trundled through the streets of Rome and out from the Porta del Popolo. The French set about destroying all the coats of arms of the pope throughout the city. Now referred to by his family name as Citizen Braschi by the French, the pope's entourage stopped in Siena, where he was offered hospitality by the Hermits of St Augustine. Some weeks later he was transferred to a monastery outside Florence. When the French declared war on Tuscany, the pope was taken northwards towards French territory. In March, the clearly ill pope was forced to make the journey across the snow-capped Alps into France. Arriving in Valence, the pope took to bed with a high fever. Once more his lodgings were to be simple. By now, in his 82nd year, Pius was worn out both physically and mentally. The end came on 29 August. As he lay dying in his bed, he repeated again and again, 'Father, forgive them, forgive them.' His body was refused burial according to Catholic rites and his coffin was not interred until December of that year, on Napoleon's specific orders. Two years later the body was disinterred and brought to Rome where it was solemnly buried in St Peter's Basilica.

Reports on the pontiff's declining health had been relayed from Valence during the summer. Upon his death, the cardinals were obliged to meet in conclave in a city where the largest number of cardinals were gathered. Rome was out of the question and Pius had indicated that Venice would be a satisfactory choice. Many of the cardinals had already made their way to Venice when news reached them that the pope had died. The conclave opened on 30 November, in the damp lagoons surrounding the island monastery of San Giorgio.

There was an air of gloom over the conclave proceedings. Not surprisingly, few, if any, had ambition to occupy the unsteady throne of Peter. The cardinals sat for three months before finally deciding on the compromise candidate, Cardinal Barnaba Chiaramonti, a Benedictine monk of aristocratic background. The emperor Francis of Austria invited the newly-elected Pius VII (1800-1823) PIUS VII to come to Vienna for his coronation, in the hopes of winning control over parts of the Papal States. The pope replied graciously but declined the offer, inviting the emperor to the coronation in Venice instead. The irate emperor then turned down a request for the coronation to be held in the domed basilica of San Marco. Pius was crowned in the monastery church on 21 March. A papal tiara, made from gold foil and Murano glass beads, was hastily put together for the ceremony. In a deliberate snub to Napoleon, Pius announced his election formally to the rightful king, Louis XVIII

Pius expressed his desire to return to Rome to celebrate the jubilee year of 1800. The Austrian emperor provided transport by sea, lest the populace stage demonstrations in favour of the newly-elected pontiff. Pius VII entered Rome to wild acclamation on 3 July, the crowds waving to welcome the return of the papacy as much as Pope Pius himself. Velvet and damask drapes were hung from the windows of the houses and the church bells pealed the news of the pope's triumphant entry. A group of enthusiastic young men unhitched the horses from the papal carriage as it entered the gates of Rome and pulled it all the way to the papal residence at the Quirinal.

Realising his need for an astute political assistant, Pius VII appointed Ercole Consalvi as his Secretary of State. Already a trusted confidant of his predecessor, Consalvi was created a cardinal in August 1800, while remaining a layman.

By now, Napoleon realised that the imprisoning of Pope Pius VI, who had died in French hands, had not been the perfect solution. He conveyed his respects to the new pope and assured him that France wanted to reach a compromise, beneficial to the church.

Pius VII was caught in a bind. By now, Napoleon was First Consul, and the pope could not risk undue offence. The cardinals advised extreme caution, as they saw it as no less than a trick to appease the clergy which had apostatised during the French Revolution. Their reservations seemed well founded, if reports that Napoleon intended creating a new, national church were to be believed. Napoleon realised the importance of religion for the stability of French society and was determined to obtain it.

Finally, after months of tedious negotiation between the French republic and the Holy See, a concordat was agreed and signed in July 1801. At first it appeared that Pius had conceded too much to Napoleon, and was resigned to accept the losses of church properties in

France. However, there was much to be gained. Catholicism was once more officially sanctioned and the pope was permitted to veto the bishops nominated by Napoleon. Progress was slow as the French Consul dallied in promulgating the decrees throughout French territories.

On 4 May 1804, Napoleon succeeded in realising a dream. The Senate in Paris voted him emperor for life. This was what Napoleon had yearned for and had laboured so hard to achieve. At last he could shake off the image of an impoverished soldier from Corsica and don the purple mantel of the imperial families of Europe.

The date for the ceremony was set for 2 December at the Cathedral of Notre Dame in Paris. No emperor since Charles V had been crowned by a pope, and Napoleon determined to have the pontiff at the coronation. For Pius, this posed a delicate dilemma. If he were to consent, he would be the laughing stock of the crowned heads of Europe. If he resisted, the church in France would suffer. Consalvi urged the pope to attend the ceremony, assuring him that the new emperor would reward the papacy for the pope's presence. After much hesitation, the pontiff decided to accept the emperor's invitation and set out on the long journey to Paris.

The pope's entourage left the Vatican in early November. Crossing the Alps onto French soil, the pope was amazed at the enthusiastic welcome he was given by the crowds. Through every village he passed, people pressed their infants towards the windows of the carriage for the pope to bless. On several occasions the pontiff stopped his carriage and stepped out to greet the people. Such was the popularity of the Italian pope that Napoleon sent an escort to speed up the journey to Paris.

The day before the ceremony, the pope discovered that Napoleon and Josephine had not been married in a religious service. The pope refused to countenance the public coronation unless the couple were married. Napoleon flew into a temper and threatened to send the pope home in chains. The problem was resolved by the intervention of Cardinal Fesch, Napoleon's uncle by marriage, who blessed the union in a quiet ceremony the afternoon before the coronation.

The painter David has left a grandiose picture of the event. The emperor stands proudly in the sanctuary, before the high altar. Napoleon is dressed in white silk with a burgundy velvet dalmatic embroidered with gold thread. He has just placed the gilded crown of laurels on his head, and holds aloft a diamond-studded tiara for Josephine who kneels before him. Behind him sits Pius, with a far-away, possibly resigned look in his eyes. The emperor had agreed beforehand with the reluctant pope that he would crown himself and then his wife with his own hands.

It was not a disrespectful gesture, but one calculated to underline the superiority of the emperor above the pope. Although Napoleon practised his religion, he separated the papacy in his mind, aware of its strong political and social power.

Napoleon desired the blessing of the pope at the ceremony to summon up the vision of the coronation of the earliest French kings. In a sense, it was to give his empire a certain prestige, which Napoleon, because of his non-aristocratic origins, felt he lacked. Ironically, the papacy was greatly enhanced by the ceremony at Notre Dame, and the pope delayed his return to Rome until early the following summer.

Relations between the two men were soon to deteriorate dramatically. That same year, Napoleon accepted the crown of Italy, which corresponded to the northern part of the peninsula. In 1806, he demanded that the pope close all ports in the Papal States, an act the pontiff adamantly refused to countenance.

Napoleon began to see the papacy as a thorn in the side of his ever-expanding empire. Early in 1808, the emperor sent a regiment, under General Miollis, to Rome with the intention of making the pope submit to his orders. The general invited the aristocracy to his residence at the Palazzo Doria and sounded them out over the proposed action. The pope soon heard about the elaborate dinner parties in the French quarters and rebuked those who had attended. Pius' attitude to the French hardened. The pontiff received the French delegation at his palace on the Quirinal Hill, in the presence of Cardinal Pacca, the Pro-Secretary of State. The French explained that the refusal of the pope to co-operate with the emperor threatened the stability of the region. Pius refused to be browbeaten. The French were breaking the concordat, the pope protested, and therefore could no longer be trusted. The pope was furious and demanded that the French delegation be escorted from the palace. Later, the cardinal recounted with evident admiration the determined stance taken by the vexed pontiff.

A year later, the emperor finally lost patience with Pope Pius and annexed the Papal States to France. Pius indignantly excommunicated all 'robbers of Peter's Patrimony', an action which led Napoleon to arrest the pope and expel him from Rome.

History seemed about to replay itself. During the night of 5 July, French soldiers scaled the walls of the Quirinal Palace. The papal guard were alerted by the cries of some soldiers who fell from a window ledge during the attack. Soon lights appeared in the chambers and corridors as the papal court was awoken. The pope was alerted to the offensive, and gave orders that no blood should be spilt to protect him. When the French gained entrance, General Radet was admitted to the Audience Hall. There, he found the pope sitting on his throne between two cardinals. Having asked Pius to abdicate as ruler of the Papal States, the general urged him to leave the Papal States of his own free will. Radet was a pious man and was reluctantly convinced that the end of the papacy was in sight. The pope refused. Radet ordered his troops to escort the recalcitrant pontiff to a carriage that was waiting in the piazza below. The elderly pontiff was obliged to dispense with his servants and ordered his guard not to interfere. The route northwards was the same taken years earlier by Pius VI. The papal party were not told where they were being taken until they arrived in Savoy, where they were lodged in a small house. Here the pope remained, living simply, without the trappings of the papal court, until the spring of 1812, when he was transferred to Fontainbleau.

The journey across the French alps, dressed in the black of a simple priest, tested the failing health of the pontiff. Twelve days later, when he arrived in Fontainbleau, he was so ill that he collapsed on descending from the carriage.

Napoleon was in Russia, about to commence a campaign to conquer Russia. As autumn turned to winter, the freezing temperatures and superior military tactics decimated the French army, and in January 1813, the emperor retreated to Fontainbleau. Here he bullied and threatened the pontiff until he signed an agreement forfeiting the Papal States and the right to nominate bishops within French territories. The pope, moreover, accepted that the seat of the papacy would once more be moved to France.

By now, Napoleon's military battles had begun to go disastrously wrong, and in March, Pius retracted the agreement he had signed under duress. 'I am,' he wrote in all sincerity to Napoleon, 'nothing but dust and ashes.' Napoleon refused to acknowledge the letter and in January of the following year, Pius was returned to Savoy. The emperor tried to negotiate with the pope, as now his dreams of dominion were crashing around him in defeat after defeat. In 1813, the battle of Leipzig marked a crushing blow for the doomed empire. Napoleon's brother-in-law, Joachim Murat, who had been appointed King of Naples, broke with the emperor and marched on Rome. By March 1814, the French were forced to retreat from the city and withdraw northwards.

In April, Napoleon was finally defeated and forced to abdicate. Allowed to keep his nominal title, he was exiled to the island of Elba.

By the spring of 1814, Pius was released from his captivity. His former Secretary of State, Cardinal Consalvi, came to visit him and organised his return to Rome. The entrance of the pope into Rome was a triumph. Trimphal arches were erected along the route the papal carriage travelled as the pope made his entrance into the city, and bells pealed from church towers. The dignity with which he had withstood his imprisonment had won the admiration of the nobility and populace alike. As he returned to the Quirinal Palace, which he had left six years earlier, the pope ordered a *Te Deum* to be sung at the Vatican.

With the Congress of Vienna in 1815, the territorial map of Europe was redrawn. The Holy Roman Empire had been mortally wounded by Napoleon in 1806, and nothing could revive it. The Papal States were returned to the pope and the rulers of Europe decided to form a loose union, or confederation. The alliance was to give Europe 40 years of peace, badly needed after the preceding 20 years of bloodshed and upheaval. Louis XVIII was installed as the king of France. The pope was obliged to take flight once more when Napoleon escaped his captors on Elba and landed by boat in France. This campaign of Napoleon was brief, just 100 days, and he was finally defeated by an allied army at the Battle of Waterloo. Pius took advantage of the public sympathy by rapidly drafting concordats with the European heads of state to restore church properties and ensure ecclesiastical rights. The last years of his pontificate were spent trying to rebuild a battered papacy. As Napoleon lay dying in his second exile on St Helens, the pope sent a chaplain with his blessing and forgiveness.

CHAPTER 18

A Prisoner in the Vatican

GREGORY XVI • PIUS IX

Revolution continued to mark Europe and its history. During the first half of the 19th century, the States of America continued to expand, growing in terms of territory, population and prosperity. The question of slavery, however, haunted the conscience of the New World.

In Europe, musicians, artists, poets and philosophers mourned the dashed hopes of the revolutions that had been so evidently left unfulfilled. Disillusionment and frustration marked artistic endeavour, which laid emphasis on the cult of the individual. The wistful quest for freedom and equality seemed to be a romantic dream, incapable of satisfactory fulfilment. Yet social progress could only be gained by the co-operation of all members of society.

In England, the population rose from 16 to 27 million in half a century. Improved technology had increased productivity, which had led to greater prosperity. A large middle class both absorbed and generated the expanding wealth. Much of this was built on child labour and a vacuum of human rights. Queen Victoria, who had a keen social conscience, tried to express her Christian principles in social improvements. Yet in the cities, life was often difficult for those chained by their social class to the lowest place, choked by the coal smoke rising from the fires on which the emerging economy was based.

As trading and conquest continued abroad, the British Empire spread. The queen's colonies were triumphantly established in India, New South Wales and Australia. By the end of the century, the proud Victorian could boast that as the sun was setting on one horizon of the empire, it was rising on another.

In January 1848, a Russian émigré in London, Karl Marx, published his seminal work, the *Communist Manifesto*. The struggle between the property-owning class and the 'working proletariat', he prophesied, could only end in revolution.

In the same month, an insurrection took place in Sicily against the Spanish rulers. Within days, the population of the Papal States petitioned the pope to be granted a constitution which would ensure their rights.

Pius IX (1846-1878) had been elected only two years PIUS IX earlier, at the relatively young age of 54. He was handsome and charming, and something of a ladies' man. There were popular rumours that he may have fathered a son. Pius was in direct contrast with his predecessor, GREGORY XVI Gregory XVI (1831-1846), a dour Venetian who had seen papal power eroded before his eyes. The reorganisation of Europe had proved to be a disappointment to Gregory. Several of the governments which arose from the Congress of Vienna appeared to be anti-Catholic. Worse still, they favoured a dangerously liberal line in granting greater freedom than their citizens had hitherto enjoyed. In response, the pope concentrated his energies on the mission territories of the church, as well as strengthening the episcopate in the United States and in England.

In 1839, Pope Gregory denounced the slave trade as corrupt and evil, and urged countries such as Spain and Portugal to ban it in their colonies. The fruits of two centuries of active proselytism in the mission territories were paying off, and now native clergy began to be ordained.

After his election to the papacy, Pius showed sympathy with liberal reformers. His cheerful character was disposed to helping people and he well understood the difficulties of the daily lives of his flock. He took a keen interest in the welfare of the citizens of the Papal States, introducing trains and labour-saving mechanical devices. His reduction of taxes earned him the grateful devotion of the people. Nor was this confined to the Catholics of the States. Jews also were given improved facilities in the ghetto and were no longer obliged to listen to sermons preached to them on Sundays. A famous case involving the raising of a Jewish boy who had been baptised Catholic caused considerable dissent, but Pius argued that he had no choice but to intervene, as not to raise the child as Catholic would be to deny his duty.

The pope's popularity was to vanish like smoke in the face of the Austrian invasion of the north of Italy. The people had presumed that the affable Pius shared the long-desired dream of a united Italy. The difficulty was that although Pius was amenable to the unification of all the other states, he did not agree that the Papal States should form an equal part of the new Italy. His predecessors had fought hard, he considered, even to the point of death for those very territories which ensured papal independence from the influence of other states. The choice of name indicated his reverence for his closest predecessors, who had suffered greatly at the hands of invaders.

In the spring of 1848, the Italian states united to drive the Austrians from the north of Italy. There was a tacit expectation of Pius' approval and even a hope in some quarters that Pius might act as the new king of Italy. Pius eschewed the covert invitation, invoking the papal claim that he could not countenance the attack of one Catholic state upon another. The Italian nationalists, by far the majority, were shocked. The refusal of the pope to be involved in a war was understandable, but this was seen as betrayal. As the summer came, the economy of the Papal States was hit by inflation. The nationalists among the citizens blamed Pius' deputy, Count Rossi, for their hardships. Pellegrino Eduardo Rossi was a native of Carrara and had become an avid supporter of Napoleon's dashing brother-in-law, Joachim Murat, when the latter became king of Rome. After Murat's fall from grace in 1815, Rossi fled to Paris, where he rose rapidly in politics. Shortly after the election of Pius, Rossi was appointed ambassador to the Holy See. The new pope was impressed with Rossi's sour determination to defend the temporal power of the Papal States, and appointed the ambassador his Prime Minister in the summer of 1848.

Some months later, on 15 November, the count was assassinated as he alighted from his carriage in front of the Palazzo della Cancelleria. The murder provoked widespread demonstrations of the citizens, who called for an improvement in the administration of the Papal States. The pope's residence, the Quirinal, was attacked and windows were broken. One of Pius' officials was killed. The pope retreated into his private quarters to contemplate what action he might take.

Some days later, Pius decided to flee to the seaport of Gaeta, 80 miles south of Rome. Dressed as a simple priest, the pope left Rome by night in a plain carriage. Gaeta lay in the territories of the Kingdom of Naples and he was assured that the Neapolitan king would grant him asylum. Encouraged by Cardinal Antonelli, his ambitious Secretary of State, the pope demanded an end to the insurrection. But no such submission was forthcoming, and a Roman republic was established under a triumvirate.

As a fellow monarch, the crowned heads of Europe had sympathy for the exiled pontiff. While Pius deliberated about moving his court to Malta, discrete soundings came from other royal courts. In the end, the thought of moving from Rome definitively was too much for the pope, who politely refused the kind invitations.

In Rome, the newly-established Republic had to defend itself from a French attack. The arrival of the French-born Giuseppe Garibaldi in April 1849, stirred up support for the revolutionaries. Dressed in a poncho and high felt hat, the bearded leader urged a stiff resistance to the French legions which were camped outside Rome. The French soldiers saw themselves as liberators from the burden of papal rule and expected little resistance from the insurrectionists.

When the assault began, however, the Romans rallied to their new leader and routed the French from the city. Garibaldi urged Giuseppe Mazzini, one of the governing triumvirs of Rome, to pursue the retreating troops, which Mazzini stoutly refused. 'Such actions,' reasoned Mazzini to Garibaldi, 'would serve only to make us enemies of the French as well as of the pope.'

A month later, French reinforcements arrived at the walls of Rome and began to engage with the untrained insurrectionists. By the end of June, the French troops had broken into the city and established their rule once more. Garibaldi retired from Rome to engage in guerrilla skirmishes which would weaken the French. His few thousand supporters were too few to match the well-drilled French troops which entered the city on 3 July.

Over the coming months, Roman resistance to the French weakened, and many of the republican leaders succeeded in escaping from the city, to brood and plot their return.

Pius bided his time, waiting for the right moment to return to Rome in triumph. The moment never came. As the French restored order in the city, Pius was persuaded with difficulty by his advisers to make a rather low-key entry. On 12 April 1850, the pope returned to the Eternal City. He chose no longer to reside at the Quirinal Palace but took up residence in the 16th-century Apostolic

Palace at the Vatican. On 18 April, the pope appeared on the balcony of St Peter's to bless the victorious French troops who had restored to him the Papal States. He was blissfully unaware that most of the three million inhabitants of the Papal States would by now have preferred if he had stayed in Gaeta.

Times had changed during the months of the pope's exile. New, revolutionary and liberal ideas were circulating, causing hope in some, confusion in others. The pope was wary of any movement towards reform and reproached himself for his earlier tolerance of liberal ideas. However, he was willing to make improvements in the government of Rome and the Papal States. Pius undertook a visit of the Papal States in 1856, and received a loyal, if not very enthusiastic welcome from the populace. In 1860, the pope blessed the first train to depart from the Roman railway station, bound for Frascati. The drains of Rome were improved and a new bridge was erected over the Tiber. Even the tobacco factory was rebuilt as a grandiose edifice. In gratitude, the pope received several boxes of his favourite snuff.

On 22 February 1859, the British ambassador, Odo Russell, wrote to the foreign minister in London, informing him of Pius' conclusion that order had been restored to the Papal States. 'Cardinal Antonelli desires me to inform Your Lordship confidentially,' wrote Russell to the Earl of Malmsbury, 'that the condition of the Papal States is so satisfactory that he has demanded, in the name of the pope, the early and complete withdrawal of the French and Austrian troops from the Papal States, and that their complete evacuation and the fulfillment of this request now rests with the governments of France and Austria.'

But Pius was rapidly becoming irrelevant in the patriotic fervour which was sweeping through the Italian peninsula.

Russia proposed a congress which would resolve the impasse, which Pius impatiently rejected. The pope confided openly that he would accept the invitation of Queen Isabella of Spain to go to live in her territories if the impending war made such a move necessary. Pius made it clear that he would preserve his neutrality in the face of the hostilities. However, in June, the Swiss mercenaries in the papal army attacked the town of Perugia, which had rebelled against the pope's rule. Several men, women and children were killed in the ensuing melee. The following months, two and a half thousand of the papal army deserted to the Piedmontese. By the end of July, Cardinal Antonelli told Russell that 'the progress of recruitment for the papal army was unfortunately rather slow, but the pope received many letters from Ireland offering him any amount of soldiers for his army. He foresaw, however, two reasons against organising Irish regiments: firstly, the cheapness of wine in Italy which might prove fatal to the Irishman and, secondly, the laws of England which might involve the pope in difficulties with Her Majesty's government if he accepted the offers made by these Irish volunteers. In consequence he had no intention of accepting them.'

The Austrians were obliged to withdraw northwards, following their defeat at the Battle of Magenta.

As fate would have it, Pope Pius was glad to have the help of the Irish. By 1860, the papal troops numbered 21,000, enlisted from several nations. In September 1860, the Piedmontese army invaded the Papal States. The pope gave orders that no resistance was to be made when the troops attempted to scale the walls. Within months, King Victor Emmanuel II had succeeded in uniting most of Italy under his rule. In March of the following year, Rome was declared capital of the new Italy.

Now deprived of his lands, the pope launched an

attack on liberalism. In 1864, Pius published an encyclical, *Quanta Cura*, to which he appended the *Syllabus of Errors*, a list of most of the liberal achievements of the century to date. Influenced by the pamphleteering tradition of the times, the Syllabus served to drive a wedge between the papacy and modern reality. Among the 80 propositions condemned were freedom of speech, religious tolerance, and the concept that the pope could and should be reconciled with modern society. It was such theories, Pius thought ruefully, which had inspired the recent insurrection. In a document published just two days before the *Syllabus of Errors*, Pius indicated that he intended to convoke a council to be held at the Vatican. Efforts to proceed with the council were hampered by the outbreak of war between Italy and the Austrians in 1866.

The council finally convened in St Peter's Basilica on 8 December 1869. Psychologically, the presence of hundreds of bishops from all over the world served to boost the prestige of the papacy. At the heart of the discussions was the theory of papal infallibility. Pius proposed the definition which would assert that when the pope spoke on matters of doctrine and morals, he was preserved by God from error. The issue was hotly debated, with strong support and violent opposition from many quarters. Not all opponents were churchmen. Governments also feared the added power such a definition might confer on the pope.

A few days before the fourth public session, a large number of the bishops of the minority left Rome with the permission of the cardinals directing the council. They believed the definition was inopportune. On Monday, 18 July 1870, the day before the outbreak of the Franco-Prussian War, 435 bishops assembled at St Peter's. The last vote was taken. All but two voted in favour of the definition. As the pope read out the new dogma in Latin, a violent thunderstorm broke over the Vatican, drowning out the pontiff's voice.

Two months later, at seven-thirty on the morning of 8 September, the Piedmontese troops invaded Rome. Breaching the Porta Pia, the soldiers met no resistance. The pope had given orders that just one token shot should be fired and then arms were to be laid down. Thus ended the Patrimony of St Peter, which had lasted over a thousand years.

Apart from the loss of Rome, the pope was in despair that his council could not proceed. When King Victor Emmanuel established his residence at the Quirinal Palace, Pius withdrew to the Vatican, where he cultivated the impression that he was an involuntary prisoner. Sympathy for the deposed pontiff grew in his self-imposed captivity. The recently invented photograph allowed images of the benevolent old man to be circulated throughout the world, increasing the devotion of millions of Catholics who had never even heard of the Papal States.

When death finally overtook Pius in his 85th year, he had been pope for 31 years, seven months and 22 days. His was the longest pontificate in history.

CHAPTER 19

The World at War

LEO XIII • PIUS X

BENEDICT XV • PIUS XI

PIUS XII

Any man who has stood at twelve o'clock at the single narrow doorway, which serves as the place of exit for the hands employed in the great cotton-mills, must acknowledge that an uglier set of men and women, of boys and girls, taking them in the mass, it would be impossible to congregate in a smaller compass. Their complexion is sallow and pallid – with a peculiar flatness of feature, caused by the want of a proper quantity of adipose substance to cushion out the cheeks. Their stature is low, the average height of four hundred men, measured at different times and different places, being five feet six inches. Their limbs slender, and playing badly and ungracefully. A very general bowing of the legs. Great numbers of girls and women walking lamely or awkwardly, with raised chests and spinal flexures. Nearly all have flat feet, accompanied with a down-tread, differing very widely from the elasticity of action in the foot and ankle, attendant upon perfect formation. Hair thin and straight – many of the men having but little beard, and that in patches of a few hairs, much resembling its growth among the red men of America.

So wrote Peter Gaskell in 1833, describing the misery caused by industrialisation in Britain. The rapid improvements in mechanical textile production, farm labour and transport meant that people were no longer central in production. Where once the person was vital for work, now machines replaced exhausted and weary hands. Iron had taken the place of flesh and muscle at the heart of the

Industrial Revolution. R. Clynes, later a Labour Party cabinet minister, recalled his unhappy childhood in a cotton mill in Oldham:

> The noise was what impressed me most. Clatter, rattle, bang, the swish of thrusting levers and the crowding of hundreds of men, women and children at their work. Long rows of huge spinning-frames, with thousands of whirling spindles, slid forward several feet, paused and then slid smoothly back again, continuing the process unceasingly hour after hour while cotton became yarn and yarn changed to weaving material. I remember no golden summers, no triumphs at games and sports, no tramps through dark woods or over shadow-racing hills. Only meals at which there never seemed to be enough food, dreary journeys through smoke-fouled streets, in mornings when I nodded with tiredness and in evenings when my legs trembled under me from exhaustion.

A somewhat rosier picture was provided by Frederick Engels in 1892, when he observed: 'If the German middle class have shown themselves lamentably deficient in political capacity, discipline, courage, energy, and perseverance, the German working class have given ample proof of all these qualities.'

The pace of industrialisation raised serious issues for politicians and nations. When Pius IX died in 1878, Cardinal Pecci was called upon to succeed him as Leo XIII LEO XIII (1878-1903). Pecci was from a minor noble family. Soon, his features, with his aquiline nose, broadly smiling mouth and shock of wiry white hair were to become familiar to the Christian world through the dissemination of lithographs and photographs.

From the beginning of his pontificate, Leo sought to protect the rights of people, albeit within a strict religious context. Leo showed himself more open and more realistic than his predecessor in dealing with the political powers of the world. Without compromising Catholic teaching, the pope negotiated with the changing political institutions. The end of the 19th century saw the states of Europe scrambling for more territories outside the continent. The monarchies, quondam foes and allies of the papacy, were in a state of flux and in some countries were soon to disappear. When Kaiser William II, the emperor of Germany, came to the Prussian throne in 1888, the pope wrote a note of congratulations. The emperor replied with a cool acknowledgement, but decades of anti-Catholic legislation under the Iron Chancellor Bismarck was about to be undone.

In a surprising volte-face, the pope encouraged French Catholics to support the Third Republic. The pope's request, however, split the church in France into two groups, the conservatives and the liberals. In the last decade of the century, many conservative Catholics were involved in the deplorable Dreyfus affair.

In 1894, papers were discovered which indited a French military officer for providing secret information to the German government. Stripped of his rank, he was exiled to Devil's Island, a penal colony located off the coast of South America. The fact that Dreyfus was Jewish stirred up anti-Semitic sentiment. Although pardoned in 1899, it was not until 1906 that Dreyfus was exonerated of his charges. The result was to polarise Catholics in France and to cause a division within the French government.

Leo shared the suspicion of communism and socialism, both of which had been condemned by Pius IX. He also denounced Freemasonry as incompatible with Catholic doctrine. More pragmatic than Pius, Leo accepted the new political reality of Italian politics. The end of the

Papal States had come and there was no realistic chance that they would ever be re-established.

In 1891, the elderly Leo XIII issued an encyclical, *Rerum Novarum*, on human labour and progress. The 19th century had seen an expansion of Catholicism through the work of missionaries. Already in 1888, the pope had urged the abolition of African slavery. Since his youth, Gioacchino Pecci had shown an interest in the welfare of people, first as an administrator in the Papal States and later as bishop of Perugia. In this document, he reflected the church's concern for the welfare of the poor. In the ground-breaking encyclical, Leo asserted the people's right to work and to earn a just wage. Employers were urged to use their property wisely and provide suitable conditions for their employees. Counselled by Cardinals Gibbon of Baltimore and Cardinal Manning of Westminster, the pope approved of unions, the forerunner of trade unions, where workers could meet to lobby for their rights. In 1886 violence between police and strikers had ended in a massacre at Haymarket in Chicago. Despite the threat of such repeated violence, the pope approved the struggle to establish such unions and condemned the exploitation of the workers and unfair competition.

The pope, moreover, spelt out the theory of subsidiarity, 'the doctrine that a higher body (such as a government agency or bureaucracy) should not assume on behalf of a lower body (for example, a community) functions which the lower body is able to perform for itself', which protected the lower-paid workers.

Apart from the assertion of the rights and obligations of the workers, the pope also significantly altered the relationship between church and state. He accepted the validity of democratically-elected governments, and broke the church's centuries-old dependence on and support of the rapidly vanishing monarchies.

On Leo XIII's death in 1903, Giuseppe Sarto, the patriarch of Venice, was elected to the papacy, taking the name Pius X (1903-1914). The son of a village postman in the northern Italian hamlet of Riese, Sarto was noted for his extraordinary piety. As pope, he devoted his energies to rooting out heresy which was believed to have infiltrated religious institutes, seminaries and universities. Pius X saw his mission as one of restoration and purification of the priesthood and fostering the devotion of the lay faithful. His interest in global politics was minimal and he left the execution of papal policy to his Secretary of State, Cardinal Merry Del Val. Nonetheless, the pope was devastated when the First World War broke out in the summer of 1914. Indeed, he died only a few weeks after the commencement of the hostilities.

The invention of the airplane in 1903 changed the world dramatically. Soon the time spent travelling was to be reduced and just over a decade later, the aircraft was to be employed in the greatest war the world had ever seen.

With the outbreak of the First World War in August 1914, Europe was engaged in a veritable conflagration which consumed old alliances and brought forth new enemies. This war was different from all others. For the first time in history, bombs could be launched into enemy territory from the air. As the war progressed, the aeronautical engineers worked frantically to produce ever more lethal weapons. By 1917, the German Curtiss H-16 appeared, armed with six machine-guns and capable of carrying 416 kg of bombs. With improved wireless telegraphy, the combatants in the air could attack with greater precision targets on the ground or at sea. Never before was the world involved in such violent confrontation.

The pontificate of Pope Benedict XV (1914-21), who succeeded Pope Pius X, spanned the period of the First

World War and the fragile peace that ensued after the signing of the peace treaties in 1919.

As the hostilities continued, Benedict pleaded for a truce at the first Christmas of the war. He hoped that this chink might allow an end to the 'suicide of Europe'. The Germans accepted the proposal, but it was rejected by the Allies. An idea of what might have come about had the papal initiative been accepted is provided for us by a soldier, an eyewitness to the event. Writing to his mother on Christmas Day, 25 December 1914, Second Lieutenant Dourgan Chater related:

> I think I have seen one of the most extraordinary sights today that anyone has ever seen. About 10 o'clock this morning, I was peeping over the parapet when I saw a German, waving his arms, and presently two of them got out of their trenches and some came towards ours. We were just going to fire on them when we saw they had no rifles so one of our men went out to meet them and in about two minutes the ground between the two lines of trenches was swarming with men and officers of both sides, shaking hands and wishing each other a happy Christmas.

Benedict, a native of Genoa, had spent most of his priestly life as a Vatican diplomat. His election to the papacy took place against the background of the outbreak of the First World War. Following the pontificate of Pius X, the cardinals realised that a skilled negotiator was needed to intervene between the belligerent sides. Accordingly, they chose the Archbishop of Bologna, Giaccamo della Chiesa, who for six years had been Undersecretary of State to Pius X. Della Chiesa has developed good relations with the ambassadors accredited to the Holy See. The new pope had been made a cardinal only weeks before the death of the pope. A short, unprepossessing man, who walked with a limp, and uneven shoulders, Benedict was unkindly called the dwarf by some members of the papal court. Indeed, he once referred to himself as 'an ugly gargoyle among the beauties of Rome'.

The pope adopted a policy of strict neutrality – or impartiality, as he preferred to call it – between the Christian nations which were at war. While he maintained his respect for the legitimate authorities, he founded a relief service at the Vatican for prisoners and victims of the war. The pope followed personally the work of the nuncios who were accredited to the warring nations, intervening with advice and suggestions as he saw fit. His diplomatic efforts to foster peace were all rebuffed by the belligerents. On 1 August 1917, Benedict issued a peace proposal. He explained his desire to be impartial and urged the warring parties to unilaterally reduce their armaments. 'Once the supremacy of law has been established,' he wrote, 'let every obstacle to the ways of communication between the peoples be removed, by ensuring through rules to be fixed in similar fashion, the true freedom and common use of the seas. This would, on the one hand, remove many reasons for conflict and, on the other, would open new sources of prosperity and progress to all.'

With the collapse of Russia in 1917, Benedict saw the possibility of the reunification of the Orthodox and Catholic Churches, and founded the Pontifical Institute of Oriental Studies. His hopes were to remain unfulfilled in the short term, although understanding between the two churches was to grow as the century unfolded.

The pope's overtures were largely ignored. When, at last, the war came to an end with the Paris Peace Conference, the Vatican was excluded from the negotiations. On 12 January 1919, leaders of 32 states, representing about 75 per cent of the world's population, attended the

Paris Conference. No invitation to the Vatican was issued to send a delegation, although Benedict was broadly in favour of the terms of the subsequent Treaty of Versailles which ensured the peace. It seemed, once more, that the Vatican was now little more than a threadbare political power, a shadow of its former glory.

While standing in a drafty corridor at the Vatican one cold January evening, Pope Benedict caught a chill. He had been waiting for over half an hour while a key was fetched to open a door. Soon afterwards he took to bed with a high fever. Within days, the pope had contracted pneumonia. On 22 January 1922, after a pontificate of seven years, four months and 20 days, Pope Benedict died. He was just 66.

The choice of the cardinals gathered in the Sistine Chapel three weeks later fell on the scholarly archbishop of Milan, Achille Ratti. As a young man, Ratti had become the chief librarian at Milan's prestigious Ambrosian Library, before becoming vice-prefect of the Vatican Library. He had come to the attention of Benedict during the war years. Benedict admired his forthright manner and his vigorous attitude to work. In the delicate aftermath of the world war, the Vatican needed a talented, well-versed diplomat who could skillfully negotiate with the emerging powers. Benedict dispatched Ratti to Poland as his representative, with instructions to improve relations with the Holy See. Little could the new nuncio imagine that as the Red Army invaded Poland, the map of Europe was to be changed radically. He had shown skill in his mission, and was rewarded with the prestigious position as Archbishop of Milan.

The new pope took the name Pius XI (1922-1939) in PIUS XI honour of his recent predecessors. Ratti's passion was mountaineering and the myopic pontiff rose to the many challenges with the enthusiasm and tenacity of the

Alpinist. Shortly after his election as pope, Pius XI set about establishing relations with the Italian state in order to overcome the impasse regarding properties confiscated during the pontificate of Pius IX. Benito Mussolini had become the Prime Minister of Italy in the same year as the accession of Pius. A commission, composed of representatives of the Holy See and the Italian government, examined the claims of both sides. Pius was dismayed when, in 1925, Mussolini established a fascist dictatorship. After four years of careful negotiation, an agreement was reached. The pope was represented by Cardinal Gasparri and the king represented by Benito Mussolini. On 11 February 1929, both parties met at the Lateran Palace, built on the site of the first donation of imperial property by the emperor Constantine in the early fourth century. The Holy See acknowledged that Italy was a legitimate kingdom and the Italian authorities agreed to the establishment of the Vatican City State, the area of 108 acres around the Basilica of St Peter's. The Vatican would continue to be the residence of the popes, but some properties in Rome, which had been seized by the Italians, were restored to the church. As a sovereign state, the Vatican was permitted to have its own government, its own ambassadors, its own coinage and postage as well as newspaper and radio communications. A lump sum was paid by the Italian state to the Holy See in compensation for properties forfeited 60 years earlier. The funds were invested primarily in Italian industrial interests. Pius' arrangement was not universally welcomed, and even some Catholics called him the 'Fascist Pope'. The concordat was to remain in force, governing Vatican-Italian relationships, until a radical revision in 1985.

But even the concordat was not enough to silence Pius. When Mussolini's troops prevented young Catholics from meeting freely, the pope rounded on *Il*

Duce and denounced him for interfering in areas which belonged properly to the church. In a stinging encyclical, *Non Abbiamo Bisogno* (*We Have No Need*), published in 1931, Pius rebuked Mussolini's interference and warned him to refrain from exerting influence on the young people.

Advised by his Secretary of State, Cardinal Eugenio Pacelli, Pius signed a concordat with Germany to ensure the church's rights. The Vatican had watched with suspicion and alarm the political and military rise of Adolph Hitler during the 1930s. Through clever propaganda, the Austrian-born leader stirred up Teutonic pride, organising monster meetings of Germans and swelling an exaggerated nationalism. Ever pragmatic, the Vatican diplomats sought to deal with the threat with compromise. In 1933, Germany and the Holy See signed a concordat, governing church administration and education. No sooner was the ink dry on the paper than Hitler began to break the promises. When the German Führer visited Rome with an entourage of 5000 attendants to meet Mussolini, Pius XI conspicuously retired to his summer residence at Castelgandolfo, some 20 miles outside the capital. Hitler was infuriated by the snub and immediately imposed a ban on German Catholics from travelling to the Eucharistic Congress held in Budapest in 1938. Although Hitler flouted the provisions of the concordat, German Catholics were legally obliged to observe them.

Meanwhile in Spain that same year, the state confiscated church property and the clergy lost their privileged status. Anarchy was narrowly prevented in 1936, when General Francisco Franco crossed from his post in Morocco and landed at Cadiz. The general declared himself a dictator in time of crisis and established a provisional government. This led to a horrific civil war, which lasted three years. In 1941, a concordat was agreed between the ecclesiastical authorities and Franco's victorious government.

From the beginning of the war, Pope Pius XI sought to preserve the neutrality of the Holy See. That, however, did not prevent him from publishing a forthright encyclical, *Mit Brennender Sorge* (With Burning Anxiety) on 14 March 1937. Pius expressed his frustration with National Socialism and saw Russian Communism as a threat to be vanquished. Five days later, he published another encyclical, *Divini Redemptoris Promissio* (Of the Divine Redeemer), condemning atheistic communism. Hitler was infuriated by the actions of the octogenarian pope and delivered frenzied addresses attacking the papacy. He tempered his language only when he realised that such anti-papal propaganda could rebound against him if it were to lower morale in the army. Pius was informed that Hitler's Nuremberg Laws deprived Jews of German citizenship and threatened their very existence in Germany. In June 1938, the pope asked an American Jesuit, Father John LaFarge, to secretly compose, in his name, an encyclical condemning racism and anti-Semitism. Working rapidly with two colleagues, LaFarge had the first draft ready by September. The working title, *Humani Generis Unitas* (The Unity of the Human Race) indicated the concern of the church with the rising tide of racism and xenophobia. He sent a copy to the pope to read. Pius was impressed with the work, and added further notes and comments prior to its eventual publication. But time was not on the elderly pontiff's side. Pius XI died in early February, 1939, and his successor, Pius XII, decided not to proceed with the publication, perhaps judging its contents inflammatory and provocative. The question has often been posed: if Pius XI had lived to see the publication of the encyclical, would history have been different?

Eugenio Pacelli ascended the papal throne in March, 1939, taking the name Pius XII (1939-1958). The new pope had spent his life in Vatican diplomacy. The first pope to have been born in Rome since 1740, Eugenio Pacelli was a member of a minor noble family. His health was so delicate as a young man that he completed most of his studies at home, rather than at the seminary. Shortly after his ordination, Pacelli was appointed to the Secretariat of State at the Vatican. In 1917, he had been appointed nuncio to Bavaria. Shortly afterwards, in 1920, he was made nuncio to the new German Republic, a position he occupied until his recall to Rome in 1929. Those years had given the shy, fastidious Pacelli a deep appreciation and admiration of the Teutonic character. The cardinals realised that in view of the impending war, it was imperative that the new pope have a clear command of European politics. For them, the perfect choice was Pius XI's most trusted adviser, who had been the latter's Secretary of State for almost 10 years.

Had the war not intervened, Pacelli's papacy may have been one of the finest in history. A brilliant linguist, the pope enjoyed nothing as much as work. Blessed with a photographic memory, he memorised his addresses in various languages and delivered them as if they were impromptu reflections. The crowds, which came from all over the globe, delighted in listening to the pope speaking in their own language. Shortly before his death, Pius began to study Arabic. On one occasion, an aide apologised for moving a microphone while the pontiff was delivering an address. The pope expressed his surprise and explained that he had not seen the hand, as he was 'reading the text'.

Pius XII had a shrewd appreciation of the emerging world of cinema and the importance of the cinematic and photographic image. His fine profile, with its high brow and sharp aquiline nose, was reproduced in countless mass-produced photographs and portraits. His large brown eyes, which suffered from a slight cross, were framed by round steel frames. Pius exerted something of a magnetic attraction. Over two and a half million people visited Rome during the jubilee year of 1950. The pope was very interested in modern means of communication and partook in a filmed documentary about his life. A celebrated clip showed the camera catching the pontiff by surprise walking in the Vatican gardens, reading his official documents. In fact the pope practised the shot four times prior to the recording. Catholics were fascinated by the details of the pope's private life, his pet canary, the German sister who ran the papal household and who even decided who gained entrance to visit the pope. In smoky cinemas throughout the world, newsreels regularly reported the activities of the 'Angelic Pastor'. The pope slept four hours at night and often whiled away the dark hours reading obscure medical journals or agricultural manuals in order to converse with those whom he met in private audience the next day.

Sadly, although Pius abhorred racism, his view of the Jews reflected a common Catholic position that was anti-Semitic. Although Pius XI had famously remarked in 1938, 'we are all spiritually Semites', many Catholics had long regarded Jews with suspicion and prejudice. Already in 1179, the Third Lateran Council had declared that the word of a Jew was not as trustworthy as that of a Christian. Some years later, Jews were obliged to wear a special hat for identification. Not until the reign of Pope John XXIII was the prayer for 'the perfidious Jews' removed from the Prayer of Intercession during the Good Friday liturgy.

In various allocutions, Pius XII admonished the warring sides to seek reconciliation and peace. His words fell on deaf ears. The nuanced language of diplomacy lost its lustre in the face of the horrific acts committed by the belligerents. Several bishops complained bitterly that the

Holy See did not effectively condemn the atrocities carried out by the Nazis in Poland.

As the war progressed, Pius seemed to have an exaggerated belief in the efficacy of his diplomacy. He tenaciously clung to his policy of impartiality, of which he was partly an architect under the pontificate of Benedict XV during the First World War. Dismayed by the aggressive advance of Nazism, he feared as much the establishment of atheistic Bolshevism in the heart of Christian Europe. Faced with the escalation of violence, he clung to the wreckage of his pre-war policies, which had long been rejected by the warring nations. The pope seemed to believe that any outright and specific condemnation would make the plight of the population even worse. Pius was aware of criticism of his perceived silence. On 2 June 1943, he addressed the College of Cardinals. 'Every word that We addressed to the responsible authorities and every one of Our public declarations had to be seriously weighed and considered in the interests of the persecuted themselves in order not to make their situation unwittingly even more difficult and unbearable.' Diplomacy, Pius seemed to insist, would win out. In veiled language, the pope defended 'people who because of their nationality or race ... who, without even fault on their part, seem destined for extinction'.

This view was shared by Ernst von Weizsacker, the German ambassador to the Vatican during World War II. In his memoirs, he wrote:

Not even institutions of worldwide importance, such as the International Red Cross or the Roman Catholic Church saw fit to appeal to Hitler in a general way on behalf of the Jews or to call openly on the sympathies of the world. It was precisely because they wanted to help the Jews that these organisations refrained from making any general and public appeals; for they were afraid that they would injure rather than help the Jews thereby.

However, it was part of von Weizsacker's mission to persuade Pius that any public denouncement would cause further harm and suffering. The dilemma which presented itself to Pius was the same one as faced the Allies against Hitler. Nor was suffering confined to the Jews. Thousands of priests and religious died in the concentration camps. Evidence has come to light in the past decade indicating that Pius knew about a plot to assassinate Hitler, and gave his tacit approval. This cannot be proven until the wartime archives are published by the Vatican. The archives, however, show that the nuncio in Berlin issued over 300 protests against the excesses of the Third Reich. Hitler, for his part, considered kidnapping the pope and taking him to captivity in Munich, a plan he abandoned with reluctance, fearing the reaction of the Catholic world.

A former inmate of Dachau, Mgr Jean Bernard, later Bishop of Luxembourg, observed:

The detained priests trembled every time news reached us of some protest by a religious authority, but particularly by the Vatican. We all had the impression that our warders made us atone heavily for the fury these protests evoked ... whenever the way we were treated became more brutal, the Protestant pastors among the prisoners used to vent their indignation on the Catholic priests: 'Again your big naïve Pope and those simpletons, your bishops, are shooting their mouths off ... why don't they get the idea once and for all, and shut up. They play the heroes and we have to pay the bill.'

At the Vatican, a bureau was set up to locate missing persons, using the web of papal links throughout the world to gather information and pass this on to family and friends. In Germany, some bishops tried to appease Hitler, while others publicly supported him. Nazi policy towards the Jews varied from country to country. Archbishop Saliege of Toulouse and Archbishop Gerlier of Lyons and Bishop Thias of Mantauban organised a rescue campaign that sheltered as many as 200,000 victims of Nazism. In Holland, the clergy stirred up fiery opposition to Nazi violence. The Jewish historian Pinchas Lapide observed:

> The saddest and most thought-provoking conclusion is that whilst the Catholic clergy of Holland protested more loudly, expressly and frequently against Jewish persecutions than the religious hierarchy of any other Nazi-occupied country, more Jews – some 11,000 or 79 per cent of the total – were deported from Holland; more than anywhere else in the West.

Church officials in Hungary issued an estimated 80,000 baptismal certificates to Jews in order to save them from Nazi authorities. In other areas of Eastern Europe, the Vatican continued to develop an elaborate escape network. These sometimes, however, favoured Nazi spies. In Bulgaria, the papal representative, Archbishop Angelo Roncalli, managed to rescue several hundreds of Jews. He issued false baptismal certificates so that Jews could flee Bulgaria. At the Vatican itself, an Irish priest, Monsignor Hugh O'Flaherty, hid hundreds of Jews and British soldiers and arranged for their escape from Italy. To all of these efforts, Pius gave his tacit approval and support. At his country residence at Castelgandolfo, some 20 miles outside Rome, the pope housed thousands of Jewish refugees, providing them with food, shelter and clothing.

Equally damning was the silence from Rome on the

ethnic slaughter in the Balkans where Orthodox, Catholics and Muslims engaged in a ferocious massacre, the embers of which conflict remained for decades, only to flare up again at the end of the 20th century.

Historians are divided over the effectiveness of the papacy's role during the war. Pope Pius supervised a rescue network which saved 860,000 Jewish lives – more than all the international agencies put together. However, it remains a sobering thought that six million Jews alone perished in the heartland of Christian Europe. How much more the Vatican could have done is impossible to calculate. That it could have done more is unquestionable.

When Pius died at Castelgandolfo in October 1958, his last moments of painful life were caught on camera and sold to the press by his discredited doctor. Thousands lined the route of the sombre cortege which made the journey from the country residence to St Peter's for burial. The crowds were horrified at the public exposition of his corpse at the Vatican. As his body lay in state before the high altar, his face turned black, the result of inefficient embalming. In his latter years, Pius became almost a recluse and was regarded as a hypocondriac by those who cared for him. Before his death, he had confided to a diplomat that he feared for the church after his death. 'After me,' he commented sadly, 'comes the deluge.'

CHAPTER 20

A New Spring

JOHN XXIII • PAUL VI

JOHN PAUL I

A French visitor once asked Pope John XXIII (1958-1963) how many people worked at the Vatican. The pontiff paused for a moment and then replied cheerfully, 'Oh, about half of them!'

Several such anecdotes recount the wit and wisdom of 'Good Pope John'. Recalling his impoverished youth in the north of Italy, Angelo Roncalli observed, 'There are three ways of ruining oneself: women, gambling and farming. My father chose the most boring!'

Roncalli, who succeeded Pius XII in October 1958, was deeply impressed by the work of Bishop Giacomo Radini-Tedeschi whom he assisted as secretary after his ordination. Pope Leo XIII's teachings were still being developed and applied and the bishop was an enthusiastic supporter of the rights of workers. During the First World War, he enlisted as an army chaplain in the medical corps. When the war ended in 1918, he taught briefly in Rome, before being sent as Apostolic Delegate to Bulgaria. He was the first papal representative to the country in 600 years. Roncalli's relations with his superiors in Rome were often strained, and after 10 years he was appointed to another obscure outpost in Turkey. His time in Turkey corresponded with the Second World War and he worked tirelessly to help the victims of Hitler's regime who lived in or passed through the state.

When the war ended, the new French government insisted that the Papal Nuncio in Paris had to be removed immediately as he had collaborated with the Vichy administration. The Vatican was obliged to find a replacement at short notice. The nuncio was, by tradition, the dean of the diplomatic corps. This was made all the more urgent by the fact that in the absence of a nuncio, the New Year's address of the diplomats would be given by the Soviet ambassador. Given Pius XII's unflinching opposition to communism, that would be unthinkable. Roncalli had hitherto enjoyed respectable obscurity and nobody could think of any reason to oppose his appointment.

Archbishop Roncalli was enchanted by Paris, with its elegant embassies and salons. The rotund figure of the gregarious nuncio was a common sight at official receptions, where he jovially chatted with anyone he met. On one occasion he was seated at an official dinner opposite a lady who sported a descending collage. Afterwards, the embarrassed host apologised to the archbishop for the table-placing. 'Not at all,' replied the nuncio, 'Don't worry. Everyone was so busy looking at me to see how I would respond that nobody looked at madame!'

After eight pleasant years in the French capital, Roncalli was created a cardinal and appointed to the patriarchal See of Venice. It was an honourable end to a life of obedient service. It was from the railway station in Venice that the Patriarch set off to attend the conclave. His return ticket was in his pocket.

When Pius XII died on 9 October 1958, 50 cardinals gathered at the Vatican to elect his successor. Pius had named a large number of non-Italian cardinals, and there was a hope that a non-Italian might be elected. On the 12th ballot, Roncalli was elected, taking the name John XXIII. He would never use the return ticket. He was almost 77. He had time to prepare a brief speech for the cardinals who had elected him, marked by simplicity and trust in God.

The cardinals may have elected John as a caretaker pope, until the church had time to adjust to the death of

Pius XII. 'I have taken John as my name,' he commented to one well-wisher, 'It is the most common of the papal names. And most of the John's had very brief pontificates.'

The two men could not have been more different. While Pius was tall and slim, John was short and fat. Pius always found the most flattering angle for the camera, John simply smiled broadly for the photographer. 'If God had intended me for the papacy,' he once quipped, 'He could at least have made me photogenic!'

People were not interested in the pope's physical appearance. His gestures spoke more loudly than words. On his first Christmas, John decided to visit Rome's prison, *Regina Caeli.* His assistants tried to dissuade him from making such an unusual visit, but the pope was adamant. 'I have always visited prisons. Now that I am pope, surely I will not change.' That visit was followed up by a visit to the children's hospital, where to John's evident delight, he was greeted by some of the young patients as Father Christmas. Realising that the pious pictures he had given the children were rather small, he sent toys to the hospital some days later.

On 25 January 1959, John announced to the cardinals gathered at the Basilica of St Paul-outside-the-walls that he intended to convene a general council. The surprise announcement was greeted by the elderly men with a stony silence. After a moment, John observed, 'We would have expected greater enthusiasm from Your Eminences.' John was to experience frustration with Vatican officials on a regular basis. When he received George Fisher, the Anglican Archbishop of Canterbury in December 1960, he was exasperated to find that the Vatican newspaper, *L'Osservatore Romano,* made no mention of the visit, 'even though they delight in printing every other tittle-tattle of Our day'.

In the event, the Second Vatican Council was to be the defining event of John's five-year pontificate. But for a time, it appeared that he might not live to see the opening session.

John realised that he was seriously ill in November 1961, when he suffered a major intestinal haemorrhage. The grim prognosis was confirmed by his doctor. The pope was suffering from cancer of the stomach. John was deeply disappointed with the news, for he realised that the council, still in its initial stages of preparation, was in danger. He charged his doctors to say nothing and swore the sisters who cared for him in the papal apartments to secrecy. Nobody was to know that he was a dying man.

John received in audience at the Vatican the daughter of Nikita Khrushchev, the Russian premier. The move broke the ice of decades. In 1962, John intervened in the Cuban missile crisis, writing personally to Khruschev and President John F. Kennedy of the United States. His appeal was received cordially by both sides. A realist, John succeeded in improving relations between the Holy See and democratically-elected governments.

Finally, in October 1962, the months of preparation came to fruition and John presided over the inauguration of the Second Vatican Council at St Peter's Basilica. It was clear by then that the elderly pope was ill. John allowed the bishops to discuss various topics in freedom, although he observed the proceedings in St Peter's Basilica on a closed circuit television in his apartments. Throughout the early months of the following year John suffered from the advancing cancer. Realising that he was dying, he nevertheless retained a resigned sense of peace. 'My bags are packed,' he assured his secretary, 'I am ready to go whenever the Lord calls me.' Pope John died on 3 June 1963. His death provoked a veritable outpouring of grief, not only within the Catholic community but from quarters not traditionally sympathetic to the popes. His breadth of vision stemmed from a simple faith and understanding of the frailty of the human condition.

The cardinals who gathered at the Vatican to elect John's successor decided that the most suitable candidate was the archbishop of Milan. Giovanni Battista Montini, who PAUL VI took the name Paul VI (1963-1778) had spent over 30 years in the Roman Curia before his surprise nomination as head of the archdiocese of Milan in 1954. For the conservatives who had been polarised by John, Montini offered a track-record of faithful and unobtrusive service. For the liberal wing, Montini was a cultured man with an open and generous attitude to a rapidly changing world. What the cardinals wanted most of all was a pope who could astutely steer the council to a safe end.

Montini was the son of a wealthy lawyer, who had abandoned his legal career in favour of journalism. The young Montini was ordained in the northern Italian town of Brecia in May 1920 at the age of 23. After further studies in Rome, he entered the Vatican Secretariat of State and in 1923, he was dispatched to the nunciature at Warsaw. He was recalled to Rome the following year by Pius XI, where he later progressed under the patronage of Cardinal Pacelli. He was nominated chaplain to the Federation of Catholic University Students, a role that exposed him to contemporary thinking and concerns In 1937, Pope Pius XI nominated him, on Pacelli's recommendation, as the Substitute for Ordinary Affairs. He was, in effect, the assistant to Pacelli, then Secretary of State. When Pacelli was elected to the papacy, he confirmed Montini's role. On the death of Pacelli's Secretary of State, Cardinal Maglione, in 1944, Pacelli reassumed his former role as Secretary of State himself and Montini became the chief assistant to the pontiff. Montini, with his deep-set grey eyes under his bushy eyebrows and wide brow, soon became as familiar at the Vatican as the pope's shadow.

In 1953, Montini was appointed archbishop of Milan, a surprising nomination as he had been appointed Pro-Secretary of State just one year previously. Breaking with tradition, Pius failed to create Montini a cardinal. Some saw this as a snub. Pius, however, in 1952 explained that he had intended to create Montini a cardinal but that the latter had declined the honour.

The new archbishop of Milan enjoyed the break from the decades of often tedious administration at the Vatican. Although personally shy and retiring, soon Archbishop Montini had won general admiration as 'the workers' bishop', making visits to factories and industrial plants. The sight of a bishop wearing a plastic safety-helmet was a novel sight indeed. His contact with university intellectuals suggested to him the importance of education, and he greatly improved the level of education within the diocese. Montini's father had become a successful newspaper editor and the archbishop himself enjoyed a favourable relationship with the press. Already at the conclave of 1958, Montini was mentioned as the rightful heir to Pacelli although he was not a cardinal. Even though according to church law a man did not need to be a cardinal for election to the papacy, for centuries the new pope had come from the ranks of the Sacred College. Just two months after his election, Pope John XXIII named 23 new cardinals. Montini's name headed the list.

On 21 June 1963, less than three weeks after the death of Pope John XXIII, Montini was elected to the papacy. Reticent in comparison with his jovial predeccessor, Pope Paul VI reconvened the council and resolved to bring it to a satisfactory end. Like John, Paul was deeply aware that the church needed to be brought up to date.

He oversaw, with careful diplomacy, a contentious reform of the liturgy. For centuries, the Mass had been celebrated in Latin, and accretions both of beauty and deformity had clung like pearl barnacles to the prow of a ship. Despite staunch opposition from some quarters, Paul proceeded to simplify the liturgy and present the public prayers of the church in the vernacular. It was a considerable risk, and for several years, those who refused to accept the changes brought about by the Second Vatican Council clung to the Latin Mass as their bulwark.

Pope Paul, ever the diplomatic pragmatist, instituted an international synod of the world's bishops to meet on a regular basis. He thus sought to give greater autonomy to diocesan bishops, clergy and faithful to carry out their Christian functions without interminable recourse to Rome. Such a belief, argued Paul, was more in keeping with the earliest practice recorded in the New Testament. Historical developments, such as the Great Schism of the East and the Protestant Reformation had led the popes to exaggerate their position as the fulcrum of the church. Paul shared John's dedication to the cause of ecumenism. Like his predeccessor, Paul realised that progress could only come about through change. 'The pope, as we well know,' observed Pope Paul, 'is without doubt the most serious obstacle on the ecumenical road.'

In 1964, as the council was ending, Pope Paul travelled to the Holy Land to make a pilgrimage of thanksgiving for the success of the council. Here he met with Athenagoras, the Patriarch of Constantinople. The two men lifted the mutual excommunications which had been imposed by their predecessors over a thousand years previously and their symbolic embrace built a bridge for stronger communications.

Paul continued the ecumenical initiative begun by John XXIII. He received the Anglican Archbishop of

Canterbury in the Sistine Chapel as 'his dear brother' and referred to the Anglican communion as a 'sister Church'. Centuries of resentment on both sides were swept away by a simple embrace.

Certainly, Paul had his critics. He was derided by some for a naïve desire for Christian unity at all costs. Others chastised him for his indecisiveness in dealing with emerging scandals in the church. In America, the archdiocese of Chicago was torn over the controversial Cardinal Cody, who was accused of spending diocesan funds on a mistress. In Europe, papal authority was flouted by Archbishop Marcel Lefebvre, whose conservative followers refused to accept much of the teaching of the council. Yet Paul could never have been described as a liberal. He wrote two encyclicals which underlined his traditional outlook. In the first, *Ecclesia Dei* (The Church of God), he gave his assurances that priestly celibacy would remain the norm of the Catholic Church. In his encyclical *Populorum Progressio* (On the Development of Peoples), he expressed his concern for the division of the world into rich and poor, and the exploitation of the Third World by the rich industrialised countries of the First World.

Yet Paul also accepted disastrous banking advice from Italian financiers who persuaded the pope to move Vatican investments from Italian stocks, where they could be negatively influenced by a change in the international economy. One of his trusted advisers, Michele Sindona, ended his own life in prison. Paul's promotion of Chicago-born Archbishop Paul Casimir Marcinkus also led to further scandal involving the Vatican finances.

The most controversial encyclical, *Humanae Vitae* (On Human Life), issued in July 1968, dealt with the dignity of the human person especially within marriage. Pope John XXIII had established a panel of experts to examine the church's teaching on contraception. The final report, presented to Paul, showed disagreement on the issue and left open the possibility that church teaching could be modified. The pope rejected the findings of the commission and condemned the use of artificial contraception.

Pope Paul wished to preserve the sanctity of marriage and argued that the contraceptive mentality would only undermine the institution of marriage. Although most accepted Paul's proposition in theoretical terms, many rejected his teaching as wholly impractical. The public dissent was mirrored by pronouncements made by some national episcopal conferences, which sought to mitigate the negative publicity of the encyclical. The Vatican responded by insisting that these ambiguous statements be clarified or withdrawn, in line with the pontiff's teaching. Paul was stung by the criticism and complained to his aides that he had been deliberately misrepresented. Notably, however, the pope issued no more encyclicals during his pontificate, and avoided further discussion of the subject. For decades ahead, the Roman authorities would seek to curb the independence of the national episcopal conferences.

If Pius XII had raised the image of the papacy to an exalted height, his disciple Paul VI sought to bring the papacy into contact with the world. He became the first pope to travel by plane and helicopter, visiting all five continents. During a pastoral journey to the Philippines in 1970, Paul narrowly escaped an assasination attempt. While making his way though a large crowd, a young man lunged at him with a dagger. The blade penetrated his white soutane but was deflected by the medal of Mary that the pope wore underneath his pontifical garments.

During a visit to the United States in 1965, Paul VI addressed a plenary assembly of the United Nations.

Here he made an impassioned plea for peace. Speaking in French, he denounced the futility and horrors of war. 'War, never again.' They were words destined to fall on deaf ears.

Almost crippled with arthritis, Paul thought of abdicating and retiring from the papal office. The weary pope deferred his decision until after the Holy Year of 1975. The events of the year proved to be extraordinarily successful and the septuagenarian pontiff struggled on until his death three years later.

Following the death of Pope Paul VI, on 6 August JOHN PAUL I 1978, 111 cardinals met in the Sistine Chapel to vote for his successor. Most of the prelates were not Italian, as the late pope had sought conscientiously to internationalise the senate of the church. After just one day of voting, the choice, however, fell on an Italian. Albino Luciani had been patriarch of Venice, and now like Pius X and John XXIII he was to be elected pope. Luciani was elected with over 100 votes, in one of the shortest conclaves ever held.

The new pope took the first double-name in the history of the papacy. He explained his unusual choice of the two names to the crowd which gathered in St Peter's Square the day after his election. 'Yesterday morning, I went tranquilly to vote in the Sistine Chapel. I could never have imagined what was to happen. As soon as the danger for me began to emerge, two colleagues beside me whispered encouragement.' The crowds in the square applauded the informality of the pope. 'When they asked what name I would take, I was surprised for I had little time to think. I thought of Pope John who consecrated me a bishop. I thought of Pope Paul, who made me go red when, in St Mark's Square , in front of 20,000 people, he took off his stole and put it on my shoulders. I was never so embarrassed! So I said, I will be called John

Paul. I do not have either the wisdom and heart of Pope John, nor the preparation and culture of Pope Paul, but I am now in their place and I must seek to serve the church. I hope you will help me with your prayers!'

The public thronged the Audience Hall of the Vatican to participate in the weekly audiences which the new pope held. John Paul seemed nervous and somewhat overawed by the dramatic change in his life. Yet he touched those who listened to his simple, extemporaneous exhortations which were so evidently sincere. Some Vatican officials were scandalised when he invited children to the podium to meet him and even share the microphone as he related stories and anecdotes. That the pope had penned a series of letters to imaginary figures in literature also puzzled them. When he referred to God as mother as much as a father, they were positively alarmed.

The pope broke with tradition by declining to have a coronation ceremony, and inaugurated his papacy by receiving the *pallium,* a white woollen stole draped over the shoulders that marks the ministry of archbishops.

During the first month of his pontificate, John Paul gave little indication of his policy. He did, however, express his disapproval that a bishop should head the Vatican bank, or Institute of Religious Works. The president of the bank was still Archbishop Paul Casimir Marcinkus. John Paul's pontificate was cut short on the night of 28 September. The pope retired as usual that evening, giving no indication of ill health. Indeed, the staff in his apartments recalled he was in good form. The pope's health, however, had imperceptibly disimproved during the month since his election. His sudden death seems to have been caused by a clot which went to his heart as he lay in bed. His body was discovered the following morning when the sister who cared for him noticed he had not taken the coffee she had left outside his bedroom for him. The discovery of the corpse threw the papal household into chaos. Cardinal Villot, the Secretary of State, was informed by Fr John Magee, an Irish priest who served as the pope's private secretary. Within the hour, Vatican Radio broadcast the news and the Secretary of State began the onerous task of notification and arranging the funeral. The suddenness of the death gave rise to conspiracy theories that various parties wanted the pope out of the way. Books and articles appeared, making outlandish claims and eroding public faith in the Vatican.

The reality was more likely to have been much more simple. The pope's physician in Venice had not handed over all the medical records to the pontiff's Vatican doctor, intending to travel each fortnight to tend to his illustrious patient. As a result, the correct medication for the pope's heart condition may not have been administered. An elderly sister, who had only settled into the papal apartments three weeks earlier, and who may have been disorientated by the events, was responsible for leaving the pope's medication by his bedside. It is also possible that John Paul, also overwhelmed by the dramatic change in his life, neglected to take the medicine at the appropriate time. It seems unlikely that we will ever know.

CHAPTER 21

Two Men from Afar

JOHN PAUL II
BENEDICT XVI

The evening of 16 October was mild. The summer had faded from Rome but the autumn scarcely heralded the winter which was shortly to begin.

Many of those who gathered in St Peter's Square had been in the piazza six weeks earlier and had witnessed the election of John Paul I.

Darkness had fallen and all eyes were trained on the small chimney that protruded from the Sistine Chapel, visible to the side of the basilica. After each ballot of the cardinals in the chapel, the votes were burned. In earlier centuries, if the vote was inconclusive, damp straw was added to turn the smoke black. If a pope had been elected, the voting papers were burned alone, and the white smoke exiting the chapel informed the crowds in the piazza. Slowly, a stream of smoke appeared from the chimney. In the glare of the TV lights, it was not possible to be sure if the smoke was white or black. Excited shouts went up. '*Il fumo é bianco!*' Other voices denied it. '*No, é nero!*'

The shouts died down but for a further 15 minutes, the spectators betted among themselves if a pope had been elected. The atmosphere in the piazza was electric. Suddenly, the great doors of the central balcony swung open. Cardinal Pericle Felice stepped out. His voice magnified by the loudspeakers, the cardinal announced in sonorous Latin the time-honoured phrase: '*Anuntio vobis gaudium magnum. Habemus papam.*' 'I announce to you a great joy. We have a pope.' The throng went wild. The cardinal paused before announcing that the new pope was Cardinal Karol Wojtyla. The crowd was stunned for a moment.

The name was not familiar and slowly it dawned that the first non-Italian pope in over four and a half centuries had been elected. The cardinal added that the new pope would be called John Paul II.

Some moments later, the new pope, vested in red and white, stepped onto the balcony. At 58, the pope was comparatively young. He had the physique of an athlete gained by years of canoeing and skiing. His rugged face showed determination and enormous energy. Traditionally, the new pope imparted his blessing in Latin and went to the papal apartments. This pope was not to be bound by protocol.

Taking the microphone in this hand, he introduced himself as 'a man from afar'. He told those gathered below that he had been called from a country with strong links to Rome and was now their bishop. However, he was new, and he asked the crowd to correct him if he made mistakes 'in your – no, our – language!' The Italians present roared their approval.

Born Karol Wojtyla in the Polish town of Wadowice, the future pope had studied drama and poetry at Krakow University. His mother died when he was a young child and he and his brother were raised by his pious father, a retired army officer. While Karol was still a boy, his brother, who had become a doctor, died during an epidemic. During the Second World War he began studies for the priesthood. After ordination he was sent to Rome to complete a doctorate in theology. Having completed a further doctorate in philosophy, in 1964 he became archbishop of Krakow, and an outspoken critic of the Polish government.

A keen scholar, the new pope was fluent in several languages. This talent would be of great value in his new ministry. It also transpired that the pope was a formidable opponent of Marxist communism. It was even rumoured that Cardinal Wojtyla had brought some communist periodicals into the conclave to while away the hours between voting sessions.

From the start of his pontificate, Pope John Paul II dived into the political waters with enthusiasm. On 24 January 1979, he accepted the request made by Argentina and Chile to mediate in solving the controversy over the Beagle Channel. The same day he received in private audience the Soviet Foreign Minister, Andrei Gromyko.

The following day, he departed Rome on his first pastoral journey. The destination was Mexico. This was more than a desire to visit the Catholics of that country. He timed his visit to coincide with the meeting of the bishops of Latin America in Puebla. For some years, Vatican officals had been worried about a new trend called Liberation Theology. It marked a departure in the pastoral care of the poor, who had so often been oppressed even by the church that wished to protect them. Initially, Pope John Paul shared the suspicion of some members of the Roman curia. In particular, he distrusted the lay administration of the base Christian communities. He was horrified by reports that some clergy favoured armed rebellion against governments, even though there was corruption at the highest levels.

However, his visits to the poor countries of Latin American and the Third World exposed the pope to the often brutal reality of institutional poverty, and in places the ineffectualness of the church in the face of such abuse.

In June of that same year, he made the first of eight visits to his homeland. The Poles, long oppressed under a communist regime, proudly greeted their illustrious compatriot as a hero. Under an enormous cross in the city of Kracow, the pope delivered a rousing homily, full of patriotic sentiment. 'It is not possible,' he told his captivated audience gathered in Victory Square, 'to understand the history of the Polish nation without Christ.'

Although the pope considered it his duty to be involved in the politics of the world, he prohibited bishops and priests from playing any role. He had unhappy memories of the war years, where Catholic clergy assumed political posts with disastrous results.

While the pope's travels gradually turned him into a popular globetrotter, he tightened his control over church discipline and administration. The appointment of the conservative German theologian, Josef Ratzinger, as Prefect of the Congregation for the Doctrine of the Faith, displayed his intransigence on matters of morals and the faith. His absences from Rome, amounting to two and a half years by 2003, necessitated a reliable and faithful staff at the Vatican.

Pope John Paul maintained a patriotic interest in his native Poland. When, in August 1980, some workers at the Lenin shipyard in Gdansk staged a 17-day strike, John Paul let it be known that he supported the action. The strike was organised in response to a rise in meat prices. Hundreds of workers defied the communist authorities by refusing to work for 17 days. After a humiliating defeat, the government was forced to recognise the rights of the workers to organise themselves in trade unions, the first to be permitted in the Soviet bloc. The movement, named Solidarity, spread like wildfire throughout Poland, and even beyond its borders. In January of the following year, the pope received in audience Lech Walesa, the shipyard electrician who had led the successful August strike. The pope offered his support, even though he urged caution and patience, virtues he had learned during his years of dealing with the anti-Catholic government.

Five months later, on 13 May 1981, Pope John Paul

entered St Peter's Square to begin a Public Audience. The Vatican authorities had transferred the weekly meetings from the Paul VI Hall to accommodate the enormous number of pilgrims who wished to see the pope. The pontiff was been driven through the flag-waving crowds on a 'pope mobile', a white jeep which allowed him stand and salute the crowd. He had reached out and taken an infant in his arms, kissed it and handed the girl back to her mother, when a shot rang out. The pope stood for a moment, and then slumped back, his fall broken by his shocked secretary, Fr Stanislaus Dziwisz, who was seated behind him. Blood began to trickle through his white soutane. He had been hit twice by an assassin. The security police immediately called for an ambulance, and the jeep roared away to the side of St Peter's where the pope was transferred to the vehicle. Realising the pope's life was in danger, the medical team brought him to the Gemelli Polyclinic. The frenzied journey was hampered by heavy traffic, but with sirens wailing wildly, the motorcade arrived at the hospital in eight minutes. On arrival at the hospital, the pope was unconscious, and his secretary administered the Sacrament of the Sick. Meanwhile two other pilgrims who had also been shot at were treated for their wounds.

There followed a five-hour operation to repair the damage done to the abdomen and intestine by the bullets. One of the projectiles had narrowly missed the pontiff's heart, having been deflected by the pope's shattered finger. Many pilgrims waited, stunned, in St Peter's Square, praying for the pope's survival. At almost one in the morning, a bulletin confirmed that the operation had been successful and that there was hope for the patient. Some days later, a taped address was recorded at the pope's bedside and relayed to St Peter's Square. The feeble voice of the pope was heard: 'I am particularly close to the two people who were wounded together with me. I pray for that brother of ours who shot me, and whom I have sincerely pardoned.'

Who was the mysterious assassin? Even as he tried to flee the scene, the gunman, Mehmet Ali Agca was brought to the ground by pilgrims gathered for the General Audience. He was arrested by the police and brought for interrogation. The 23-year-old Turkish terrorist, with links to the Grey Wolf Organisation, claimed to have acted on behalf of Bulgarian government authorities, who were pressurised by the KGB to get rid of the Polish pope. Soon, word spread that the communists were afraid of the influence John Paul was exerting on the Polish Solidarity Movement. But slowly the pope recovered. Although weakened in body by his injuries, he was indomitable in spirit. In September, he issued an encyclical, *Laborem Exercens* (On Human Work), which pointedly dealt with the rights and obligations of employers and employees. The occasion was the 90th anniversary of the publication of Leo XIII's revolutionary encyclical, *Rerum Novarum*. The pope listed the fallacies in both the socialist and capitalist systems when carried to extreme. He asserted the principle of the priority of labour over capital. 'This principle directly concerns the process of production: in this process labour is always a primary efficient cause, while capital, the whole collection of means of production, remains a mere instrument or instrumental cause.' The document showed the world that the Holy See could compose important, intelligible arguments to support the social teaching of the church. The communist regime could not fail to sense that the gauntlet had been defiantly thrown down.

John Paul continued to offer his support for the workers who were struggling to achieve their basic human rights. Time and time again, the pope played on the name of the trade union, offering, his 'solidarity' in their difficulties.

In December, the new leader of the Communist Party in Poland, General Jaruselski, declared a state of martial law and outlawed Solidarity. Pope John Paul intervened by writing to Leonid Brezhnev, President of the Soviet Union. In his letter, the Slav pontiff observed: 'The events which have taken place in Poland over these past months have been caused by the ineluctable necessity of the economic reconstruction of the country, which requires, at the same time, a moral reconstruction based on the conscious engagement, in solidarity, of all the forces of the entire society.' The message was clear. The pope would continue to fight publicly for the oppressed peoples. The authorities may have lamented that Agca had missed the target dressed in white.

The remainder of the decade was dramatic not only for Poland, but for all the satellite countries of the Soviet Union, who were influenced by the events unfolding in Poland. The outlawed movement continued to garner members, soon in their millions. From Rome, the Polish pope became more and more explicit in his denunciations of totalitarian regimes.

As pastor of the Universal Church, the pope could not simply be engaged in politics behind the Iron Curtain. Always ready to welcome visitors and pilgrims to the Vatican, John Paul was also determined to travel to bring his message to those who otherwise might not hear him. In 1994, outside Manila in the Philippines, the largest crowd ever to gather for a religious ceremony – almost four million – gave the pope a rapturous welcome.

During John Paul's pontificate, the number of Catholics passed the billion mark. The travels of Pope John Paul not only exposed the papacy as an international corporation to the world, but exposed the pope to the diversity of cultures. Through modern means of communications, Pope John Paul's face became one of the most familiar on the planet. His longevity ensured that, as other world leaders left the world stage, his remained a voice which continued to confront, to encourage, to scold and exhort. 'Every papal visit,' John Paul explained, 'is an authentic pilgrimage to the living sanctuary of the People of God.' Not everywhere was the pope's message welcome, and sometimes John Paul must have realised that his worlds fell on deaf ears. Already in his first year as pope, he had visited six African countries, France, Germany and a twelve-day visit to Brazil. The pope carefully selected his visits, and over a quarter of a century, was to visit many countries on more than one occasion. Nowhere was either too far or too hazardous, the pope considered, for a visit of the Successor of Peter. With great reluctance the pope abandoned a trip planned to Mongolia in August 2003 due to his failing health. The strain on the pope's physical resources were redoubled after the assassination attempt. Although a team developed the germs of his addresses into scripts the pope would deliver, John Paul learned several new languages, even if only phonetically. During a visit to Japan, the pope surprised his audience by addressing the crowds in Japanese.

Although John Paul was convinced that his vocation was primarily to preach the gospel, he was not unaware of the political aspect. He also tried to initiate a dialogue with the Chinese authorities which, through most of his pontificate, was fruitless. But closer to home, he witnessed an unprecedented development. In April 1988, Mikhail Gorbachev made an overture to the leaders of the Russian Orthodox Church to end decades of persecution by the communist regime. In December, Gorbachev meet with the American President, Ronald Reagan, and suggested that the Cold War, a euphemism for the political situation following the Second World War, be brought to an end. Early in 1989, Solidarity was legalised by the Polish government, at Gorbachev's suggestion. During that summer, tens of thousands of citizens of the German Democratic Republic were given permission to cross the border into Austria. This was to lead to an avalanche of 50,000 refugees reaching the Federal Republic until the fall of the Berlin Wall in November. Two weeks later, Mikhail Gorbachev and his wife, Raisa, made an official visit to the pope. The Russian couple were received with all honours and the pope was evidently moved by the historic occasion. While Raisa was accompanied by a monsignor to the Sistine Chapel, the pontiff and the Russian leader engaged in a dialogue which lasted an hour and a half. Central to the pope's dialogue was the right of people to religious freedom. For 70 years, John Paul's predeccessors had railed against the Soviet authorities. The Slavic pope succeeded with reasoned arguments to obtain a dramatic change. As the two leaders took their leave of each other, Gorbachev issued a surprising invitation to the pope to visit the Soviet Republic. The pope was taken aback, not having dared hope for such a gesture. In the event, the Soviet Union was to disintegrate before the opportunity presented itself to avail of the invitation.

As the pope watched his illustrious visitors leave the library where the meeting had taken place, the monsignor who had accompanied Raisa to the Sistine Chapel asked the pontiff how the visit went. 'It was providential,' he replied impishly, 'The next time they come, I will take Raisa to see the Chapel and you stay and talk to Gorbachev!'

The pope also appreciated the political impact which religions have on the world. Already in 1986, he invited the leaders of the world's religions to Assisi, the town of St Francis, to pray for peace. Addressing the assembled leaders, he noted 'that in the great battle for peace, humanity, in its very diversity, must draw from its deepest and most vivifying sources where its conscience is formed and upon which is founded the moral action of all people'. He pragmatically noted that 'peace, where it exists, is always extremely fragile. It is threatened in so many ways and with such unforeseeable consequences that we must endeavour to provide it with secure foundations.'

This was to be the first of three such gatherings at Assisi. In response to the bombing of the Pentagon and the World Trade Centre in New York in September 2001, the pope invited leaders once more to the small Umbrian town in January 2002. This time, the crisis was more acute. The pope was joined by Muslims, Hindus, Buddhists, Shintoists, Jews, Orthodox, Pentecostalists, Lutherans, Methodists, Quakers, among others. A month after the meeting, the pope wrote to all heads of states, enclosing the text of a common declaration made by the various religious leaders who attended the event. In it the participants condemned 'every recourse to violence and war in the name of God or of religion and we commit ourselves to doing everything possible to eliminate the root causes of terrorism'.

As a boy, Karol Wojtyla had grown up with the Jews of his neighbourhood in Wadowice. Jerzy Kluger was a classmate and the two boys often played soccer together. They remained friends until the horrors of the Second World War disrupted their lives and separated them. Karol Wojtlya remained in Poland, while his friend left the country having served in the Polish army.

Three decades were to pass before Kluger found out what had happened to his boyhood friend. After the war, he settled in Italy. In 1965, while driving in Rome, he heard a radio report that mentioned Cardinal Karol Wojtlya, who was in Rome attending a session of the Second Vatican Council. He wondered if the cardinal might be a relative of his childhood friend, and could give him news of his whereabouts. He did not even know if Karol had survived the war.

After several phone calls, Kluger managed to track down the cardinal, to his temporary residence at the Polish College. The two could hardly believe their fortune on their tearful reunion. They remained friends even after Wojtyla was elected pope. 'I call him Lolek, and he calls me Jurek, as we did when we were children,' Kluger replied to curious questions. Into old age, the two men met in the Vatican for dinner twice a month, reminiscing about their childhood, the way the world was, and dreaming of how to make it better.

John Paul, given his background, was deeply concerned to improve Jewish-Christian relations. He visited Rome's synagogue in 1986, the first pope to do so since the time of Peter, even though the distance from the Vatican to the Jewish temple is only a mile. He also asked Kluger to help the Vatican establish full diplomatic relations with Israel, the negotiations for which dragged out until 1994.

Since the beginning of his pontificate, John Paul fostered relations between other faiths, most especially the three monotheistic religions. His respect for the values of Islam was evidenced again and again during his visits around the world. Speaking before a crowd of 50,000 young Muslims in Casablanca in 1985, the pope told his listeners that Muslims and Christians shared many values. 'Christians and Muslims generally have understood each other badly. Sometimes in the past we have opposed each other and even exhausted ourselves in polemics and wars. I believe that God is calling us today to change our old habits. We have to respect each other and stimulate each other in good works upon the path indicated by God. In a world that desires unity and peace, but which experiences a thousand tensions and conflicts, believers should foster friendship and union among humanity and the people who comprise a single community on earth.'

On the eve of the invasion of Iraq in March 2003, Pope John Paul met with political leaders from Germany, Spain, Italy, Great Britain and America in the hopes of dissuading the powers from attacking Iraq. He also met with the Iraqi Prime Minister, Tariq Aziz, addressing a personal letter to Sadaam Hussein in the hopes of averting war. The pope refused the acknowledge the legitimacy of what the Allies called a 'preventative war,' dismissing the term as empty and arrogant propaganda.

If the pope had suffered from an attempted assassination, he nevertheless continued to courageously condemn the selfish spiral of violence that threatened to destroy whole groups of people. He continuously appealed to the belligerents during the wars in the ex-Yugoslavian republics in the mid-1990s. In 2003, the elderly pontiff travelled to Croatia, Bosnia and Slovenia to urge the population to be reconciled.

The pope also took a courageous stand against the Mafia and other minor terrorist groups who rang corrupt rings of crime in the south of Italy. On a visit to Sicily in May 1993, the pope fiercely denounced the corruption in society. 'No man, no human association, no Mafia can change or trample on the things that belong to God.' Two months later, the Mafia responded by detonating bombs at the Church of San Giorgio in Velabro and at the Cathedral of San Giovanni in Laterano.

After the fall of communism, the pope was equally vocal in his criticism of capitalism, and the various other ideologies that reduced people to the sum of their possessions. He roundly condemned the scandal of the arms trade and the abuse of children in rings of prostitution.

The latter years of John Paul's pontificate saw the once-robust and athletic pope bend into a frail old man, scarcely able to shuffle a few steps without great difficulty. Bowed by Parkinson's disease and severe arthritis, he became a shadow of his former self. His spirit remained, however, indomitable. Dismissing rumours that he might abdicate, in 2003, his passed into history as the third longest pontificate in history.

In early February 2005, Pope John Paul was admitted to the Gemelli Polyclinic suffering from an acute breathing problem. Alarms bells sounded throughout the world's media. Although he was discharged from hospital ten days later, he was obliged to return in March when a tracheotomy was performed to help his breathing. He returned to the Vatican shortly before Easter at the end of March but was unable to participate in any of the ceremonies. On his last public appearance from his study window on Wednesday, 30 March, he tried to mouth a blessing. But his once-famous baritone voice had deserted him. He lifted his arms helplessly and traced a blessing above the tear-filled crowd gathered below. It was the last time the world was to see the great communicator. That evening, his condition worsened, triggering a vigil which lasted in St Peter's Square until, three days later, Pope John Paul died.

Here was a pope who had used the media to accompany his pontificate and carry his message further than any of the 263 popes had ever done before him. John Paul was a master of words and gestures. After his death, an estimated three million people filed past his body as it lay underneath the great cupola of St Peter's Basilica. His funeral was attended by some 200 heads of state and government and leaders of all the world's major religions, the largest such gathering in history. With such a tribute, the great and the simple acknowledged the magnitude of his influence on world history.

It was difficult to guess if the media had fostered the worldwide attention on his last years or if his pontificate had captured the imagination of the media. It was the variation of the old conundrum: which had come first, the chicken or the egg? What was certain was that the pontificate of the Polish pope had attracted greater global attention than ever before.

Pope John Paul had been called 'God's politician'. The pope would have no doubt understood the phrase in its original sense, a person concerned for the needs of people – God's people. As Pope John Paul led the Catholic Church into the third millennium, he may have looked back over the sweep of 2,000 years.

Speaking at St Peter's to mark the twentieth anniversary of his pontificate, John Paul wondered aloud about his stewardship of the church. 'Jesus asks the question: "When the Son of Man comes, will he find faith on earth?" This is a question which challenges everyone, but in particular the successors of Peter. I cannot fail to ask myself a few questions today. Have you observed all this? Are you a diligent and watchful teacher of faith in the church? Have you sought to bring the great work of the Second Vatican Council closer to the people of today? Have you tried to satisfy the expectations of believers within the church and that hunger for truth which is felt in the world outside the church?'

For many, the pontificate of the Polish pope was disappointing and frustrating. His uncompromising views on contraception, divorce, homosexuality, the ordination of women and celibacy of the clergy dismayed and angered many. Others simply continued their life's journey outside the church, abandoning an institution which seemed

265

to them singularly out of step with the needs of contemporary humanity. The pope accused the modern world of embracing a 'culture of death' wherein abortion and euthanasia were increasingly accepted and practised. At the end of his pontificate, he rallied forces to include a mention of Christianity's historical place in the European Constitution. His efforts failed, as did his attempts to discourage governments from changing the very meaning of marriage to include same-sex relationships. Meanwhile, scandals involving clerical pedophiles and the horrific and arrogant treatment of victims by some church authorities were handled by many church authorities with stupefying incompetence. Such tardy action caused bitter disappointment and disillusionment among even the most ardent faithful. The appointment of Cardinal Bernard Law to a prestigious sinecure in Rome had infuriated Catholics in Boston, the diocese from which he was forced to resign over his feeble handling of pedophile priests. Only late in his reign did Pope John Paul manage to address the issue directly, but for many victims and others, it was too little, too late.

While the number of Catholics rose to 1.3 billion during John Paul's pontificate, millions abandoned the church or joined other religions. While some people saw John Paul as a benevolent, fatherly figure, others saw him as an authoritarian dictator, unwilling to listen to constructive criticism. Only time can put his pontificate in focus. Ultimately, evaluations of John Paul's pontificate will have to take into account his human nature and the limitations imposed by history.

* * *

BENEDICT XVI Gathering in the Sistine Chapel on 18 April 2005, 115 cardinals from 52 countries voted to elect the 265th successor to Peter. Never before in the history of the papacy had world attention focused on a papal election. Television stations had booked space on terraces overlooking the Vatican for several years. Some stations, anxious to broadcast Pope John Paul's funeral and the subsequent conclave, paid €15,000 a day to the proprietors of these prestigious buildings.

Speculation was rife as to who would succeed in the papal line. As commemorative issues poured out from magazine and newspapers houses, attention turned to the cardinals gathering in Rome for the obsequies and subsequent conclave. Cardinals from less than a third of the countries of the world would enter the conclave to elect a new pope, whose election would have enormous consequences for global history.

From the number of cardinals, less than a dozen were really *papabile*, or likely to be elected. Would it be an African, the first to be elected since the pontificate of Gelasius (492-96)? Or would the cardinals elect the first Latin American? After a long pontificate, some twenty-six-and-a-half years, it was doubtful if the cardinals would elect another 'young' pontiff.

In the late afternoon of the following day, white smoke began to billow from a chimney installed above the Sistine Chapel. The votes of the fourth ballot were being burnt. This was the traditional signal that the conclave was over and a new pope had been elected. Those gathered below in the Square squinted into the grey sky to determine which colour the smoke might be. Then the great bells of St Peter's began to toll. A new pope had been elected. Bells throughout the city began to ring in unison, alerting Romans and visitors alike of the news. People began to make their way hastily to the Vatican. On radio and television stations throughout the world, programmes were interrupted to announce the decision. The Arabic station Al Jazeer broke into its schedule to show scenes from Rome, a gesture unthinkable a quarter of a century earlier. As the piazza filled, the windows overlooking the Square opened and a red carpet was draped from the balcony, final confirmation that the pope would shortly appear. The crowd was nearly wild with excitement and anticipation.

Within the hour of his election, the world saw the new pope step onto the Loggia of Benedictions at the centre of St Peter's Basilica. The 78-year old Bavarian, Joseph Ratzinger, chose the name of Benedict XVI. He did not take the name John Paul III in order both to avoid comparison with his immediate predecessor and to emphasise that he was the successor to Peter of Galilee. The cardinals had evidently chosen a 'safe' elderly European candidate, surprising to many after a lengthy Polish pontificate. The fact that the new pope had been a well-known theologian, prolific writer and member of the Roman curia had given him an elevated profile. Never had an international theologian of such standing become pontiff. Introducing himself to the crowd as a 'humble servant in the vineyard of the Lord', the new pope confided himself to their prayers and support. Within moments the catch-cry began to circle the Square 'Benedetto!' followed by a handclap reminiscent of a football stadium.

Once more in the space of three weeks, kings, queens, presidents and prime ministers made their way to the Vatican to participate in the Inauguration Mass of the new pope. As Prefect of the Congregation for the Doctrine of the Faith for the quarter of a century preceding his election, Joseph Ratzinger had earned a reputation for strictly guarding the faith. Many Catholics had abhorred the legalist way in which they perceived some doctrine to have been presented by his office. But the new pope now had to assume a directly pastoral role, seeking to unite rather than cause division. It was a formidable task for the shy and retiring German, especially after the charismatic Karol Wojtlya. Thanks to the media, it was fascinating to see how Joseph Ratzinger, a totem pole for conservatives, gradually metamorphosed into a gravity force for dialogue with other Christians and world faiths, with whom he pledged to work 'for the good of humanity'.

On a breezy Sunday morning, 24 April, Pope Benedict celebrated Mass for the Commencement of the Petrine Ministry. The old ceremony of coronation had been dispensed with by Pope John Paul I in 1978, and this was the first time the new ceremony was performed. Pope Benedict specifically approved the rite just a day after his election, abandoning the title *inauguration* in favour of *Commencement of the Petrine Ministry as Bishop of Rome*. There was a distinct reason Pope Benedict made the change. It was to reflect his belief that he was successor to Peter, rather than simply to Pope John Paul. Moreover, before the Mass commenced, the new pope and the patriarchs of the Orthodox Church descended to the tomb of St Peter beneath the baldachino of Bernini. Here they paid homage to the prince of the apostles and then processed to celebrate Mass in front of the façade, to the sung rhythm of invocation of the saints. After the gospel had been sung in Latin and Greek, the pallium was bestowed on the pontiff. The wide woollen band embroidered with five red crosses dates back to the period before Christianity was divided. The choice of the pallium was new. Rather than the truncated version hitherto used, the pallium was modelled on an ancient pallium which dated back to the early centuries before the division of the church. He also received the Fisherman's Ring, a gold band which once was used to seal papal documents. It is a low-relief of St Peter, casting his net. Formerly the ring was used only to seal documents. Now it would be worn as a symbol of Peter by his successor. As the pallium recalled the pope's role as shepherd, the ring was a reminder of his link with Peter, the fisherman of Galilee.

Speaking at the Mass to Elect a New Pope in St Peter's the morning the conclave opened, it fell to Cardinal Joseph Ratzinger as Dean of the College of Cardinals to celebrate the Mass and deliver the homily. Noting that for several decades there has been upheaval in society, he warned against the dictatorship of various ideologies which diminished responsibility and placed the individual at the centre of their own universe.

How many winds of doctrine we have known in these last decades, how many ideological currents, how many fashions of thought? The small boat of thought of many Christians has often remained agitated by the waves, tossed from one extreme to the other: from Marxism to liberalism, to libertinism; from collectivism to radical individualism; from atheism to a vague religious mysticism; from agnosticism to syncretism, and so forth.

Every day new sects are born and we see realised what St Paul says on the deception of men, on the cunning that tends to lead into error (cf Ephesians 4:14). To have a clear faith, according to the creed of the church, is often labelled as fundamentalism. While relativism, that is, allowing oneself to be carried about with every wind of 'doctrine', seems to be the only attitude that is fashionable. A dictatorship of relativism is being constituted that recognises nothing as absolute and which only leaves the 'I' and its whims as the ultimate measure.

For the new pope, Cardinal Ratzinger indicated, the challenge was to offer the measure of Christ to help the world avoid a selfishness which can so easily stifle and has often smothered the aspirations and achievements of humanity. Within twenty-four hours, the task had fallen to him to cast out the net of Peter.

* * *

The papacy began on the shores of the Lake of Galilee, when Jesus entrusted the care of his followers to Peter. With blustering enthusiasm, Peter dedicated himself wholeheartedly to tending to the needs of the very first followers of Christ, even to the extent of dying with them under the first imperial persecution of Nero. His successors also faced the risk of death and persecution, until in the fourth century the papacy was endowed by the generous gesture of Constantine. That gift may have been the very undoing of the church. Money sadly brings greed and corruption, and the subsequent history of the papacy was filled with the lights of glorious achievement and the shadows of shameful failure.

Nevertheless, the papacy has endured as the oldest non-hereditary monarchy in the world. The influence of the popes has waxed and waned. As the third millennium progresses, the popes will continue, no doubt, to have an influence on the development of humanity. The fisherman's net will be cast again and again. And so the story continues.

CHAPTER 22

The Papacy and Music

Writing in the early seventh century, St Isidore, bishop of Seville, lamented 'unless sounds are held in the memory by man they perish, because they cannot be written down'. Since time immemorial, music has been passed from one generation to another. As it is transmitted from one performer to another, it undergoes subtle changes. Political upheavals can radically change the lives of musicians and affect the music of a people. Such happened the musical heritage of the Roman Empire and now only faint echoes survive in the music adopted by the Christian church.

In the earliest times, books were limited to the highly educated classes and only a fraction of the population was literate. Memorisation was essential. Already in the late sixth century, Pope Gregory the Great (590-604) had fostered musicians attached to his residence at the Lateran to provide music for the liturgies. Over a century later, Pope Gregory II (715-731) reorganised a school which Gregory the Great had set up. Administered by monks, the school provided training for generations of youths, the *schola puerorum* who wished to serve God through music. The pupils were exclusively boys. By that stage women, in the form of deacons, had been entirely excluded from the liturgies, and henceforth only men would take part in the ceremonies. The boys began their studies at the age of five and spent several years memorising the complicated melodies which took the form of elaborate music to accompany the Divine Office and the Eucharist.

Other dioceses, taking note of Rome's burgeoning

musical talent, established their own *schola cantorum*, where singers could be trained. Under Charlemagne's rule, these spread throughout the Holy Roman Empire, effectively the heart of Europe. One such foundation was founded at Pomposa, a Benedictine abbey near Ferarra. The headmaster of the choir school was a certain Guido, a native of Paris. Guido was born c.995 and moved to Pomposa as a relatively young man to become a monk.

Medieval theorists saw music as a branch of mathematics. It was a belief which the Greeks had held, and with the rediscovery of the richness of Greek thought in the late Middle Ages, music went through something of a Renaissance. Guido wrote a number of scholarly texts on music, notably on rhythm. While many authors compiled obscure texts on method and theory, Guido had to struggle with a group of clearly unruly boys. This may have played a part in Guido's decision to leave Pomposa for the relatively calmer atmosphere of Arezzo. However, the fact that most important progress was made in the ninth century north of the Alps may have stung some of Guido's Benedictine confrères. Here Guido developed an ingenious method to help his singers visualise their notes and pitch. Later called Guido's Hand, the conductor held up his hand and pointed to the positions of his fingers or gaps. This was later transferred to written notation on a set of four lines, or a stave. It thus became the forerunner of modern musical notation.

In Rome, Pope John XIX (1024-33) heard of Guido's simple but effective invention. The pontiff had been 'consul, dux and senator' before being elected pope in a single day. A member of the powerful Tuscolani family, John was a rather ineffectual ruler, but evidently interested in music. Hearing of Guido's gifts, the pope summoned him to Rome. Guido recounted the meeting in a letter.

'Pope John, who governs the Roman Church, heard of

our song-school's reputation. He heard in particular of our books of antiphons so boys could sing songs they had never heard. He was greatly astonished and sent three messengers to bring me to him. The pope was most glad to see me and asked me a great many questions. He turned over the pages of the antiphonary as if it were some great prodigy. He did not move from the place where he sat until he had learned to sing one versicle that he had never heard. What more is there to say? I had to leave Rome soon, the summer fevers in those wet and swampy places were death to me. We did agree, however, that when the winter returned I would return to explain our work to the pope and his clergy.'

Although other methods of writing had been used for a century before Guido's invention, none of these enjoyed enduring success. Guido also invented the sol-fa method of singing, which is still in use today. It was employed to help the boys learn the tones and semitones used in music. He adapted it from a hymn in honour of St John the Baptist. He had observed that each line began on an ascending note:

UT queant laxis
REsonare fibris
MIra gestorum
FAmuli tuorum
SOlve pollutes
LAbii reates, Sancti Joannes.

The pope's enthusiasm ensured that Guido's method received widespread support and papal endorsement. A century later, polyphony began to develop; it emerged in France from a method called *organum*. This involved singing a second line above or below the Gregorian melody and did not require to be written down. Polyphony, with its divergent rhythms, however, needed notation, and Guido's invention was to pave the way for centuries of magnificent polyphony patronised by the church.

Such growth did not always attract papal approval and in 1332, Pope John XXII (1316-1334) issued a bull condemning the excesses of modern polyphony:

> Certain disciples of the new school prefer to devise new methods of their own rather than singing in the old way. Moreover, they deprave it with descants and sometimes pad out the music with upper parts made out of profane songs.

John indicated a problem which would not go away so easily, namely the mixing of secular tunes with sacred music. There was no shortage of criticism, however, of the developing mishmash of styles. Composers often based their settings of the Ordinary of the Mass on love songs or war tunes. *The Armed Man* was one such setting which was very popular, provoking an outraged worshipper to make a violent rebuttal: 'What has this to do with our Christ? How is the armed man agreeable to the peaceful Lamb of God?' But that was not the only source of irritation. By the sixteenth century, music had developed further with elaborate settings which stretched the liturgy beyond the patience of congregations. Martin Luther urged composers to provide music easily sung and performed.

By the middle of the century, the church was obliged to call a council to deal with the valid challenges provided by the reformers. The Council eventually convened under the leadership of Pope Paul III (1534-49). The pope was an enthusiastic supporter of music. In his service were several fine singers and composers such as Cristóbal de Morales, who toured in the pope's entourage. During the period 1536-1543, de Morales travelled extensively with the pope throughout northern Europe, where his music made an enormous impression.

Some years later, Pierluigi da Palestrina joined the papal choir in the service of Pope Julius III (1550-1555). He was dismissed a few months later when a new pope, Paul IV (1555-1559) discovered that he was married, a state which excluded him from membership in the choir. An effort to simplify the Mass was made by Palestrina. In his *Missa Papae Marcelli*, dedicated to the pontiff who lived less than a month, Palestrina tried to make the words of the Mass intelligible for the singers and listeners. The legend runs that Palestrina submitted this Mass to a committee of cardinals which had been delegated by the Council of Trent. The cardinals were charged with the decision of banning polyphony entirely from the liturgy in favour of Gregorian chant. So impressed were the cardinals that they relented in their decision and granted permission to continue the use of polyphony. While he was commended for allowing all the words of the text to be heard intelligibly, he was also invited to participate in a revision of Gregorian chant, which was published in 1614.

When opera developed in Italy in the early seventeenth century, it gained immediate and enthusiastic approval from the public which packed theatres throughout the Italian peninsula. Churchmen sought to cash in on the flowering of the new musical style. One of the earliest composers to set Latin texts based on biblical texts was Giacomo Carissimi, who dominated the seventeenth century. Patronised by cardinals and the papal court, Carissimi produced works known as oratorios – as they first were performed in the *oratori*, or chapels. Oratorios were based on Old Testament figures such as Daniel, Job, Jonah and Jephtha. These were presented during Lent, when the popes forbade the performance of operas during the sacred season. A century later, George Frederick Handel turned to oratorio when opera was similarly prohibited during Lent by the Bishop of London.

The popes continued to play an important part in the patronage of music, even if the more elaborate and adventurous music was performed outside the Papal States.

In his obituary notice for Wolfgang Amadeus Mozart, written in 1793, Friedrich von Schlichtegroll related the following episode from the Italian visit the protégé made in 1770. It was Ash Wednesday, and Leopold Mozart accompanied his son Wolfgang to hear the famous Sistine Chapel Choir at the Vatican.

On Wednesday afternoon they accordingly went at once to the Sistine Chapel, to hear the famous *Miserere*. And as according to tradition it was forbidden under ban of excommunication to make a copy of it from the papal music, the son undertook to hear it and then copy it out. And so it came about that when he came home, he wrote it out. The next day he went back again, holding his copy in his hat, to see whether he had got it right or not. But a different *Miserere* was sung. However, on Good Friday the first was repeated again. After he had returned home he made a correction here and there, then it was ready. It soon became known in Rome, and he had to sing it at the clavier at a concert. The castrato Christofori, who sang in the Chapel, was present.

The setting of the *Miserere* was that by Gregorio Allegri. The *Miserere*, or Psalm 50, alternates verses of Gregorian Chant with polyphonic passages which reach a high C, a rare combination of the time. For that reason, the music was jealously guarded by the choristers.

Word soon leaked that Mozart had made a copy of the

famous work. Even Pope Clement XIV (1769-1774), an enthusiastic musician, heard of the rumour. He summoned Leopold and his talented son and, to the amazement of all, bestowed on the child the Cross of the Order of the Golden Spur.

* * *

Of all the strange influences the popes may have had on music, by far the most curious was their fostering of the male castrati. As far back as antiquity, boys were castrated to preserve the puerile timbre of their voices. The operation was usually performed before the child was seven. There is evidence of castrati in Constantinople in the early Christian centuries. However, they did not enjoy much success and the practice died out in the early Middle Ages. With the development of polyphony from the twelfth century onwards, boys had difficulty reaching and maintaining certain pitches. The Spanish developed falsettos, a male who sang in an unnaturally high register. Since women were prohibited from singing in the liturgy, these falsettos supplied the higher lines. But not everybody was in favour of castrati or falsettos. In 1498 the emperor Maximilian replaced the castrati with boys. The choir still exists to day as the famous Vienna Boys Choir.

Already in Avignon during the fourteenth century, castrati were employed to sing in the papal choir. Music was confined to the chapel, and palace records detail lists of the money paid to the musicians to entertain at feasts. The first record of a castrato singing in the papal choir dates to 1562 under Pope Pius IV (1559-1565), although he was delicately described as a falsetto. The practice was by no means unique to Rome. Already in the 1560s Orlando di Lassus employed six castrati to sing at the emperor's court in Munich. The first acknowledged castrati to sing in the papal choir were Pietro Folignati and

Girolamo Rosini, who enrolled to sing for Pope Clement (1592-1605) in 1599. In the following year, upwards of two million pilgrims visited Rome during the Jubilee year. They participated in the ceremonies at the Vatican where they heard the new singers. Many musicians were struck by the power of the voices which soared into the vaults of the new basilica which was slowly rising from the debris of the Constantinian building.

By the seventeenth century the castrati were openly acknowledged as such and took pride in their vocal possession. The Most Serene Republic of Venice was proud of its musical tradition, and offered generous emoluments to castrati who sang in its churches. With the growing popularity of opera in the century, Pope Innocent XI (1676-1689) issued an edict forbidding women to sing on stage within the Papal States. This paved the way for the castrati to perform on stage and make a career independent of the church. The pope had also unwittingly opened the way for the castrati to attract the attention of an even wider public. Half a century later, when Handel was seeking singers to perform in his operas, and later his oratorios, he travelled to Italy for the specific purpose of contracting castrati. The most famous of these, Farinelli and Senisino, were feted on the London stage. Public opinion gradually turned against the practice of castration during the nineteenth century. There were horror stories of boys being kidnapped from their homes to undergo the barbaric operation. It is estimated that almost 3000 children were castrated between the sixteenth and nineteenth centuries, the majority of them in Italy. Of that, only a minority succeeded in making a successful career in church or on the stage.

The church was the last European institution to abandon the castrati which it had promoted. The service of the castrati was formally abolished by the Vatican in

1903. The last castrato of the Sistine Choir was Alessandro Moreschi who died in 1922. There still exists a recording which he made in later life, a sad and melancholic voice which still causes astonishment when heard today, a century after his voice had faded.

The Papal Succession

St. Peter (c.32-c.64)
St. Linus (c.66-c.78)
St. Cletus (c.78-c.91)
St. Clement I (c.91-c.101)
St. Evaristus (c.101-c.109)
St. Alexander I (c.109-c.116)
St. Sixtus I (c.116-c.125)
St. Telesphorus (c.125-c.136)
St. Hyginus (c.136-c.142)
St. Pius I (c.142-c.155)
St. Anicetus (c.155-c.166)
St. Soter (c.166-c.174)
St. Eleutherius (c.174-c.189)
St. Victor I (c.189-c.198)
St. Zephyrinus (c.198-c.217)
St. Callistus I (c.217-22)
St. Urban I (c.222-30)
St. Pontian (230-35)
St. Anterus (235-36)
St. Fabian (236-50)
St. Cornelius (251-53)
St. Lucius I (253-54)
St. Stephen I (254-58)
St. Sixtus II (257-58)
St. Dionysius (260-68)
St. Felix I (269-74)
St. Eutychian (275-83)
St. Caius (283-96)
St. Marcellinus (296-304)
St. Marcellus I (306-08)
St. Eusebius (c.309-10)
St. Miltiades (311-14)
St. Sylvester I (314-35/6)
St. Marcus (336)
St. Julius I (337-52)
Liberius (352-65)
St. Damasus I (366-84)
St. Siricius (384-99)
St. Anastasius I (399-401)
St. Innocent I (401-17)

St. Zosimus (417-18)
St. Boniface I (418-22)
St. Celestine I (422-32)
St. Sixtus III (432-40)
St. Leo I (the Great) (440-61)
St. Hilarius (461-68)
St. Simplicius (468-83)
St. Felix III (II) (483-92)
St. Gelasius I (492-96)
Anastasius II (496-98)
St. Symmachus (498-514)
St. Hormisdas (514-23)
St. John I (523-26)
St. Felix IV (III) (526-30)
Boniface II (530-32)
John II (533-35)
St. Agapetus I (535-36)
St. Silverius (536-37)
Vigilius (537-55)
Pelagius I (556-61)
John III (561-74)
Benedict I (575-79)
Pelagius II (579-90)
St. Gregory I (the Great) (590-604)
Sabinian (604-06)
Boniface III (607)
St. Boniface IV (608-15)
St. Deusdedit (Adeodatus I) (615-18)
Boniface V (619-25)
Honorius I (625-38)
Severinus (640)
John IV (640-42)
Theodore I (642-49)
St. Martin I (649-53)
St. Eugene I (654-57)
St. Vitalian (657-72)
Adeodatus (II) (672-76)
Donus (676-78)
St. Agatho (678-81)
St. Leo II (682-83)

St. Benedict II (684-85)
John V (685-86)
Conon (686-87)
St. Sergius I (687-701)
John VI (701-05)
John VII (705-07)
Sisinnius (708)
Constantine (708-15)
St. Gregory II (715-31)
St. Gregory III (731-41)
St. Zachary (741-52)
Stephen II (752)
Stephen III (752-57)
St. Paul I (757-67)
Stephen IV (768-72)
Adrian I (772-95)
St. Leo III (795-816)
Stephen V (816-17)
St. Paschal I (817-24)
Eugene II (824-27)
Valentine (827)
Gregory IV (827-44)
Sergius II (844-47)
St. Leo IV (847-55)
Benedict III (855-58)
St. Nicholas I (the Great) (858-67)
Adrian II (867-72)
John VIII (872-82)
Marinus I (882-84)
St. Adrian III (884-85)
Stephen VI (885-91)
Formosus (891-96)
Boniface VI (896)
Stephen VII (896-97)
Romanus (897)
Theodore II (897)
John IX (898-900)
Benedict IV (900-03)
Leo V (903)
Sergius III (904-11)
Anastasius III (911-13)
Lando (913-14)
John X (914-28)
Leo VI (928)
Stephen VIII (929-31)

John XI (931-35)
Leo VII (936-39)
Stephen IX (939-42)
Marinus II (942-46)
Agapetus II (946-55)
John XII (955-63)
Leo VIII (963-64)
Benedict V (964)
John XIII (965-72)
Benedict VI (973-74)
Benedict VII (974-83)
John XIV (983-84)
John XV (985-96)
Gregory V (996-99)
Sylvester II (999-1003)
John XVII (1003)
John XVIII (1003-09)
Sergius IV (1009-12)
Benedict VIII (1012-24)
John XIX (1024-32)
Benedict IX (1032-45)
Sylvester III (1045)
Benedict IX re-elected(1045)
Gregory VI (1045-46)
Clement II (1046-47)
Benedict IX re-elected (1047-48)
Damasus II (1048)
St. Leo IX (1049-54)
Victor II (1055-57)
Stephen X (1057-58)
Nicholas II (1058-61)
Alexander II (1061-73)
St. Gregory VII (1073-85)
Blessed Victor III (1086-87)
Blessed Urban II (1088-99)
Paschal II (1099-1118)
Gelasius II (1118-19)
Callistus II (1119-24)
Honorius II (1124-30)
Innocent II (1130-43)
Celestine II (1143-44)
Lucius II (1144-45)
Blessed Eugene III (1145-53)
Anastasius IV (1153-54)
Adrian IV (1154-59)

Alexander III (1159-81)
Lucius III (1181-85)
Urban III (1185-87)
Gregory VIII (1187)
Clement III (1187-91)
Celestine III (1191-98)
Innocent III (1198-1216)
Honorius III (1216-27)
Gregory IX (1227-41)
Celestine IV (1241)
Innocent IV (1243-54)
Alexander IV (1254-61)
Urban IV (1261-64)
Clement IV (1265-68)
Blessed Gregory X (1271-76)
Blessed Innocent V (1276)
Adrian V (1276)
John XXI (1276-77)
Nicholas III (1277-80)
Martin IV (1281-85)
Honorius IV (1285-87)
Nicholas IV (1288-92)
St. Celestine V (1294)
Boniface VIII (1294-1303)
Blessed Benedict XI (1303-04)
Clement V (1305-14)
John XXII (1316-34)
Benedict XII (1334-42)
Clement VI (1342-52)
Innocent VI (1352-62)
Blessed Urban V (1362-70)
Gregory XI (1370-78)
Urban VI (1378-89)
Boniface IX (1389-1404)
Innocent VII (1404-06)
Gregory XII (1406-15)
Martin V (1417-31)
Eugene IV (1431-47)
Nicholas V (1447-55)
Callistus III (1455-58)
Pius II (1458-64)
Paul II (1464-71)
Sixtus IV (1471-84)
Innocent VIII (1484-92)
Alexander VI (1492-1503)

Pius III (1503)
Julius II (1503-13)
Leo X (1513-21)
Adrian VI (1522-23)
Clement VII (1523-34)
Paul III (1534-49)
Julius III (1550-55)
Marcellus II (1555)
Paul IV (1555-59)
Pius IV (1559-65)
St. Pius V (1566-72)
Gregory XIII (1572-85)
Sixtus V (1585-90)
Urban VII (1590)
Gregory XIV (1590-91)
Innocent IX (1591)
Clement VIII (1592-1605)
Leo XI (1605)
Paul V (1605-21)
Gregory XV (1621-23)
Urban VIII (1623-44)
Innocent X (1644-55)
Alexander VII (1655-67)
Clement IX (1667-69)
Clement X (1670-76)
Blessed Innocent XI (1676-89)
Alexander VIII (1689-91)
Innocent XII (1691-1700)
Clement XI (1700-21)
Innocent XIII (1721-24)
Benedict XIII (1724-30)
Clement XII (1730-40)
Benedict XIV (1740-58)
Clement XIII (1758-69)
Clement XIV (1769-74)
Pius VI (1775-99)
Pius VII (1800-23)
Leo XII (1823-29)
Pius VIII (1829-30)
Gregory XVI (1831-46)
Blessed Pius IX (1846-78)
Leo XIII (1878-1903)
St. Pius X (1903-14)
Benedict XV (1914-22)
Pius XI (1922-39)

Pius XII (1939-58) John Paul I (1978)
Blessed John XXIII (1958-63) John Paul II (1978-2005)
Paul VI (1963-78) Benedict XVI (2005 –)

Select Bibliography

Barry, C.J., (ed) *Readings in Church History*, Westminster, Newman Press, 1960-65.

Brown, R., *Peter in the New Testament*, New York, Paulist, 1973.

Collins, P., *Papal Power*, Fount.

Cullmann, O., *Peter, Disciple, Apostle, Martyr*, Philadelphia, 1953.

Gill, J., *Byzantium and the Papacy, 1198-1400*, London, 1979.

Davis, R., *The Book of the Pontiffs*, trans, 2 vols, Liverpool University Press, 1989, 1992.

Duffy, E., *Saints and Sinners, A History of the Popes*, Yale University Press, 1997.

Duschene, L., *The Early History of the Church*, 3 vols, London, 1904-29.

Granfield, P., *The Papacy in Transition*, Dublin, 1981.

Hay, D., *The Church in Italy in the Fifteenth Century*, London, 1977.

Housely, N., *The Italian Crusades: the papal-Angevin alliance and the Crusades against Christian lay powers 1154-1343*, Oxford, 1982.

Kelly, J. N. D., *The Oxford Dictionary of the Popes*, Oxford, 1986.

Kirschbaum, E., *The Tombs of St Peter and St Paul*, London, 1956.

Küng, H., *Infallible? An Unresolved Inquiry*, London, 1994.

Mollat, G., *The Popes of Avignon*, London, trans, 1963.

Richards, J., *The Popes and the Papacy in the Early Middle Ages 476-752*, London, 1979.

Tanner, N., *Decrees of the Ecumenical Councils*, London, 1960.

Walsh, J. E., *The Bones of St Peter*, New York, 1982.